A CONSTITUTION TO KEEP

Praise for *Liberty After Freedom*

'What makes Alva's book special is its attempt to answer the question that has puzzled both legal experts and students of law, as to why the drafters of the Constitution gave up the "due process" guarantee in the context of exceptions to be made to the right to personal liberty, and their decision to opt for the much more supine phrase, "except according to procedure established by law".'
—*The Week*

'The book demonstrates how a simply written sentence in intelligible English becomes a site of ideological contestation and a strong framework of rights in India. The book is also about the beauty of the argumentative Indian mind and a peek into the thinking of our founding fathers. It must be read by anyone interested in the making of the idea of India.'
—*Hindustan Times*

'Alva has collated diverse materials, in what must have been an arduous task, and presented views on both sides. Alva's well-put-together book gives us the genesis of Article 21, which needs to be known by judge, lawyer, law-maker and layperson alike, in order to appreciate not only the past, but the present as well.'
—*Business Standard*

'Rohan J. Alva's *Liberty After Freedom* enquires into the fascinating history of one such instance of changed meaning: the fate of "due process" in Article 21 of the Constitution. Alva's presentation of the proceedings of the Assembly allows us a rare glimpse into the full arc of a single provision's evolution. Alva's investigation reveals the limits of speculating on the motivations of the drafters and the understanding of

Celebrating
30 Years of Publishing
in India

the members of the Assembly regarding the implications of the drafting choices they voted on.'

—*The Telegraph*

'Rohan J. Alva's debut work is an eye-opener regarding the migration of the present Article 21 from the "due process of law" to the "procedure established by law." *Liberty After Freedom* is an important addition to the existing academic writing on Indian Constitutional history. To lawyers, law students and legal academics, the familiar phraseology of the right to life and personal liberty clause is almost taken for granted, finding mention in so many judgments of the constitutional courts. Alva has brought to bear an impressive grasp of legal history to shine light, however, on the arduous journey that Article 21 undertook to reach its present form. Through meticulous research, Alva shows how fragile the Article was at its inception, and how important it is for citizens to continue to ensure that this most important of rights remains protected, so that it, too, may in turn protect us in the future as it has done in all the years gone past.'

—**K.K. Venugopal, Attorney General for India**

'*Liberty After Freedom* is an ambitious and fascinating account of how India's post-World War II Constitution, consciously drafted to resist American-style judicial hostility towards Progressive-era economic regulation, was nonetheless later interpreted to protect substantive liberty interests, such as privacy. Alva sheds interesting historical and comparative light on the well-nigh irresolvable conflict between a society's commitment to protecting the fundamental rights of individuals and constraining the power of unrepresentative and politically less-accountable judges.'

—**Michael Klarman, The Charles Warren Professor, Harvard Law School**

'The extraordinary story of due process in India must be told, and there is no one better to tell it than Rohan J. Alva. This monumental book is simultaneously a rich legal history excavated from the annals of India's Constituent Assembly, a careful doctrinal analysis of the domestic law of due process, a global escapade through the great constitutional democracies of the world and a manifesto for an evermore just reading of the Indian Constitution. *Liberty After Freedom* places Alva in the pantheon of the most thoughtful contemporary scholars of India's democratic constitution.'

—**Richard Albert, Professor of World Constitutions and Director of Constitutional Studies, The University of Texas at Austin**

A CONSTITUTION TO KEEP

SEDITION *AND* FREE SPEECH *IN* MODERN INDIA

ROHAN J. ALVA

HarperCollins *Publishers* India

First published in hardback in India by HarperCollins *Publishers* 2023
4th Floor, Tower A, Building No. 10, Phase II DLF Cyber City,
DLF Gurugram, Haryana – 122002
www.harpercollins.co.in

2 4 6 8 10 9 7 5 3 1

Copyright © Rohan J. Alva 2023

P-ISBN: 978-93-5629-665-7
E-ISBN: 978-93-5629-666-4

The views and opinions expressed in this book are the author's own and the facts are as reported by him, and the publishers are not in any way liable for the same.

Rohan J. Alva asserts the moral right
to be identified as the author of this work.

All rights reserved. No part of this publication may be reproduced, stored in a retrieval system, or transmitted, in any form or by any means, electronic, mechanical, photocopying, recording or otherwise, without the prior permission of the publishers.

Typeset in 11.5/15.7 Minion Pro at
Manipal Technologies Limited, Manipal

Printed and bound at
Thomson Press (India) Ltd

This book is produced from independently certified FSC® paper
to ensure responsible forest management.

For
Mumma, Baba, and Kuki

Contents

	Prologue	ix
1	Disaffectionately Yours, Sedition	1
2	Half a League, Half a League, Half a League Onward	27
3	Wounded Vanity	52
4	The Many Lives of the Prince	80
5	Thunder and Lightning	108
6	The Prince Is Dead, Long Live the King	125
7	The Decisive Distinction	148
8	Reinvention	158
9	Triumph of Democracy	182
10	Putting the Soul in a Lifeless Article	210
11	The Value of Political Speech	229
12	Beware the Ides of March	241
13	Truly Free Political Speech	261
14	Avoiding a Pyrrhic Victory	283
	Epilogue	299
	Notes	307
	Index	358
	Acknowledgements	369

Prologue

TALK OF SEDITION IS ALL AROUND US. IT IS WRITTEN ABOUT IN newspaper columns[1] and in prominent magazines.[2] It is rumbustiously discussed in television debates. It is a divisive issue in Parliament.[3] As classically understood within the scheme of the Constitution of India, sedition is the crime of using the power of words to actually bring about events which result in the destabilization of the entire Indian State.

Yet, sedition has been invoked against college students,[4] members of Parliament,[5] journalists,[6] protestors,[7] cartoonists,[8] schools,[9] elected representatives hoping to chant religious scriptures as a mark of political protest,[10] and, those making hoax phone calls to delay the departure of a train.[11]

Over the years, events such as these have reverberated internationally.[12] In recent times, the call of liberalism demanding that the law on sedition be done away with has reached a veritable crescendo. Prominent public intellectuals have been outspoken against this law because it is considered too heavy a fetter on the right to speak, write and express oneself freely.[13]

How fragile the Indian republic must appear if one is to only note the bewildering number of prosecutions that have been launched for sedition in the twenty-first century itself. They run into the thousands.[14]

The law on sedition is contained in Section 124A of the Indian Penal Code (IPC). It is a law which has reigned now for over a century and a half. In its essence, Section 124A outlaws any expression which seeks to excite disaffection against the government. To be accused of sedition is a dangerous thing. The maximum sentence for sedition is life imprisonment, which makes it one of the most serious crimes in India.[15]

In 2021, none other than the highest court of the land decided to intervene. It categorically expressed doubts on whether the law on sedition had a place in a democracy, and agreed to examine whether it violates the Indian Constitution.[16] In another instance, the Supreme Court took adverse notice of the shocking spectre of media houses being booked for sedition and decided that it was time that new guidelines were properly formulated to ensure that the freedom of the press is upheld.[17]

On 11 May 2022, in the intense summer, as the sun reached high noon, came some cool respite. The Supreme Court directed the states as well as the Union government to desist from pursuing any case involving sedition, until it decided whether the law is constitutionally valid.

In reaching this decision, the Supreme Court took note of the Attorney General for India's grievance that there were all too many instances of the law on sedition being misused. It also took note of the fact that the Government of India had indicated that it would revisit the feasibility of the law itself, in view of the many concerns that had been voiced against it.[18]

Effectively, the Supreme Court suspended the operation of Section 124A. Nevertheless, the question of whether this law is constitutional is yet to be decided. It continues to remain on the statute books. The respite, although much welcome, is only temporary. In the face of this, it becomes more important than ever to critically evaluate whether the law on sedition is consistent with the Constitution of India.

What is sedition? What is its provenance? How did the law on sedition take root in India? How was it used against the greatest nationalist leaders? Is there any justification for the persistence of such a law in modern India? What is the constitutional vision which decisively establishes the incompatibility of such a law with the fundamental right to the freedom of speech and expression guaranteed by the Indian Constitution? This book seeks to answer these timely and relevant questions, which every Indian should be asking.

A Badge of Honour

Sedition is not a problem of the twenty-first century. It is a scourge that has afflicted India for close to two centuries now. It was first thought of in the early 1800s. A young Thomas Babington Macaulay, only thirty-seven, had arrived on the shores of India sometime in 1834 with a singular agenda—that of 'reforming' the state of Indian law.

Macaulay had no special love for India or for Indians. His disdain reached its pinnacle in his Minute of 2 February 1835, in which he had infamously remarked that although he knew not a word of Sanskrit, no one 'could deny that a single shelf of a good European library was worth the whole native literature of India and Arabia.'[19]

Macaulay was a member of the Indian Law Commission that was set up to make laws. In 1837 the Commission presented the Governor-General with the first draft of the Indian Penal Code (IPC). Macaulay did most of the work in the Commission, and it is from the mind of Macaulay that the IPC sprang forth. In modern times, Macaulay is sometimes praised as a genius whose enduring gift to India is the IPC.[20] However, his disdain for Indians manifested most greatly in the law on sedition.

In the IPC, he made it a crime for any person to 'excite disaffection' against the British government. It was a law whose singular purpose was to ensure that Indians remained unquestionably obedient to the British government.

Although the IPC only came into force in 1860, sedition somehow slipped through the gaps and remained out of the statute books till 1870, the year when it was re-introduced by a legislative amendment. It would become Section 124A in the IPC. Despite its belated entry into the IPC, it still remained virtually inactive for over two decades thereafter.

Towards the end of the nineteenth century, and after a series of fraught experiments, the British government realized that the best way of crushing the press, of silencing dissent and keeping the nationalist leaders in check, was to prosecute them for sedition.

All that the British government had to do was to simply accuse anyone who expressed the slightest discomfort against British rule of exciting disaffection against the British government in India. Harbouring any feeling other than (unrequited) affection, loyalty and admiration for the British was treated as the crime of sedition.

The law on sedition directly and fatally attacked the freedom of speech and expression, and more particularly the freedom of the press, to critically discuss the politics of the day. Saying, writing or expressing anything negative about the British government was a high crime. This is the enduring gift of Macaulay.

Nevertheless, there was no shame in being labelled a seditionist. The greatest leaders of the Indian independence movement, such as Mahatma Gandhi, Bal Gangadhar Tilak and Jawaharlal Nehru, cheerfully and proudly wore their convictions for sedition on their sleeves.

Most famously, in his sedition trial in 1922, Gandhi coined a new name for Section 124A. He called it 'the prince' in the Indian legal system; the one law which was specifically 'designed to suppress the liberty of the citizen.'[21]

Tilak was convicted twice for sedition. Each time he was prosecuted, Tilak proudly proclaimed his commitment to attack the foundations of British rule in India. Indeed, his first conviction for sedition in 1897 played an outsized role in shaping how the law on sedition was to be applied against nationalist leaders.

Jawaharlal Nehru was twice convicted for sedition. In October 1930, Nehru was arrested for sedition for the 'no-tax campaign' he started in Allahabad (present-day Prayagraj in the state of Uttar Pradesh) where he demanded that Indians must not pay any tax to the British. During his trial, Nehru openly claimed that he was guilty of sedition against the British government in India, and of exciting disaffection against colonial rule. He was convicted on 24 October 1930.

Four years later, Nehru was once again in the cross hairs of sedition for his speeches in Calcutta (present-day Kolkata in the state of West Bengal), which trenchantly attacked British imperialism. He was arrested for sedition but again pleaded guilty and openly claimed that he hoped to 'put an end to foreign domination'. This time too, Nehru was convicted for sedition and sentenced to two years in prison.[22]

Sedition also led to many firsts. In the 1940s, my paternal grandfather, Joachim Alva, a firebrand orator, was prosecuted for sedition for a series of articles he wrote and printed in *Forum*, a journal published by him. When he was hauled up before the Bombay High Court, my grandmother, Violet Alva, donned her legal robes and successfully defended her husband before Justices Chagla, Weston and Lokur.

Never before had a woman argued a case before a Full Bench of any high court in pre-independent India. Violet Alva is today recognized as one of the greatest women in the history of independent India.[23]

That Joachim Alva's profile on the Lok Sabha website prominently mentions that he was 'Prosecuted for sedition'[24] shows that those who fought for India's freedom considered being charged with sedition against British rule as the highest compliment that could be paid to them.[25]

It was a badge of honour.

The Endurance of Legacy

This book begins by laying out and critically evaluating the history of sedition between 1837 and 1945. The singular purpose which animated the law on sedition was the preservation of British sovereignty in India, by creating a climate of fear and repression. Indubitably, the ultimate aim was to use sedition to ensure the permanence of British rule.[26] As the Mahatma's grandson, Gopalkrishna Gandhi, wrote, 'Patriotism and sedition had become, for the Raj, synonymous and were to be dealt with typically, by Section 124A of the Indian Penal Code.[27]

From there, the book moves on to examine the dramatic developments which occurred in the Constituent Assembly between 1946 and 1950.[28] The Assembly was the body which had the supreme responsibility of preparing a written Constitution for independent India.

At one moment it appeared that the Assembly was poised to let sedition remain a crime in free India. But leaders like Sardar Vallabhbhai Patel in 1947, and K.M. Munshi in 1948, stood firm and ensured that sedition received a fitting burial.

The Indian Constitution came into being on 26 January 1950, and at its moment of birth, the Indian republic asserted the idea that sedition could not be a fetter on the freedom of speech and expression. Freedom was truly in the air.

For a whole host of reasons and almost immediately, the implementation of the Constitution posed enormous difficulties. To overcome them, the Constituent Assembly, which became the provisional Parliament between 1950 and 1952 (the year in which the first general elections were held), brought forth the First Amendment to the Indian Constitution in June 1951.

By this amendment, the Constitution underwent a dramatic transmogrification. Importantly, the article pertaining to the restrictions that can be imposed on the freedom of speech was amended, and new articles which sought to permanently save land reform laws from legal challenges, were made a part of the Constitution.

In recent years, truly outstanding scholars of the Indian Constitution have written on the relationship between free speech and sedition. They are of the view that it is the First Amendment which brought sedition back to life.[29]

There is some credence to their arguments. In 1962, the Supreme Court announced that sedition was specifically resurrected by the First Amendment. That decision upheld Section 124A. However, as we shall see, nothing in the First Amendment can be construed as reviving sedition and the Supreme Court was in error when it held that sedition was revived in 1951.

For some time now, the dominant narrative has been that sedition, although abandoned by the Constituent Assembly in 1950, was brought back to life exactly a year later; a narrative sustained because of the Supreme Court's decision. Nothing can be further from this.

The Value of Political Speech

Whatever may be our conception of the limits of the freedom of speech and expression, we must acknowledge that sedition *is* a crime and a restriction on free speech in India. How, then, do we confront it? Which principles convincingly demonstrate the futility of a law on sedition? What are the heuristic tools which establish that Section 124A is unconstitutional?

This book propounds the normative idea that the freedom of speech and expression enumerated in the Indian Constitution, at its core, guarantees free political speech.

Political speech is conceived of as including such speech and expression which is directed against the government and contains substance which seeks to bring about a progressive transformation of the status quo.[30] Indeed, on account of its invaluable role in preserving democracy, its function in transforming public opinion, and the power of this right to inaugurate political change and keep elected officials accountable, led the Supreme Court to emphatically announce that the freedom of speech and expression is the '*most precious of all the freedoms guaranteed by the Constitution*.'[31]

The framework which this book proposes can be summarized thus: speech and expression, in whatever manner and tone, which involves a discussion of governmental affairs and advocacy for bringing about changes, is immune from routine regulation.

To establish this normative framework, the book draws on global political theory, Indian constitutional history, as well as modern Indian and global jurisprudence. In sum, the book argues that political critique of governmental affairs is above matters of State regulation. Laws cannot be made to regulate the discussion and advocacy of political issues.

At first blush, it may appear that to think that political speech is immune from all restrictions is fundamentally incompatible with the scheme of the freedom of speech and expression contained in the Constitution. That is because the Constitution authorizes the State to impose reasonable regulations on free speech on certain specified grounds, such as public order. As such, the default position appears to be that no form of speech and expression is beyond the purview of regulation.[32]

Nevertheless, as the book shows, political speech falls in that category of rights which can fend off almost any attempt at being controlled by the lawmaking power of the State precisely because of the 'value' that it adds to Indian democracy. The vitality of the Indian republic depends entirely on ensuring that the people of India are well empowered to articulate their thoughts and hold those who are in power democratically accountable.

To allow sedition to hang like the sword of Damocles over the heads of the Indian people is to give the kiss of death to political speech, and in turn to Indian democracy itself. Ensuring the survival of Indian democracy is the greatest justification for doing away with the law on sedition and unleashing the full potential of the freedom of speech.

Section 124A, and indeed the law on sedition, belongs to the domain of a colonial despot and a totalitarian regime which did not concern itself with fundamental rights and representative government. It has no place in India, which has assiduously nurtured the ideal of governments being democratically elected.

As the Supreme Court rightly noted in its 11 May 2022 judgment—when it suspended the operation of Section 124A—this is a provision of law which is 'not in tune with the current social milieu and was intended for a time when this country was under a colonial regime.'[33]

It is the constitutional duty of citizens to question and critique the politics of the day. What is more, the right of citizens to engage in political speech is specifically guaranteed by the Constitution. It is not the duty of the citizens to whisper only sweet nothings about their state of being. If that be so, then there would be no need for the Constitution to contain a right guaranteeing the freedom of speech and expression.

The very purpose of giving free speech rights a place of prominence in the pantheon of fundamental rights is to allow citizens to peacefully dissent and disagree through political discussion, and to imagine alternative visions of political ideals.[34] The principal reason for elevating free speech to this exalted position in the constitutional scheme is on account of the fact that it is this right alone by which Indian democracy can survive.

As we shall see, the founders of the Indian Constitution had precisely this vision in mind when they gave shape to the free speech guarantee. As such, Section 124A is wholly unconstitutional because its tentacles reach deep into the heart of Indian democracy and stifle free political speech.

Of course, speech which seeks to bring about imminent and inevitable consequences that harm the security of the State can be regulated. But in thinking of how such speech ought to be regulated, political speech which contributes to political discourse must not be easily curtailed by the simple invocation of State security interests. The State must always convincingly establish that there is a demonstrable and imminently inevitable harm to State security that is to be prevented.

As the book proposes, only that kind of speech which seeks to directly and imminently bring about this particular harm can be regulated. The emphasis lies on prevention of an imminent harm to State security, since this standard furnishes narrow and strict grounds by which free speech can be curbed.

More pertinently, this standard is far better than curbing free speech on the basis that it has a 'tendency' of causing some harm. Far too many problems arise when people are prosecuted for sedition only on the basis that their words have a tendency to cause some disturbance.

At the heart of the free speech guarantee in the Constitution lies political speech. Granting political speech absolute protection is perfectly compatible with the scheme set out by the Constitution.

Since 1837, India has had to wage an arduous battle against the scourge of sedition. It is only fitting that in its seventy-fifth year of Independence, India is finally able to throw off the shackles of Empire.

1
Disaffectionately Yours, Sedition

THE STORY OF SEDITION IN INDIA BEGINS WITH THE FRAMING OF THE Indian Penal Code (IPC), and its story, in turn, begins with the Charter Act of 1833. The East India Company had begun to trade with India after receiving a royal charter in 1600, and over the centuries the trading rights of the Company had been periodically extended.[1] The British Parliament, by the Charter Act of 1833, extended the royal charter granted to the East India Company for conducting its operations in India. But through the Charter of 1833, the Company's hold over India was loosened even more. For, twenty years earlier, the East India Company's right to enjoy a monopoly over commercial trade with India had been brought to an end by the Charter Act of 1813.[2]

Although, under the Charter Act of 1833, the Company was allowed to control its territories in India, these territories were now held 'in trust'[3] for the British Crown. The Charter Act also stipulated that the Company wind down its commercial operations; but it could still exercise 'administrative and political powers'.[4] Before 1833, the Charter Acts had designated Governor- Generals for the different presidencies in India. But under the Charter Act of 1833, there was to be one Governor-General for India, who would be in a Council. That Council was to have four members. The fourth member in the Council was to be a law member who would advise the Governor-General on lawmaking.[5]

The emphasis on a law member being a part of the Council was enormously portentous. At the time of the Charter Act of 1833, there were at least five different legal systems in existence in India. There were the special laws which were applicable in the Presidency territories; there were British laws made applicable to certain territories; regulations enacted by the Governors since 1793; there were special regulations which were applicable in the Madras Presidency; and, finally, the code prepared by Mountstuart Elphinstone for the Bombay Presidency.[6]

Importantly, under the Charter, the Governor-General-in-Council was conferred with pre-eminent powers to frame a general body of laws for India.[7] A specific clause in the Charter Act (Section 53) expressly announced that a system of law must be introduced which is uniform in its application, in that it applies to all persons in all the British territories in India. To that end, the Charter Act required the Governor-General to constitute a Law Commission, which would be tasked with the responsibility of framing such a general and uniform body of laws.[8]

Henceforth, the laws made in India would be known as 'Acts'.[9] What the Charter Act hoped to do was replace the motley collection of various local laws and regulations with one general law which would be the only law applicable in the territories in India under British control.[10] The ultimate purpose of this enterprise was to achieve the 'comprehensive consolidation and codification of Indian laws.'[11]

In keeping with the mandate of the Charter Act of 1833, the Governor-General appointed an Indian Law Commission, which was to survey the state of the law in India and present its recommendations to the Governor-General.[12] A four-member Law Commission comprising Thomas Babington Macaulay, Charles Hay Cameron, John Macpherson Macleod, and George William Anderson was constituted. It was to be their responsibility to craft laws for India, which could then be enacted.[13] The Commission was headed by Macaulay.[14] Indeed, it was Macaulay who had played a pivotal role in convincing the British Parliament of the need for codifying the laws in India.[15]

Macaulay arrived in India in 1834, and although initially the Commission thought it would be best to recommend a law which introduced uniformity in the realm of civil procedural law, it was soon decided to first frame a general body of criminal law for India.[16] The Commission began working towards this goal in 1835.

On 14 October 1837, the Commission presented its version of the IPC to the Governor-General of India, Lord Auckland. This was the first draft of the IPC. After several rounds of revisions, the IPC was finally enacted in 1860.[17] Although the Commission had four members, it was Macaulay who would come to draft almost the entire IPC and leave his lasting imprimatur on it. For this reason, even today the IPC is often referred to as Macaulay's Penal Code.[18]

The Report submitted by the Commission on 14 October 1837 makes for interesting reading.[19] It narrates that by the middle of the 1800s, the East India Company was finding it difficult to administer the criminal law in India. There was absence of a general body of criminal law, and a vast array of personal law regulated the realm of criminal culpability. There also existed sharp distinctions in the way in which criminal law was construed and understood in Bombay, Bengal, and Madras.

By the nineteenth century, the East India Company had reached a moment in time where it felt the need for a general law—a Code, so to speak—which would contain the criminal law. These and other reasons led the Commission to believe that Indian law was in a state of utter neglect, which necessitated a complete overhaul.[20]

The image which this Report conjured was that of England being the progenitor of the classical forms of codifying laws, and that the level of perfection it had attained in organizing laws was to be transplanted to India.[21] In other words, the Report gave the impression that India needed to follow the British model, where laws were systematically codified. This simply was not true, and in recent years this narrative of the Report has come under serious challenge.

At the time the Indian Law Commission was dispatched to India, it was English criminal law which was in a state of disarray. In England, immense public opinion had rallied against the Bloody Code, a reference to the '200 statutes that punished virtually every criminal act with death.'[22] As a result, crimes persistently increased because courts and juries were unwilling to send to death every defendant brought before them.[23]

Public outcry against an unstructured and haphazard legal system led to the enactment of the Peel Acts of 1829[24]—which were a set of eight laws 'that consolidated and amended over 200 statutes.'[25] But even that proved unsatisfactory.[26] In 1832, a Parliament backed Royal Commission was established. Its report of 1834 must have made painful reading for the British because its unmistakable conclusion was that English law was plagued with uncertainty, confusion and, above all, a total lack of coherence.[27]

No firm solution could be arrived at, and the British experiment with simplifying criminal law continued well into the late 1800s.[28] This was the state of disarray of English law from which Macaulay and his fellow members in the Law Commission emerged. It was this which led the Law Commission to introduce, in India, a model of a Code which Britain was actually in urgent need of; a Code that 'reflected the needs and ideas appropriate to England's criminal justice system,'[29] and not the other way around.[30] In the ultimate analysis, what the Commission attempted to do in India was 'modernize its own [British] primitive criminal justice system.'[31]

It is also a mistake to think that Indian law was always inferior. Take the example of homicide. According to scholars such as James Fitzjames Stephen, a notable English jurist who would be an important *dramatis personae* in making sedition a crime in India, the definition of homicide under Islamic Law was extraordinarily intricate and layered. Compared with it, the definition of culpable homicide and murder in the IPC was considered its 'weakest part' because there was no clear way to discern when and when not murder was committed.[32]

There is some truth in this assessment. In modern times, even the Indian Supreme Court has bemoaned the fact that confusion of a rather profoundly unsolvable level still prevails each time the courts encounter provisions in the IPC dealing with homicide. 'The question of whether in a given case a homicide is murder,' the Supreme Court lamented in September 2021, 'has engaged the attention of courts in this country for over one and a half century, since the enactment of the IPC; a welter of case law, on this aspect exists, including perhaps several hundred rulings by this court.'[33]

In defining homicide in the IPC, Macaulay made some allowances for Western practices which were in vogue at that time, such as drafting an exception which did not treat death caused with the victim's consent as murder, but as a lower level of homicide (which did not amount to murder). This was to ensure that a death caused in a duel, which in the Western world was a popular way of resolving disputes, was not treated on par with cold-blooded murder.[34]

Macaulay's arrival on Indian shores in 1834 had been eventful for another reason. It marked the culmination of the grand utilitarian project of developing a legal system for India. As far back as 1793, the progenitor of the idea of Utilitarianism, Jeremy Bentham, was very keen on 'framing the law system of India.'[35]

Macaulay was a dedicated disciple of Bentham, and traces of Bentham's influence are to be found in the IPC. Using simple terms like 'defamation' when dealing with the offence of hurting a person's reputation, rather than using technical terms such as 'slander' and 'malice' and providing for a sliding scale of punishments, in keeping with the degree of the crime, bear the imprint of Bentham.[36]

There does, however, seem to be some difference of opinion over whether Macaulay intended on using India as a site for demonstrating an improved version of English criminal law. Macaulay had himself disclaimed the idea that the IPC was to be an example of an advance over English law; he deemed it to be a truly novel and independent creation. But others, such as Whitley Stokes, were convinced that the IPC was English law, '*shortened, simplified, made intelligible and precise.*'[37]

Essentially, there is considerable truth in the view that crafting the IPC was less about importing best practices from England to India and more about holding up a mirror to the island's own legal system mired in chaos. So much so that even the reconstituted

Indian Law Commission comprising Charles Hay Cameron and Daniel Elliot, in their report of 23 July 1846, did not agree with the suggestion that Macaulay's draft of the IPC was extraordinarily novel. It had admittedly borrowed many principles from the legal codes of many countries.[38]

At any rate, even the Indian Law Commission had trenchantly condemned the state of English criminal law. In their report of 14 October 1837 which accompanied the initial version of the IPC, the Commission labelled 'English criminal law . . . as *requiring extensive reform*,'[39] and a system of law, 'which has just been pronounced by a Commission composed of able and learned English lawyers *to be so defective that it can be reformed only by being entirely taken to pieces and reconstructed*.'[40]

Moreover, as a general matter too, the process of codification of laws in India was treated by leading Utilitarian thinkers, including James Mill and indeed Macaulay himself, as events which must ultimately culminate in the reformation of the state of English law. All this, therefore, clearly demonstrates that it was England which would benefit by learning from the Indian experiment in codification.[41]

Perhaps no one put it better than James Fitzjames Stephen, and no one condemned English law more, when he proclaimed:

> The Indian Penal Code is to English criminal law what a manufactured article ready for use is to the materials out of which it is made of.[42]

Masterpiece in Uncertainty

In drafting the IPC, inspiration had been sought from all quarters, including the French Code as well as the Louisiana Code. For the Law Commission, the enterprise of framing the IPC merited a broad scope of inquiry where the best practices from other countries would be studied in order to decide the lessons that could be drawn from them.[43]

However, the IPC was not just a motley compilation of actions and conduct which were to be criminally culpable. Rather, it was a piece of legislation which was to be a 'Statute book and a collection of decided cases.'[44] The former was achieved by defining offences as well as the punishments that were to be imposed. The latter was achieved by enumerating numerous 'Illustrations' to many of the provisions in the IPC. The use of Illustrations, which were hypothetical fact patterns of the kind of conduct which a particular provision in the IPC made an offence, would help those called upon to administer the IPC to view 'the law in full action.'[45]

However, there was no room for judicial discretion to give the IPC a meaning not intended by the plain words. Invoking Roman Law, the Indian Law Commissioners ruled out the possibility of the IPC being understood creatively.[46] The IPC meant what it said.[47] As we shall see, in the context of sedition this lofty ideal suffered a series of stunning setbacks, with the British administration in the late 1800s expressing its disdain for the vagueness with which Macaulay defined sedition.

In the initial draft of the IPC prepared by Macaulay, a separate chapter was devoted to 'Offences against the State' (Chapter V).[48] In listing offences against the 'State' uppermost in the IPC and before offences against persons, Macaulay followed the classification of offences obtaining in the French Penal Code.[49]

Macaulay was writing in the 1830s, a time at which India was still under the administration of the East India Company, which had under its control some territories only. There was no 'State' yet to speak of, for India had not yet been brought directly under the British Crown. That would happen in 1858.

Ensconced in Chapter V was the crime of sedition. Clause 113 made it a crime to say, write or express anything which excited, or attempted to excite, feelings of disaffection against the government which the East India Company had established. The punishments were extraordinary, because they swung between being particularly harsh (banishment for life from the territories under the control of the East India Company) to being comparatively soft (simple imprisonment for three years).[50]

Macaulay may have been a Utilitarian whose mission was to infuse legal certainty and predictability when it came to the making of laws. On the true scope of legislation, Macaulay had famously remarked:

> Our principle is simply this; uniformity where you can have it, diversity when you must have it; *but in all cases certainty*.[51]

Yet, although the IPC has been praised as a law whose provisions 'are defined with precision,'[52] it does not take skilful training to note that Macaulay's Clause 113 was a masterpiece in uncertainty.

The most obvious problem with Clause 113 was this: what did disaffection mean? The clause itself did not define it, and neither was a definition forthcoming from anywhere else in the IPC. Did disaffection mean that people did not hold the government in love and affection, or did it mean something much more sinister? This complicated things because it belied the main purpose of making the IPC, which was to ensure that uncertainty over the meanings of words and phrases used in a statute would no longer linger.

Contrary to all canons of codification, the offence of sedition would end up creating fertile ground for the invention of thus far unknown standards which constituted disaffection. These standards would perhaps always be unknowable due to the vagueness which inhered in that one word—disaffection.

The use of Illustrations across the IPC was intended to clarify the scope of a particular clause; to give a practical example of actions which constituted that particular offence.[53] Curiously, however, no Illustration was appended to Clause 113. Macaulay did not even provide an example of a hypothetical situation of the kinds of words and expressions which were to be treated as sedition. There was, simply put, no objective standard by which one could glean the nature of the offence of sedition.

Further, the crux of the crime of sedition was not that one was successful in inducing people to lose their affection for the government. The crime of sedition was to make an attempt at committing it. Whether that attempt succeeded or failed was a different matter. Whether a person's seditious words were ignored, not understood, or simply not heard by others made no difference to either guilt or punishment.

The only relevant factor was that a person attempted to excite disaffection against the government. What was also missing from Clause 113 was a causal link to the consequences. Even if a person were to do nothing more than succeed in convincing another to lose their affection for the government, the punishment of banishment for life loomed large.

It is a different matter that in England, the law on sedition had developed along a different course, and not as widely as what was proposed by Macaulay in Clause 113 of the draft version of the IPC.[54] In England, in the 1800s, convictions for sedition were on the wane because the law required some evidence that the seditious speech or expression resulted in disorder.[55] Moreover, sedition was treated as a 'political offence,'[56] and after the passage of the Reform Act of 1832, sedition cases were no longer pursued.[57] As James Fitzjames Stephen said:

> Since the Reform Bill of 1832, prosecutions for seditious libel have been in England so rare that they may be said practically to have ceased.[58]

More importantly, when it came to sedition in England, to speak against the Crown would not to be treated as sedition if such speech or expression was unaccompanied by 'incitement or encouragement to use physical force or violence.'[59] If at all an uprising resulted as a consequence of the speech in question, only then could the speech be treated as sedition. And this was punishable with a two-year jail term.[60] As James Fitzjames Stephen put it:

> In *one word, nothing short of direct incitement to disorder and violence* is seditious libel.[61]

Nonetheless, Macaulay and his fellow members in the Indian Law Commission believed that making the IPC was a process of refinement and overcoming the problems which plagued English law.[62] If the absence of seditious speech and expression setting off a chain reaction of violent events was an obstacle in obtaining convictions in England, then the process of refinement perhaps called for eliminating this obstacle in India and doing away with the need for establishing causation from the offence of sedition altogether.

Perhaps the solution thought of was to draft the provision of sedition in such a way that the prosecution would not be burdened with the responsibility of having to establish that the seditious act led to something tangible in order to successfully obtain a conviction.

Effectively, in this new avatar of sedition in the IPC, Macaulay separated the act of seditious expressions from the consequences which followed it. By a clever sleight of hand, Macaulay made the expression of critical ideas itself the crime of sedition in India. As a result, speaking against British authority in India was converted into the crime of sedition. This sleight of hand becomes all the more suspicious because in its classical understanding, which James Fitzjames Stephen endorsed and which is oft-cited, the Latin word 'seditio,' which is the root word for sedition, meant *'an actual riot rather than an act of displaying a seditious intention.'*[63]

In one sense, Macaulay's law on sedition hearkened back to medieval England when the Star Chambers, in a decision in 1606 in the case of *De Libellis Famois*, had said that sedition meant, among other things, 'conspiring with others to incite hatred or contempt for persons in authority in which the truth and falsity of libel was immaterial.'[64] Making the expression of critical ideas itself the high crime of sedition in India was a malevolent inventive step which sprang forth from the mind of Macaulay.

All this was perhaps morally wrong and inconsistent with English law. But, after all, 'the legislator [w]as the sword-arm of the eighteenth-century despot,'[65] and seen in this light, there was no need for Macaulay to have defined sedition in narrow terms or as it was understood in England, because that was not his duty. The IPC demanded obedience from the subjects, and Clause 113 was a step in obtaining that obedience on pain of banishment for life.

The fact that the people of India, under the control of the East India Company, must remain obedient towards the British administration regardless of every consideration was explicitly alluded to. For the Indian Law Commission, the moment anyone made an attempt at questioning the motives of the government, the offence of sedition was committed. As the Commission saw it:

> We may here observe that an imputation which is not defamatory may under certain circumstances, be punishable on *other grounds*. Such an imputation may be intended to excite disaffection. *If so, though not punishable as defamation, it will be punishable as sedition.* An attack made, in good faith, on the public administration of the Governor of a presidency, will in no case be a defamation. *But if the author of it designed to inflame the people against the Government*, he will be liable to punishment under clause 113.[66]

The Forewarnings

There were many problems with Clause 113 and the comments which were received displayed the full extent of the contradictions which plagued this utilitarian project of codification. Macaulay left India after submitting the IPC in 1837 and went on to become a member of Parliament soon after his return to England. It then fell to the reconstituted Indian Law Commission comprising Charles Hay Cameron and Daniel Elliot to review the IPC in light of the comments received, which they did and in respect of which they submitted two reports.[67]

In the second report of the Indian Law Commission of 24 June 1847,[68] the Commission took note of the comments received on Macaulay's provision on sedition contained in Clause 113. Not only had it come in for heavy criticism, but it had also been excoriated by those who were part of the British administration in India.

That the provision on sedition, in Clause 113, was not happily worded and could not be treated as a model of clear legislative drafting was something which G. Norton, the Advocate General of Madras, pointed out. The Commissioners had attempted to introduce a clear-cut description of sedition, but 'the composers of the code,' Norton observed, were 'as unfortunate as all others have been in that effort.'[69] An instance of this failure was the absence of a graded system of punishment in Clause 113. The most harmless words and expressions could result in banishment for life. This, more than anything else, demonstrated the failure of Macaulay in defining laws with clarity.[70]

Other functionaries in the British administration too were unhappy with Clause 113. For Hudleston, a justice in the Sudder Court in Madras, Clause 113 was 'wholly indefensible.'[71] J. Cochrane, the East India Company's Standing Counsel, placed his finger on a different problem which Clause 113 would spawn: it would be weaponized to launch an assault on the liberty of the press. Importantly, for Cochrane, it was a subversion of public policy to make it a crime to say critical things against the government, when it was unaccompanied by violence.[72] As we shall see, Cochrane's prediction about the true impact of sedition in the IPC would prove to be prophetic, and deserves to be read and reread:

I think that as a mere matter of public policy, every Government should *avoid punishing mere words*, unless such be accompanied by acts injurious to the interest of the State. *But this clause does not only apply to words, but is in fact a direct attack on the public press.* The expression 'as is compatible with a disposition to render obedience,' which is the qualification of the clause, appears to me of *a very dangerous tendency, and calculated to place men's rights and liberties in the discretion of each particular judge.*[73]

In the face of all this criticism, the Indian Law Commission stood firm. For them, Clause 113 was perfectly clear: any discussion on government affairs was permissible so long as it did not cross the line by exciting disaffection against the government. This meant that the people must still obey the government and hold it in high esteem.[74]

Yet, this still did not clarify the plain meaning of disaffection, and the fact that the Law Commission spent copious amounts of time explaining the meaning of that one word, 'disaffection,' brought to bear the eternal controversies which legislative enterprise brings with it. For this process was far removed from the simple exercise of only stating the law in clear terms which could be comprehended by anyone who encountered it. Although denied by the Law Commission, it had become increasingly clear that the meaning of Clause 113 was far from crystal clear.

The Precursor

The IPC saw the light of day only in 1860 and was brought into force in 1862. When it came into effect, there was a surprising absence. Macaulay's Clause 113 was not present in the IPC. Only later did it come to light that the absence of sedition was not an act of progressive lawmaking to create breathing space for free speech, but because of an error which none of the principal actors involved in the making of the IPC had taken notice of.

Exactly a decade after the IPC was enacted, the British administration began setting the wheels in motion to bring back sedition in the IPC. By that time, the landscape of Indian polity had transformed. India had witnessed the Great Revolt of 1857. The ruthlessness and cruelty with which the revolt had been crushed between May and September of 1857 was unparalleled. The Mughal emperor of India, Bahadur Shah, whom the rebels claimed as their leader, was exiled to Burma.[75] Towards the end of 1857, India was no longer a mere outpost for the British. By Queen Victoria's Proclamation of 1858, India became a British colony and a crown jewel (both literally and metaphorically) in the British Imperial Crown.[76]

After the Great Revolt of 1857, the British government in India found renewed vigour in enacting laws and crushing the freedom of speech and expression. Indeed, for some time there had been some resistance to the enactment of the IPC itself. The Revolt of 1857 jolted the British administration out of its inertia, spurring the Governor-General to quickly enact it. Which is why, although the IPC lay dormant for over two decades after the Indian Law Commission had submitted the first draft in 1837, it was enacted into law within three years of the Revolt of 1857.[77]

A month into the Revolt, the Governor-General, Lord Canning, introduced the Gagging Act, which applied to all newspapers in India, whether English or vernacular. The term 'vernacular' was used to refer to publications in Indian languages. In bringing forth this law, Canning deserves full credit for being unpretentious and not hiding his disdain for the press and, more generally, for the liberty of speech.

The Gagging Act was an extraordinary measure to control the press, which the British believed was inflaming distrust against the government. But its enactment was also a moment of grim irony. As one commentator observed at that time, it was impossible to imagine that during the Crimean War, the British government would have moved to disband *The Times* for its writings on British war efforts. Moreover, the irony was further compounded by the fact that in England, the Revolt of 1857 was discussed in some detail in the press with vituperative attacks launched on Lord Canning and the ability of the British administration to govern. But in India, any criticism of the government was to be met sternly.[78]

The Gagging Act of June 1857 (Act XV of 1857) was an oppressive piece of legislation. It made it a crime for anyone to keep a printing press and publish anything without the prior authorization of the Governor-General. If one printed anything without first obtaining a licence, the government could walk in and seize all the printed material. Further, the Governor-General could at any time order a freeze on any publication. Violations of that order would result in punishment, besides confiscation of all the printed material.

The Gagging Act also had other stipulations, such as requiring those who were licensed to print and publish anything to prominently display their name and place of printing on that publication. Licensed printers and publishers were also required to transmit a copy of each publication to the magistrate.[79]

The true intent behind the Gagging Act was revealed a week after it came into force. In Bengal, a notification laying down the conditions under which permits could be given for keeping a printing press spelt this out in its very first clause:

> That no book, newspaper, pamphlet, or other work printed at such press, or with such materials or articles, shall contain any observations or statements impugning the motives or designs of the British Government, either in England or India, or in any way *tending to bring the said Government into hatred or contempt, to excite disaffection* or unlawful resistance to its orders, or to weaken its lawful authority, or the lawful authority of its civil or military servants.[80]

This, more than anything else, showed that the communication of ideas could not be treated as a licence to criticize the government. Such a broadly worded prohibition, which, incidentally, was not part of the text of the Gagging Act itself, imposed onerous restraints on anyone publishing any material from shining a penetrative light on governmental conduct. The effect of this new law was felt almost immediately. Established publications such as *Friends of India* and *Bengal Hukuru*, one of India's oldest journals, succumbed to the Gagging Act.[81]

Laws such as the Gagging Act and the accompanying notifications showed that the response of the government was episodic. By its own terms, the Gagging Act was to be in force only for a year.[82] There was no general law that could be deployed to curb speeches, writings and expressions which brought the government into disrepute. Moreover, even in the aftermath of the Revolt of 1857, unsuccessful prosecutions had been launched against newspapers 'under the common law for libel and sedition.'[83]

Viewed from this perspective, it is not difficult to imagine that once the British Crown assumed paramountcy over India in 1858, there was a need to have a general and expansively worded law that would, for all time, be available to crush any sort of speech or expression which remotely showed the government in a poor light. If the Gagging Act was a temporary measure, then a more permanent measure had to be thought of to control the minds of freethinking Indians. The stage was thus set to bring back sedition.

Correcting the Blunder

In 1870, the Governor-General's Council would deliberate on incorporating a provision in the IPC which made sedition a crime.[84] On 2 August 1870, the Council of the Viceroy and Governor-General of India met in Simla to discuss legal affairs. On that day, James Fitzjames Stephen, a member of the Council, proposed that certain amendments had to be made to the IPC in order to meet urgent developments.[85] One of the other members in the Council was John Strachey. His son, in 1897, as a judge of the Bombay High Court, would try the nationalist Bal Gangadhar Tilak in one of the earliest cases on sedition.

One of the amendments which was Stephen's handiwork and of which he was proudest was to make it easier to punish people who conspired to wage war against India. The singular reason for introducing this new provision was the Revolt of 1857.

Under this new provision, which would become Section 121A in the IPC, convictions could be obtained easily on showing that a person had knowledge that actions were afoot to wage war against the Crown in India, even if the person did nothing in respect of these supposed acts.[86] The Revolt of 1857, said Stephen, was 'as great a crime as could well be committed.'[87] That is why extraordinary punishment had to be inflicted on even those who may possess some knowledge of events such as these.[88]

With Section 121A, however, there was a gap in the IPC, since those who used words and expressions to criticize the government could not be brought to book swiftly, so to speak. It is for this reason that immediately after proposing Section 121A, Stephen proposed an amendment to bring in sedition—Clause 113 from Macaulay's draft of the IPC. This would eventually become Section 124A in the IPC.

The very absence of sedition, according to Stephen, was due to an 'unaccountable mistake.'[89] Stephen told the Council that when the IPC was being finalized, there had been some talk of modifying Macaulay's Clause 113. Although those changes had not been agreed upon, the IPC in 1860 came into existence without this provision on sedition. No one could understand or take stock of exactly how this blunder occurred.[90] Even Stephen, who appeared to be mortified about this occurrence during his address to the Council, did not know how this had happened.[91]

In bringing sedition back into the IPC, Stephen was not making a mere editorial correction. The fact that Stephen proposed the introduction of sedition just after he claimed that the 1857 Revolt was a 'great crime' demonstrated that there certainly was a causal link between the events of 1857 and the desire of the British government to acquire greater and permanent powers to crush anyone who said anything critical of it.

Stephen intended on bringing back Clause 113 from Macaulay's draft IPC. But in defending it, he erred. Stephen seemed to think that Macaulay's version of sedition protected speech which was merely critical of the government and only punished such speech which was intended to induce the people to use force against the government.[92] This, as we have seen, was not the case, at least not by its plain words. In fact, Macaulay's draft on sedition was heavily criticized precisely because it did not require a causal link between disaffection being created against the government and actual disorder ensuing.

Ironically, Stephen's description of sedition is something which Macaulay would have himself disapproved of. In the utilitarian project of lawmaking, the people were supposed to be bound by what was stipulated in the law and not by what people conceived it to mean. If for the British, India was the land where they could engage in endless experimentation with how best to make laws,[93] then all that had to be taken into account was the chemical reaction which occurred after mixing two compounds; not what the reaction would be or ought to have been. Seen in this light, Stephen's idea that Macaulay's draft on sedition did not punish mere speech, words or expression alone was entirely misbegotten.[94]

There was an urgent need to empower the British government to act against anyone who brought it into disrepute, and Stephen admitted this in November 1870, when the Council discussed the Select Committee's report on the proposed amendments to the IPC. The absence of sedition was a 'great defect,' because bringing the government into disrepute could not be dealt with sternly and quickly and had to be dealt with as a lesser class of offences, namely as an act of abetment.[95]

Since warring against the Crown was a high crime, Stephen believed that those who uttered words to exhort people to rebel against the government, or at least intended for others to do so, should also be considered to have committed a high crime. And this was the advance which Macaulay's draft on sedition made.[96]

As Stephen told the Council, sedition in England was governed by statute, the Treason-Felony Act, as well as by common law under the doctrine of seditious libel. Stephen attempted to persuade the

Council that Macaulay's Clause 113 was both an advance and an improvement over its English counterpart.

According to Stephen, it was an advance because, in England, under the Treason-Felony Act, only those who wrote about their ill-feelings against the Crown and the government could be punished. But in India, what was material was not one's personal feelings, but whether others were induced to hold the English administration in disaffection.[97]

This was also seen by Stephen as an improvement. In England, the crime of seditious libel asked the question whether there was a 'plain tendency to produce public mischief by perverting the mind of the subject and creating a general disaffection towards the Government'.[98] But in Macaulay's provision of sedition, which Stephen wanted to make a part of the IPC, it was noted that anyone could be critical of the government as long as obedience to the government was not affected.[99] What Stephen cleverly did not allude to was that unlike its English counterpart, sedition in India would be punishable even if the recipient of seditious speech took no heed of it.

Stephen's emphasis lay on obedience, and it revealed more than anything else the sinister design behind his desire to make sedition a crime in the IPC. His time in India had instilled in him an insatiable appetite for ensuring 'obedience to benevolent and right-minded rulers.'[100]

'Obedience,' however, was not just an objective term but had a moral dimension. Would the subjects in India have to withstand the most oppressive practices which the British could imagine without once asking whether one was morally required to comply? As we shall see, it was the demand for obedience which would prove to be a flashpoint in the nationalist movement, and inevitably the fate of the greatest fighters of the freedom movement would be intertwined with sedition.

The biggest problem with Macaulay's draft on sedition was that disaffection had not been clearly defined. Stephen admitted that although 'disaffection' may not have a precise or a specific connotation, all words cannot always have the clearest meanings. Almost entirely abandoning Macaulay's utilitarian project of attaining legal certainty, Stephen presented a remarkable defence in favour of vagueness:

> But all human language was more or less vague. In a general way, *everybody knew what disaffection was*, but in that and every other word of the sort, *there must be a good deal of vagueness* from the imperfection of the human mind itself.[101]

The vagueness of the word 'disaffection' would become an important tool for the British to ruthlessly crush a whole variety of writings and speeches that questioned governmental conduct.

Stephen's amendment bringing back sedition was opposed because it would become a tool to silence the press.[102] In reply, Stephen presented a remarkable rebuttal. He believed that there was no such thing as complete freedom, and therefore there was no question of freedom of the press. There was only an unclaimed zone in which a person could say or write something, so long as that zone was not claimed by the law—which was why Stephen believed that 'liberty of the press was mere rhetoric.'[103]

Stephen was candid in condemning the press. Being a journalist was a good thing, Stephen remarked, provided you were loyal. And continued loyalty would act as a restraint on exciting people against the government. If a journalist were not loyal, then 'he could not complain of being punished.'[104]

However, just before the amendment bill moved by Stephen would be voted on, he suddenly raised the spectre of India tottering on the verge of violent instability, which is what had necessitated the retrieval of Macaulay's law on sedition. This was in stark contrast to his opening remarks to the Council in November 1870, at which time Stephen had proclaimed that 1870 was the right time to bring back Macaulay's draft on sedition because India was in a state of peace.[105]

Stephen now told the Council that since October 1870, a Wahabi Conspiracy was afoot, which aimed at whipping up public support against the government. To countenance a development in which public opinion was being mobilized against the British government, Macaulay's law on sedition was needed more than ever. The transcript of Stephen's speech in the Council records:

> A man was convicted and sentenced to transportation for life, substantially for committing the very offence at which this section was directed: it was preaching *Jehad* or holy war against Christians in India. ...[t]his person was in the habit, for weeks and months and years of going from village to village, and preaching in every place he came to that it was a sacred religious duty to make war against the Government of India.[106]

With Stephen now telling the Council that a civil war was about to be waged against the British government and that making seditious speech an offence was the only way to prevent things from deteriorating irretrievably, it was only inevitable that any speech and writing aimed at exciting disaffection against the

British government in India would become a crime. And it did on 25 November 1870, when the Council voted on Stephen's amendments to the IPC.[107] Macaulay's Clause 113 became law, albeit with some variations, and was now codified in Section 124A of the IPC.[108]

Stephen's Untruth

For more than a century and a half, Stephen's claim about the Wahabi Conspiracy necessitating a provision such as Section 124A has had some staying power and is accepted as being the obvious justification for introducing Section 124A.[109] But Stephen's claim was misleading.

In the years which followed the Revolt of 1857, the British had conjured up a so-called Wahabi Conspiracy, which the south Asian historian Julia Stephens calls 'The Phantom Wahabi,' which needed to be put down with extreme ruthlessness.[110] Matters came to a head during the trial of Amir and Hashmadad Khan—the Khan Brothers—accused of financing jihadi fighters in the North West Frontier. They were incarcerated in prison for over a year and a half before being released in 1871, but were soon rearrested under the new Section 121A, which punished any act of waging war against the British Crown.[111] Along with a few others, the Khan Brothers were tried in Patna in 1871.[112]

During that time, public opinion began to form in favour of the Khan Brothers. One reason for this was the enactment of Section 124A. Although ostensibly passed as a means of quelling the alleged Wahabi Conspiracy, it was increasingly viewed as a law which could be used against anyone, including the press, and not just against those who were part of the conspiracy. Remarkably, the sectarian justification for making sedition a crime gave way to collective opprobrium being poured on the British administration.[113] The 9 August 1870 edition of *The Times of India* gave voice to this angst by proclaiming, 'Such a mountain, a very Himalaya, has been made out of this Wahabee molehill.'[114]

Ultimately, in the case of the Khan Brothers, only one of them (Amir Khan) was convicted and sentenced to transportation for life, but that sentence was not carried out. Furthermore, some of the others who were convicted along with the Khan Brothers were acquitted when they appealed their conviction. This entire sordid episode culminated in 1877, when Amir Khan was formally pardoned in the days leading up to Queen Victoria's anointment as India's Empress.[115]

James Fitzjames Stephen had played grand mischief and succeeded. Section 124A was on the statute books, and it was only a matter of time before the wheels of injustice would begin to grind slowly but surely.

2
Half a League, Half a League, Half a League Onward

The Initial Years

AT THE TIME MACAULAY PROPOSED TREATING SPEECH AND expressions critical of the British government as the crime of sedition itself, Cocherne, the East India Company's Standing Counsel, had warned that such a law would be enormously harmful to the interests of a free press.[1] And that is precisely what happened. With Section 124A in hand, the British launched an unprecedented campaign to not only prosecute but also persecute the press, and in the process crush the freedom of speech and expression.

The first major case on sedition took place in 1891, twenty years after the Viceroy's Council had voted in favour of Section 124A. The case came from Calcutta.[2] Facing trial was Joginder Chunder Bose and his associates who ran the Bengali newspaper

Bangobasi.³ The charge levelled against them was that between March and June of 1891, *Bangobasi* had published articles which excited, and attempted to excite, disaffection against the British government of India.

One of the articles in question dealt with the destruction caused by the famine in India and criticized the government for failing to remedy the plight of the hungry. The other articles had criticized the Age of Consent Bill of 1891.⁴ That was a law which amended the IPC and increased the age (from ten to twelve) at which girls could give consent for sexual intercourse. The passage of the law had been opposed by those who hoped to preserve the orthodoxy of culturally permissive practices.⁵

These articles did not give a call to arms but spoke of the lived experiences in India. And some of the articles in *Bangobasi* were not off the mark. At the turn of the twenty-first century, the globally renowned medical journal *The Lancet* (the journal is of ancient vintage and its first issue was released in 1823) published a report on the state of health of the Indian population. The report painted a depressing picture.

Drawing on the Third Census Report, it pointed out that India had been ravaged by famine and blighted by the plague, and because of this, between 1891 and 1901, India's population grew at a very slow rate.⁶ The people were in a state of utter misery towards the end of the nineteenth century,⁷ and the articles in *Bangobasi*, which lamented the misery faced by the people of India, furnished the first major case on sedition.

As we saw, all that Section 124A required for the purpose of conviction was an attempt to excite disaffection against the government, and nothing more. This was seized upon by the prosecution, who tried to convince W.C. Petheram, the Chief Justice of the Calcutta High Court who was hearing that case, that the jury must focus only on whether an attempt was made to raise disaffection against the government.⁸

During the trial, there seemed to be some confusion on how the case ought to proceed. The defence argued that the articles had been published anonymously and it was only the author who could be tried for sedition, and not those who published the articles. The defence also attempted to stop the Chief Justice from instructing the jury on how Section 124A was to be understood; that was a matter for the jury to decide.

This was the first major case on sedition, and perhaps realizing he had a tabula rasa before him, Chief Justice Petheram was adamant that he would lay down the law by instructing the jury on the true meaning of that nebulous word: disaffection.⁹

With this, Chief Justice Petheram converted himself into a linguist. 'Whenever the prefix "dis" is added to a word,' Chief Justice Petheram told the jury, 'the word formed conveys an idea the opposite to that conveyed by the word without the prefix.' Applying this formula, Chief Justice Petheram declared that '[d]isaffection means a feeling contrary to affection.' One may not entirely approve of what the government does, but one must not cease to be affectionate towards the government. To stoke 'dislike' and 'hatred' against the government were good examples of what disaffection meant. In Chief Justice Petheram's formulation, '[i]t is quite possible to disapprove of a man's sentiments or action and yet to like him.'¹⁰

Chief Justice Petheram believed that under Section 124A, the offence was committed the moment a person used the power of their words to reduce the degree to which the government was liked. There was not, and there never would be, the need to see or establish whether the defendant had succeeded in that endeavour. In Chief Justice Petheram's view, a person would be 'guilty of the offence . . . though no disturbance is brought about by his words or any feeling of disaffection in fact, produced by them.'[11]

Nonetheless, Chief Justice Petheram was lost in his search for meaning. At various points in his instructions to the jury, he suggested different standards of what 'disaffection' could be taken to mean. At one point he instructed the jury to consider whether the articles in question 'excite feelings of ill-will,' and whether they endeavoured to bring the government into 'hatred and contempt of the people.'[12] At another point, he told the jury that one of the factors that must be weighed is whether the articles 'excite[d] feelings of enmity against the Government.'[13]

Chief Justice Petheram had begun to mix up disaffection with words such as 'hatred,' 'contempt' and 'ill-will.' He had not only twisted Section 124A beyond recognition but had also contrived a meaning for disaffection which defied logic, for none of these interpretations were anchored in the text of Section 124A. Unknown to Chief Justice Petheram, however, this formulation would prove cataclysmic. As we shall see, it resulted in the complete overhaul of Section 124A in 1898; an overhaul by which these very words would be introduced in Section 124A.

At the time at which the Viceroy's Council had discussed Section 124A in 1870, James Fitzjames Stephen had made a concession: one may say something critical against the British government, but the people's desire to obey the government must remain unwavering. That was the balance which Stephen thought Section 124A struck. This balance had meant that one could discuss governmental matters in seriously critical terms. But even this sliver of hope was dissolved by Chief Justice Petheram, because now the high crime of sedition was only whether one had attempted to raise dislike against the government.

Eventually, the jury weighed the case and were unable to return a unanimous verdict of guilt against the defendants, because they may have viewed these articles as proper criticism of governmental policy.[14] Ultimately, the charges were abandoned by the prosecution after Bose and the others who allegedly committed sedition formally apologized.[15] Bose's trial was only the start of the chapter, and Chief Justice Petheram's interpretation of 'disaffection' would come to play an outsized role in the cases that were to come.

Bal Gangadhar Tilak's First Trial

The next major case on sedition occurred at the opposite end of the country, in Bombay.[16] This time too, the court's ire was drawn towards the press. Bal Gangadhar Tilak ran the immensely popular newspaper *Kesari*, which was published in Marathi. In June 1897, *Kesari* carried articles describing the Shivaji coronation festival which took place in the city of Poona in the second week of that month. The government viewed the articles in the *Kesari* not simply as a description of Shivaji's reign and his many achievements, but rather as tales which were meant to bring to light the misdeeds of the British government and which deserved a strong response. *Kesari* also contained articles which berated the way the British government was dealing with the plague, which at that time had caused vast destruction.[17] For these articles, Tilak was put on trial for sedition.[18]

About a week after the articles were published in the *Kesari*, W.C. Rand, the president of the Plague Relief Committee, was assassinated in Poona, just as he departed from a venue where a celebration had been organized in honour of Queen Victoria's Diamond Jubilee. Tilak was also in attendance that fateful night and was shocked when he learnt of the assassination. However, with Rand's death, the government moved swiftly to prosecute Tilak for sedition. This was the immediate cause for Tilak's sedition trial.[19]

Incredibly, during Tilak's trial, the prosecution advanced a strange, if not a daringly flippant, argument. Rand had been killed soon after the publication of the articles. Although the prosecution suggested that this event should be taken into consideration when judging the effect of the articles, they were unable to present even a shred of evidence directly linking the publication with the assassination. It was, therefore, left to the jury to decide whether any causal link ought to be drawn between the articles and the assassination, despite the absence of any evidence pointing towards such a link.[20]

The prosecution came up short when trying to link Tilak with the assassination, but it was the prosecution, and not the defence, which was apparently entitled to take the benefit of this shortcoming. Incidentally, the British government decided to prosecute Tilak for sedition because it was unable to obtain any proof that linked Tilak with Rand's assassination.[21]

At the time he was being tried, Tilak's stature as someone who fought for the welfare of Indians had risen immensely. He was regarded as a leading public intellectual and as someone who could handle the British on their own terms.[22] For this reason, Tilak's trial became more than a simple domestic matter.

In August 1897, the House of Commons discussed the affairs of India, and among other things the trial of Tilak, hoping that he would receive a fair trial in the Bombay High Court.[23] And hope was needed. As the House of Commons was told, 'the Anglo-Indian Bar had in a cowardly manner, declined to defend him on his trial.'[24] Indeed, after Tilak was released on bail following his arrest he found it difficult for a Bombay-based advocate to take up his case. Fortunately, Rabindranath Tagore rushed to Tilak's aid by securing the services of Pugh, a Calcutta-based barrister who then represented Tilak in the Bombay High Court.[25]

Tilak was tried by Justice Strachey in the Bombay High Court. Strachey had an intimate connection with Section 124A. His father had been a member of the Viceroy's Council when the section was added to the IPC in 1870. Now, as a High Court judge, he was in a position to expound on the true meaning of disaffection. Justice Strachey had to instruct the jury as to what Section 124A meant, and since he was insistent that the jury had to follow his instructions alone, it fell to him to define disaffection.[26]

Inspired by Chief Justice Petheram in the *Bose* case, Justice Strachey launched into a creative interpretation of disaffection. '[D]isaffection means,' Justice Strachey commanded the jury, 'the *absence* of affection. It means hatred, enmity, *dislike, hostility, contempt*, and every form of *ill-will* to the Government.'[27] Here we can see that, like Chief Justice Petheram, Justice Strachey too began to use adjectives and different terms to collectively define disaffection.

Justice Strachey, however, made an error. By saying that disaffection was the *absence* of affection, he had created the lowest possible bar for treating something as seditious. Even the most harmless discussion of governmental affairs on someone's part may lead to their being considered as not holding the government in fond affection. According to Justice Strachey, that was enough to be treated as sedition. In the *Bose* case from Calcutta, Chief Justice Petheram may have contrived a new meaning for sedition, but Justice Strachey had now mangled Section 124A beyond recognition.

This bizarre formulation must be illustrated to truly appreciate its impact. Suppose a person met an acquaintance and told them that they disapproved of the government or the manner in which it implemented policy decisions. As soon as these words left the person's mouth, the crime of sedition would be deemed to have been committed—at least according to Justice Strachey. There may be no ill-will, no contempt, and no hatred on the part of the person expressing their disapproval.

Feeling less affectionate towards the government now became the crime of sedition. With this new formulation of 'disaffection,' almost any defence that could be raised against a charge of sedition was potentially excluded. Under the scheme of Section 124A, it made no difference whether a person had successfully created disaffection. An attempt to create disaffection against the government, whether it resulted in success or failure, was the same offence. That is why Justice Strachey decided to spend some time impressing upon the jury that 'you *must* convict him even if there is *nothing to show* that he succeeded'.[28]

Once the jury was instructed that the failure to excite disaffection was as great a crime as actually exciting it, it was left to Justice Strachey to prevent the jury members from thinking about whether the articles in question had actually resulted in something unlawful. 'Whether any *disturbance or outbreak was caused* by these articles,' Justice Strachey reminded the jury, 'is absolutely *immaterial*.'[29]

This was Justice Strachey's second move. He had to completely dissociate the views expressed in the articles from the consequences they led to, or rather the absence of them. And once that was done, it was the article alone which had to be viewed in isolation.

Thus far Justice Strachey thought that he had toed the line which Chief Justice Petheram had drawn on the meaning of the crime which Section 124A spoke of. But Justice Strachey's real contribution, if it can be called that, came in expounding on the meaning of the solitary Explanation in Section 124A.

The Explanation stipulated the class of speech which was not treated as seditious. All that it said was that if one expressed 'disapprobation' for governmental conduct, then such expression would not be seditious, provided that obedience was still rendered to the government.

The Explanation contained rambling sentences which heaped exception upon exception. Seeking to untangle the language used in the Explanation, Justice Strachey instructed the jury that Section 124A would not apply to speech which critically discussed a governmental measure. It would be seditious if the speech criticized *the* government itself.

Thus, if the publications in question were an 'attack . . . on the Government itself, its existence, its essential characteristics, its motives, or its feelings towards the people,' then there was no question of treating them as merely expressing disapprobation. They had to be treated as positively exciting disaffection.[30]

The plague which had ravaged India at the time played a central role in the case. Justice Strachey was keen to tell the jury that criticism of remedial measures being taken to tackle the plague, or criticism about the law enacted to deal with the plague—the Epidemic Diseases Act (1897)—would be treated as a crime of sedition.[31]

In this portion of Justice Strachey's instructions, there were a lot of moving parts, and it was clear that the door was closing fast on what could be legitimately expressed by Indians against the British government in India. To question the 'foreign origin' of the government, to allege that the government is the source of 'every sort of evil and misfortune,' to indulge in 'accusing it of hostility or indifference to the welfare of the people,' were, in Justice Strachey's instructions, clear traits of sedition, which Section 124A punished.[32]

With this, Justice Strachey revealed his hand. The ultimate goal of Section 124A was to ensure complete obedience from the subjects of the British government. With that in mind, Justice Strachey instructed the jury that it would be calamitous if the press were allowed to become the medium through which the people of India would come to 'hate their rulers.'[33]

Unlike in the *Bose* case, the jury in Tilak's case returned with a verdict of guilty (by a majority of six to three).[34] The jury comprised three Indians and six Europeans, who evidently voted along racial lines.[35] Perhaps the trial would have resulted in Tilak's acquittal if the jury had had Indians in the majority.[36]

Tilak's credentials were impeccable, for he was a member of the Legislative Council. But that did not stop the jury from sentencing Tilak to eighteen months in jail.[37] Nevertheless, Tilak did not take the conviction lying down and applied to the Full Bench of the Bombay High Court, for leave to appeal his conviction before the Judicial Committee of the Privy Council in England.

Before the Full Bench of three judges headed by Chief Justice Farran, Tilak attacked what was obviously the weakest part of Justice Strachey's instructions to the jury: that 'disaffection' in Section 124A meant 'absence of affection.'[38] Justice Strachey was part of the Full Bench, and when faced with this, he decided to offer an apology.

He admitted that using the word 'absence'—when he said that disaffection meant absence of affection—was not a 'fortunate word to use.' Justice Strachey went so far as to say that the 'word "absence" does not *accurately represent my meaning.*'[39] Justice Strachey knew that he had blundered. This apology was extraordinary, but it was extraordinarily disingenuous.

As Justice Strachey was nearing the end of his instructions to the jury in Tilak's trial, the defence had contended that Justice Strachey's formulation that 'disaffection means absence of affection,' was not supported by Chief Justice Petheram's interpretation of Section 124A in the *Bose* case from Calcutta. At that time, Justice Strachey had brushed aside this argument by observing that 'no good purpose would be served,' by revisiting the definition of disaffection set out by him. The exchange between Tilak's counsel and Justice Strachey is recorded thus:

> *Pugh:-* . . . Then there is a third point in regard to the Charge. It is a question as to the meaning of the term 'disaffection,' and this is of very great moment. . . . What I desire to put before the Court is as to the meaning of the term 'disaffection.' Your Lordship has put it that disaffection is simply want of affection, afterward explaining it by ill-will, dislike and enmity. The point, I take it, is that disaffection is the absence of affection. . . . The point I ask to have reserved is whether your Lordship's direction to the jury that disaffection means simply want of affection in any degree towards British rule or its representatives, is correct.
>
> STRACHEY, J.:- I held that disaffection was a common term embracing all these others.
>
> *Pugh:-* My point is that disaffection does not mean, as Sir Comer Petheram put it, 'the contrary of affection.'
>
> STRACHEY, J.:- I have considered the various points which Mr. Pugh has asked me to reserve. I am of the opinion that no good purpose would be served by reserving them, and I decline to reserve them.[40]

Now that Tilak had pointed out this obvious flaw to the Full Bench, Justice Strachey decided to offer a feeble apology for this obvious error. Justice Strachey's instructions to the jury had been patently wrong and he had been told so very clearly during the trial. But the damage had been done, because the jury had returned a verdict of guilty. Chief Justice Farran, writing the judgment for the Full Bench did not feel that Justice Strachey had made an error and declined Tilak a certificate to appeal his conviction in the Privy Council.[41]

Tilak and the Privy Council

Undeterred, Tilak filed an appeal before the Privy Council and sought special permission for his appeal to be heard. In the Privy Council, Herbert Henry Asquith, who would become the British Prime Minister in 1908, represented Tilak.[42] On 19 November 1897, the Privy Council heard arguments on Tilak's petition. The transcript of the arguments made by Asquith run into over twenty-five closely printed pages because Asquith had clearly found glaring errors in Justice Strachey's instructions to the jury.[43]

One of the first things which Asquith pointed out was the sterling role that Tilak played in combating the plague—something that Justice Strachey had completely disregarded. Asquith told the Privy Council that Tilak had led efforts in convincing the people in Poona to cooperate with the authorities who undertook measures to combat the plague. He had even set up a hospital. Asquith argued that although Tilak was critical of some of the measures that had been taken, he had done much to help fight the plague.[44]

Asquith also took 'grave exception'[45] to Justice Strachey's efforts to prejudice the jury against Tilak. Asquith told the Privy Council that Justice Strachey repeatedly referred to Rand's assassination as being a fact that had a material bearing on Tilak's prosecution, even though the prosecution brought nothing on record as evidence to link Tilak with the assassination. Yet, this reference was made for the singular purpose of biasing the jury against Tilak:

> In fact, he [Justice Strachey] had no right to take judicial notice of the fact that this murder had occurred, but to speak of a state of tension and excited feeling as having gone on for a considerable time, and culminated in a murder which took place a week after the publication of these articles, and to say that without really any evidence before the Court to justify the statement was, we contend, on behalf of the petitioner, very seriously to prejudice the case.[46]

Asquith was highly critical of Justice Strachey misdirecting the jury in Tilak's trial, when he wrongly instructed them about how Section 124A was to be understood. The point raised by Asquith was that whatever had been published in the *Kesari* which led to the sedition trial was at best a 'severe comment' on what Tilak believed were instances of 'social and political abuses.' In doing so, Tilak did not commit a crime because as a 'public journalist,' it was his right to publish such comments on government measures—a right recognized not only in British India but also in England.[47]

Asquith argued that to say that the offence of sedition was committed when a person by the power of their words leads another to dislike the government resulted in 'manifest injustice.'[48] The injustice perpetrated by Justice Strachey was that whatever balance Section 124A contained was upended, if the court only focused on how the criticism was worded rather than on the consequences which followed.

The correct method by which Section 124A had to be understood, according to Asquith's arguments, was that after examining the critical comment the court had to still judge whether the people to whom it was addressed intended to subvert the government. If that did not occur, then all critical comments against the government were positively saved by the Explanation to Section 124A.

This argument had immense intuitive appeal. According to Asquith it was incorrect to launch a prosecution for sedition unless it was shown that the writings led the reader to take steps where they actively tried to subvert public order.[49]

As he argued in the Privy Council, this was the only way in which Section 124A had to be interpreted, especially in light of the Explanation contained in it. In other words, if persons were prosecuted simply for expressing critical comment, then the liberty of speech and the freedom of the press could not possibly exist:

> The learned Judge has treated that as though it meant the moment you got a comment on specific and particular acts, if your comment is hostile and if the object of your comment is to make the people to whom it is addressed share your feelings, that would fall within the scope of the penal part of the clause.

Asquith then added:

> Surely the real, the essential thing about the explanation, that which gives it its real meaning and sting, is not the

use of the word 'measures,' but the words that follow. *The criterion suggested here is not the subject-matter criticised, but is the object of the criticism.*[50]

Asquith had presented the Privy Council with a solution to properly balance Section 124A so that critical comments against governmental action would not be stifled unnecessarily under the garb of sedition. As Asquith argued, sedition had to mean something more than 'disapproval or dislike.'[51] For this reason Asquith criticized Justice Strachey for having misdirected the jury, which had resulted in a legally unsustainable conviction.[52] Asquith's arguments had far-reaching implications because they balanced out the rigours of Section 124A by emphasizing the role played by the Explanation in the provision.

Asquith had persevered, but unsuccessfully. After hearing Asquith for some time, the judges of the Privy Council conferred and the Lord Chancellor in a short summary decision announced that the Privy Council had decided not to interfere with Tilak's conviction.[53]

Amba Prasad

The third major case on sedition came from Allahabad, in the case of *Queen-Empress v. Amba Prasad*.[54] This case was heard by a Full Bench of three judges led by Chief Justice Edge, who also authored the judgment. Prasad's case was a little different from the ones we have seen so far. Prasad was the proprietor and publisher of a newspaper, *Jami-ul-ulam*.

He was convicted for sedition by the Moradabad Sessions Court in 1897 for an article published in his newspaper.[55] When brought to trial, Prasad had pleaded guilty, but since the sentence imposed was eighteen months of rigorous imprisonment, Prasad appealed to the Allahabad High Court, hoping that this sentence would be reduced.[56]

Chief Justice Edge quickly recognized that a proper understanding of Section 124A had proved elusive chiefly because of the Explanation contained in that section.[57] 'If there be any difficulty as to the true meaning of Section 124A of the Indian Penal Code,' said Chief Justice Edge, 'it is caused by the Explanation which forms part of that section.'[58] But he also acknowledged that the welter of cases on Section 124A, including *Bose's* and *Tilak's*, had all struggled to accord a coherent meaning to the word 'disaffection.' So Chief Justice Edge took it upon himself to present a synthesis of all the different views that had been taken.[59]

'[F]eelings of hatred, dislike, ill-will, enmity or hostility towards the Government,' Chief Justice Edge declared, were cognate words for 'disaffection,' and that ultimately what has to be seen is whether the inclination to obey the government is affected or not. But Chief Justice Edge also decided to give Section 124A his own spin. For the purposes of Section 124A, held the Chief Justice, disaffection really meant 'disloyalty.'[60]

Now, yet another form of disaffection was introduced—disloyalty—which was unsupported by the text of Section 124A. What this also showed was that, in the years since Section 124A was on the statute book, not a single court could clearly say what really constituted 'disaffection.' And, because disaffection had a nebulous meaning, no one could objectively identify when the lines of permissible speech and expression were crossed.

Chief Justice Edge also used this opportunity to drive another nail in the coffin of free speech. When it came to sedition, it was immaterial what the speaker intended when he said or wrote something. It was inconsequential whether or not the words had a ring of truth to them, and it was equally inconsequential whether the speech or writing could have in fact led to the excitement of disaffection.[61]

This was an audacious declaration. The level of looseness that Chief Justice Edge attained when it came to judging whether sedition had been committed was an achievement in itself. Now there was no legal requirement to see whether the seditious material had some impact on those who came into contact with it. But there was one final blow yet to come.

When the High Court reviewed the trial court record, Chief Justice Edge declared that Prasad had rightly pleaded guilty to the charge that he had published seditious articles. Otherwise, the *'only possible defence open to him was that of insanity'*.[62] What this meant was that once it was alleged by the prosecution that an article in a publication was seditious, there was no scope to defend oneself by arguing that the intent was altogether different, that the recipient of the material was not excited to harbour disaffection, and that the seditious speech or writings did not result in any disorder.

The *only defence available*—and this is important and merits re-emphasis—was to plead that one was *insane* at the time one said or wrote something which was allegedly seditious. If one was remotely within one's senses, there could be no escape from conviction.

A Delayed Start

Although sedition entered the IPC in 1870, the major cases on sedition did not occur until the close of the nineteenth century. One explanation for this may be that from the time the British

Crown assumed paramountcy in India in 1858, the British administration in India embarked on a series of experiments to control the press.

As we saw, in the aftermath of the Revolt of 1857, Lord Canning had enacted the Gagging Act. Although the Act was in force for only a year, the passage of the law had caused widespread discontent because, along with the local press, even the English press felt stifled by the Act. Even those most sympathetic to the British cause had termed it as nothing short of 'a garrotte [sic].'[63]

For some time thereafter, the British administration contemplated starting their own government newspaper in order to put forth the official version of events, but that project was not seriously pursued.[64] Then, in 1867, the Press and Registration of Books Act was brought into force in order to regulate printing presses, newspapers as well as books.[65] But this law was not able to fully deal with publications which the British thought contained seditious material.[66] Incidentally, this law remains in force even today, which is why in a newspaper we see the details of the editor and of where it is published.

By the 1870s, the press had grown at a rapid clip and over 150 papers were in publication all over India, which cumulatively enjoyed an impressive readership. Intent on curbing the criticism that the British administration was subjected to in the press but hoping to avoid the mistakes of the past, the Viceroy, Lord Lytton, brought forth the Vernacular Press Act in 1878.

The Act began by proclaiming that the local press, dubbed as the press which published in 'Oriental languages,'[67] had been publishing material which was 'likely to excite disaffection'[68] against the British administration. Since these publications were read by 'large numbers of ignorant and unintelligent persons,'[69] it became essential to empower the authorities to 'control . . . such publication.'[70]

It created a layer of regulations where publishers could be asked to execute a bond and made to promise that they would not publish anything which was, for instance, 'likely to excite disaffection.' Moreover, publishers in some circumstances had to obtain prior permission and have the material vetted before it could be published.[71] This was nothing but blatant censorship of the press. If any publisher published anything which the Act did not allow, the entire capital of the publisher stood forfeited.[72]

Since English publications fell outside the ambit of this Act, quick thinking was resorted to by the vernacular press. *Amrita Bazar Patrika*, a popular Bengali publication which was supposed to be the main target of the Vernacular Press Act, converted itself into an English publication to ensure they were beyond the reach of the law. The Act had other effects, such as the founding of *The Hindu*, in 1878, which began as a weekly English newspaper, in the Madras Presidency and quickly acquired an excellent reputation.[73]

The Vernacular Press Act rocked public opinion and the matter swiftly reached the British Parliament. In his speech of 23 July 1878 in the House of Commons, Gladstone, the great defender of the liberty of the press, denounced the Act as creating a noxious class distinction between the vernacular press and the English press, because something could be said in English but not in the local languages.[74] Finally, Lord Ripon, who was Viceroy from 1880 to 1884, repealed the Vernacular Press Act in 1882.[75]

Another experiment was launched in 1891, when the British administration issued a notification stipulating that nothing could be published without the prior permission of the 'Political Agent.' To contravene this order meant that the publisher could be banished. The Indian National Congress, which had only recently been founded, strongly denounced this particular notification.[76] It was in this background that Section 124A of the IPC was pressed into service in the 1890s, since the other experiments of the past had been short-lived.[77]

Reconstructing Sedition

In the years in which Section 124A was applied, the courts had thrown up a mixed basket of results. Towards the end of the nineteenth century, the British government in India realized that there was one certainty when it came to Section 124A—not a single court had been able to provide a clear-cut definition of disaffection.

What the courts had provided, however, were a bewildering array of words describing feelings which meant disaffection (absence of affection, hatred, enmity, contempt and disloyalty). In order to coalesce all these varying interpretations in one place, the British government decided to entirely recast Section 124A.

A further impetus for reconstructing the law on sedition came from the fact that the solitary Explanation to Section 124A, which provided the circumstances in which the expression of disapprobation against the government would not be treated as sedition, had frustrated many plans for prosecuting newspapers for sedition.

Due to the complicated wording of the Explanation, the government as well as the advisors were often unclear as to whether the publications in question were saved by the Explanation to Section 124A. As a result, not many sedition trials took place after 1870.[78]

On 21 December 1897, M.D. Chalmers, a member of the Council of the Governor-General of India, moved a bill to amend the IPC and the Code of Criminal Procedure.[79] In that bill, Chalmers put forth an entirely new provision to replace Section 124A.

When moving this amendment, Chalmers told the Council that experience had now taught the government that there was a need to restate the law on sedition in clearer terms. Macaulay's draft on sedition, which James Fitzjames Stephen had so assiduously fought for, was not considered a 'model of clear legislative drafting.'[80] 'When the law is codified,' Chalmers told the Council, 'the codes should be as explicit as possible.'[81] Indeed, Chalmers went so far as to say that after reading the arguments for the defence in Tilak's trial, it was clear that the law on sedition could be 'expressed in clearer and less equivocal terms.'[82]

To that end, Chalmers unveiled a brand-new Section 124A. In one fell swoop, Macaulay's utilitarian project of expressing the law in clear terms was not only condemned by the British administration but also stood entirely unravelled. Macaulay had made a complete mess, and Chalmers proclaimed that he would clean up that mess by recasting Section 124A.

Drawing on the decisions of the three high courts (Calcutta, Bombay and Allahabad), Chalmers put into the new Section 124A language which spelt out that speech, writings and expressions that brought the government into hatred and contempt, apart from exciting disaffection, would be treated as sedition. To clarify the meaning of disaffection, Chalmers added a new Explanation. Inspired by Chief Justice Edge's decision in the *Amba Prasad* case, Chalmers defined disaffection to include 'disloyalty and all feelings of enmity and ill-will.'[83]

A second Explanation was also added. It stipulated that discussion of governmental measures, in order to seek a change in them, which were not accompanied by efforts to bring the government into 'hatred, contempt or disaffection,' would not count as sedition.[84]

This new version of Section 124A was meant to put curbs on the liberty of the press, and this was made clear by Chalmers. He told the Council that to control the spread of seditious writings, the government had pondered on whether to revise Section 124A and amend it to make clear the law on sedition or to enact a law along the lines of the Vernacular Press Act of 1878.[85]

The government opted for the former because they wanted a strong law that would apply to all publications and not just to those published in Indian languages. Unlike the past experiments, the law on sedition would have a degree of permanence to ensure that it endured. Nonetheless, Section 124A was still treated as a benevolent step. 'Every man is free to speak, write and print whatever he pleases,' Chalmers said in the Council, but warned that one must always remain 'within the law.'[86]

There was another important reason behind the overhaul of Section 124A, and for doing away with Macaulay's confusing version on sedition.

Chalmers wanted to ensure that what was punished was seditious intention and not the actual act of sedition. As we saw, in England when prosecutions were launched for sedition, courts insisted on some evidence that something harmful or disorderly ensued because of the seditious speech or writings. This was not to be the case in India. Chalmers thus proclaimed that it was seditious intention that was made the crime of sedition under Section 124A. And seditious intent, just like in England, had to be presumed. As Chalmers saw it:

> In England, words spoken or written without seditious intent constitute a criminal offence, and the intent

is presumed from the natural meaning of the words themselves, without reference to the actual feelings of the person who used them. In other words, the law applies a purely objective test.[87]

In fact, Chalmers praised the high courts for their decisions in which they had consistently resisted the idea that seditious intention was not to be an offence only due to the fact that 'resort to actual violence' had not been propagated in the speeches and writings in question.[88]

However, whatever Chalmers said about Section 124A was not to be treated as dispositive when it came to its interpretation. He clarified this in his address on 18 February 1898, when the Council was debating the new Section 124A.[89] He stated:

> To discover what the law is, when its meaning is contested, you must look at the language of the Act itself, and, if that language has been interpreted by the Courts, you must look to the interpretation of the Courts.[90]

During the proceedings in the Council on 18 February 1898, Chalmers agreed to add a third Explanation to Section 124A, which would clarify that if one expressed disapprobation against any governmental measure, that would be permissible so long as disaffection, hatred or contempt was not excited.

The addition of this third Explanation, seemingly expressed in simpler language what 'disapprobation of governmental measures' meant. This addition was evidently made to allay the fear that journalists and publishers would be hounded. But it proved inadequate in calming the restive voices in the Council.[91]

Allan Arthur, a member of the Council, pointed out that it was possible for one to excite contempt against the government, but still remain loyal. If contradictions such as these were not corrected, no one could really believe that Section 124A would be directed only against extreme forms of seditious speeches and writings.[92]

Another member, Gangadhar Rao Madhav Chitnavis too believed that it was impossible to rule out situations in which fair criticism was treated as sedition.[93] The Maharaja of Darbhanga, a newly elected member in the Council, suggested that Section 124A must contain the word 'intentionally,' in that the offence of sedition is committed only when the person intends to excite disaffection. Without the requisite intent, it was the ordinary law of defamation that ought to apply.[94]

When Chalmers had spoken in the Council, he took an odd example to defend the law on sedition. He had likened speech and expression in India to be as dangerous as smoking a cigar near the gunpowder room in a fort. This alarmist conception, in Chalmers's view, justified the need to crush anyone who spoke of the government in less than affectionate terms.[95]

This example by Chalmers, however, was utterly self-defeating. What it suggested was that only such action must be punished which results in an immediate and explosive consequence. Taken to its logical conclusion, then, only such speech and expression ought to be punished, under Section 124A, when the excitement of disaffection resulted in immediate and inevitable violent reactions. Logically, every sort of speech or writing exciting disaffection could not fall within the definition of sedition.

This fallacy in his argument neither occurred to Chalmers nor did it detain him. Instead, he confidently proclaimed that all instances of speech and expression exciting disaffection ought to be punished. 'Language may be tolerated in England which it is unsafe to tolerate in India,' Chalmers told the Council, 'because in India it is apt to be transformed into action instead of passing off as harmless gas.'[96] The sinister design which informed Chalmers's new Section 124A was to banish all Indians from the public sphere so far as their desire to express anything critical against the British government in India was concerned.

Ananda Charalu, a member of the Council, took Chalmers to task for his patronizing outlook. This illustration and line of reasoning visibly irked Charalu, because what Chalmers had done was designate the whole of India as a tinderbox which was ready to explode any moment. '[T]he bulk of the population who are said to be ignorant, credulous and highly impressionable,' said Charalu, 'constitute his inflammable material.'[97] In Charalu's view, with this outlook, there would no place which could be treated as a free space where one could give voice to their feelings. As he told the Council:

> The result then is this. Public speakers and public writers are gravely told to shun the haunts of men and the people at large and publish their utterances where there will be none to hear or read or none will care to hear or read. Is this not, in plain and honest English, a virtual denial of the right, by piling up imaginary fears and fancying powder magazines where none exist?[98]

Many others too expressed their disquiet with Section 124A, but after a spirited and heated debate, the Council, on 18 February 1898, voted in favour of it.[99] By Section 4 of the Indian Penal Code (Amendment) Act, 1898, the new Section 124A entered the picture.[100]

3

Wounded Vanity

———•———

CHALMERS'S SECTION 124A EVIDENTLY TREATED ONLY SEDITIOUS intention as the offence of sedition. But Chalmers had told the Council that ultimately it would be the court's interpretation, and not his views, which had to control the meaning of sedition in the IPC.

In the 1900s, the new Section 124A generated two lines of decisions. On the one hand were a set of cases in which the judiciary treated anything which spoke of the government in less than favourable terms as sedition. In these cases, the high courts followed the triumvirate of the *Bose–Tilak–Prasad* decisions in order to calibrate Section 124A as a powerful tool to silence anyone who may question the sovereignty of British imperial power.

The British government in India *was* the government established by law. And although disputing the provenance of this claim to sovereignty would become the focus of the nationalist movement, anyone who so much as expressed a whisper of some sort of change was guilty of sedition. The relationship created was that of a superior British government with its subjects—the people of India. In doing so, the courts used Section 124A as a tool to protect and preserve the sovereignty of the British government in India.[1]

In the second line of cases that emerged, the judiciary tolerated harsh criticism of the government. This was accompanied by a move towards reading Section 124A as not punishing seditious intent, but as a provision which punished sedition only when there was a tendency of violent outbreaks ensuing because of seditious speech or expression.

Such cases allowed the so-called seditious speech and writings to pass of as 'harmless gas.' These two lines of cases sometimes occurred in parallel, with a moment of time being reached when the liberal line of cases actually redefined what sedition meant.

Sedition and Preservation of Sovereignty

Emblematic of the first set of cases was a decision of the Bombay High Court in the *Bhaskar Bhopatkar* case.[2] Bhopatkar printed a paper called *Bhala*. In 1905, the paper carried an article titled 'A Durbar in Hell,' which described a fictional European ruler who was to choose the cruellest successor he could find. For this article, a prosecution under Section 124A was launched against Bhopatkar.[3]

In his instructions to the jury, Justice Batty pointed out that disaffection is a feeling which is really used to 'express a feeling which can only exist between the ruler and the ruled.'[4] In fact, this was such an obvious proposition that he cautioned the jury by saying, 'You do not need to be reminded that it is of the essence of Government in India that it is British Government and British Rule.'[5]

Establishing Section 124A as a means of protecting British sovereignty achieved many important goals. It legitimized the prosecution of those who used strong language against the government. It emboldened courts to do away with ordinary safeguards, by insisting that the publisher of a journal would be guilty of sedition even if the published article was not authored by them. Justice Batty emphatically instructed the jury that the defence that '[t]his is not my own work' was not a defence which could be deployed by a publisher in their trial for sedition.[6]

It was no longer necessary for the prosecution to prove the charge. In a reversal of normal law, the burden of proof was entirely shifted on to the defendant to prove that they were not guilty. The prosecution was unburdened from proving the charge of sedition beyond a reasonable doubt.

There was an obvious tautological fallacy in Justice Batty's instructions. If one had to make an attempt to excite disaffection, then it was necessary to have the intent of doing so. By that logic, one who only published something which carried seditious material could not have made an attempt to excite disaffection, without the prosecution establishing that the publisher had the requisite intent. But Justice Batty reversed the burden of proof, and it no longer became the prosecution's job to establish whether the charge of Section 124A could stand against the publisher.

The demolition of such safeguards was necessary, if not paramount, to obtain swift convictions for sedition. And finally, the position of all Indians as subjects was sanctified by the high court by infantilizing the people as those who were possessed of an excitable disposition, were bereft of reason and not gifted with the maturity of temperament, which were the hallmarks of the

British. Essential then, anything mildly critical of British rule was to be treated as potentially setting off a revolutionary firestorm in India.[7]

Tilak's Second Trial

The preservation of sovereignty was also a theme in Bal Gangadhar Tilak's second trial for sedition.[8] In 1908, Tilak was tried for sedition in the Bombay High Court for certain articles published in his newspaper, *Kesari*. On 12 May 1908, the *Kesari* published an article titled 'The Country's Misfortune,' and on 9 June 1908, the *Kesari* published an article titled 'The Remedies Are Not Lasting.' The call for granting swaraj to India appeared in the first article where it noted that the 'demand for *Swarajya*' was now becoming a battle cry among the people.[9]

The general tenor of the articles was that the British government were engaging in extremely oppressive behaviour such as enacting arbitrary laws which banned public meetings. As a result of this, the articles warned that the people of India were restive and that they could no longer silently endure these indignities.

The backdrop of these articles was a failed assassination attempt. In the town of Muzaffarpur,[10] Khudiram Bose had planned to assassinate Douglas Kingford, a magistrate who had acquired notoriety in the eyes of the public. Bose decided to bomb the railway car which was carrying Kingford. But on that fateful day, the railway carriage in which he threw the bomb was carrying not Kingford but the wife and child of Pringle Kennedy, a barrister. The articles in the *Kesari* alluded to this and noted that although Bose himself had been remorseful of his actions, no one could now deny that the people of India were willing to take extreme steps in order to fight the oppressive regime of the British government in India.[11]

Section 124A's role in preserving British sovereignty hovered over the trial. Tilak enjoyed the rare distinction of being tried under the old Section 124A as well as its new version which entered the IPC in 1898. But, this case was also ironic.

The judge who was trying Tilak's case, Justice Davar, had been Tilak's defence counsel in his first sedition trial in 1897, before Justice Strachey in the Bombay High Court. Now the roles were reversed. Tilak's former defence lawyer would try him for sedition. Incidentally, Davar was also the lawyer who defended Bhopatkar in the Bombay High Court before Justice Batty.

In his instructions to the jury, Justice Davar channelled the preservation of sovereignty argument with aplomb. He told the jury that only those who hate the 'good Government of the Country' can resort to acts of violence and murder. And, therefore, 'if they had proper feelings,' Indians would be a peaceful lot.[12] This was tied in with Justice Davar's idea that it was the 'bounden duty' of those who were subjects of the imperial Crown to submit themselves to the law.[13]

Section 124A, Justice Davar reminded the jury, was agnostic about consequences. It was immaterial whether violence or rebellion had ensued as a result of the seditious utterances. All that mattered was whether an attempt was made to excite disaffection, enmity and hatred against the government.[14]

Justice Davar's most pernicious contribution came in completely eliminating truth as a defence to a charge of sedition. Once the prosecution alleged that a publication harmed the good feelings that people had for the government, then whether the article was entirely libellous or entirely true was immaterial for the purpose of conviction. It was not for the jury to decide whether

Tilak spoke truth to power. All that mattered was whether the government's reputation was affected.[15] 'Whether the statements in the articles are true or not,' said Justice Davar, 'it is not for you to judge.'[16]

One of the articles Tilak had published, and for which he was on trial, had demanded swaraj for Indians. The article had warned that if the people were denied swaraj, some may resort to hostile acts to achieve it.[17] Interestingly, neither Justice Davar nor Tilak were strangers to calls for swaraj being treated as sedition.

In Tilak's first sedition trial in 1897 before Justice Strachey in the Bombay High Court, one of the articles in question spoke of attaining swaraj, which in the transcript of the judgment of the Bombay High Court was translated as '[l]iterally, "one's own government", native rule.'[18] In fact, it is Tilak who coined the slogan, 'Swaraj is my birthright and I will have it.'[19]

Tilak's fight to attain swaraj for India had put him in the cross hairs of Section 124A, and in 1897 Justice Davar, then as Tilak's lawyer, had defended him against the charge of sedition. But now, in 1908, as a justice of the Bombay High Court, it revolted him that Tilak could insist on swaraj, a demand which he now deemed seditious. Since Tilak continued to raise this demand, a heavy penalty had to be inflicted.[20] The jury returned a verdict of guilty by a majority of seven (Europeans) to two (Indians).[21] Since it was not a unanimous verdict, Justice Davar had to decide whether he agreed with the majority. He ruled that he did.[22]

At this moment, Tilak addressed the court in a short speech which since then has attained iconic status:

> All that I wish to say is that in spite of the verdict of the Jury I still maintain that I am innocent. There are higher powers that rule the destinies of men and nations and

I think it may be the will of Providence that the cause I represent may be benefited more by my suffering than by my pen and tongue.[23]

In sentencing Tilak, Justice Davar accused him of having a 'diseased mind' and a 'perverted mind' which produced articles 'seething with sedition.'[24] He thought it would be a good thing if Tilak was made to leave the country for some time and thus sentenced him to transportation for six years.[25] To serve out his sentence, Tilak was transported to Mandalay (in present-day Myanmar).[26]

Remarkably, Justice Davar invoked Tilak's sedition trial from 1897 to accuse him of having learnt nothing. 'Ten years ago,' he told Tilak, 'you were convicted.'[27] But in the decade which followed Tilak's first conviction for sedition, his resolve to fight for India's interests and to hold the British government accountable had only strengthened.

This did not please Justice Davar. 'Your hatred of the ruling class,' Justice Davar said to Tilak, 'has not disappeared during these ten years.'[28] Justice Davar could not help himself when he condemned Tilak's style of journalism as a 'curse on the country.'[29]

Tilak's trial and conviction, and Justice Davar's unrestrained attack on Tilak, proved politically calamitous for the British government. Upon Tilak's conviction, John Morley, the then Secretary of State for India, shot off a letter to the Governor of Bombay, Lord Sydenham, chiding him for initiating the prosecution, because with the trial Tilak's stature had only increased in the eyes of the people.[30]

Interestingly, the short speech delivered by Tilak upon his conviction lives on today in a physical form. In the 1950s, the Bombay High Court unveiled a tablet outside the courtroom in the High Court where Tilak had been tried. Inscribed on the tablet are the words Tilak had spoken upon being convicted for sedition. The tablet was unveiled by Chief Justice M.C. Chagla.[31]

Gandhi's Sedition Trial

The reliance on Section 124A as a means of enhancing the appeal of the sovereignty of the British government in India took centre stage in Mahatma Gandhi's trial for sedition. In his trial, Gandhi presented a masterly critique of sedition.

In 1922, Gandhi was prosecuted for sedition for three of his articles published in *Young India*, a paper of which Gandhi was the editor. The articles—'Tampering with Loyalty,' 'The Puzzle and Its Solution' and 'Shaking the Manes'—were published between September 1921 and February 1922. News of Gandhi's arrest for sedition travelled far and wide.

The headline in the 11 March 1922 edition of *The New York Times* screamed, 'GANDHI ARRESTED ON CHARGE OF SEDITION.'[32] According to the news report, it was the 'London newspapers' that exerted enormous pressure and consistently called for Gandhi's arrest.[33]

Gandhi's trial took place in Ahmedabad at the Shahi Baug Circuit House and before Judge Broomfield.[34] Gandhi was tried along with Shankarlal Banker, the publisher of *Young India*.[35]

In fact, even before the charges were read out, Gandhi proclaimed that he would be more than willing to plead guilty to the charge of exciting disaffection against the British government in India. As the court went through the preliminary steps of examining the evidence and the witnesses in order to commit the case to trial, Gandhi proclaimed:

I simply wish to state that when the proper time comes, I shall plead guilty so far as disaffection towards the Government is concerned. It is quite true that I am Editor of the *Young India* and that the articles read in my presence were written by me, and the proprietors and publishers had permitted me to control the whole policy of the paper.[36]

Before Judge Broomfield, Gandhi's trial commenced at 12 noon on 18 March 1922.[37] Sir Thomas Strangman, the Advocate General of Bombay, was deputed to lead the prosecution even though Gandhi himself decided not to avail the services of a lawyer.[38] Strangman had already cut his teeth in trying cases of sedition. He had been part of the legal team of the prosecution in Tilak's first sedition trial in 1897 in the Bombay High.

The moment the charge of committing sedition for the articles in question was read out, Gandhi as well as Banker pleaded guilty.[39] 'I plead guilty,' Gandhi told Judge Broomfield, 'to all the charges.'[40]

Gandhi's trial was not without its share of theatrics. Ordinarily, when a person admits to committing a crime, a full-fledged trial is no longer required. But Strangman was of a sporting type, and despite Gandhi saying he was guilty of exciting disaffection against the British, Strangman insisted that Judge Broomfield nevertheless try the case against Gandhi. Strangman felt this way because he believed that the crime Gandhi was accused of had a serious impact on public interest.[41]

Judge Broomfield was unimpressed with Strangman's pleas. He felt that once Gandhi had pleaded guilty there was no need for a trial and the court could straight away decide the punishment that should to be imposed. At the end of this theatrical episode, it appears that 'Gandhi smiled at this decision.'[42]

Strangman had clearly wanted to use these proceedings not to try the case against Gandhi but to launch a political attack against him, for Strangman's accusations focused on alleging how Gandhi constantly questioned the authority of the British government and encouraged others to do so.[43]

Gandhi, in turn, used the trial to launch a blistering political attack against the British government. Gandhi had a brilliant mind and knew that his trial had generated immense public interest. That was the reason why when Judge Broomfield asked Gandhi if he would like to simply place his defence statement on record (perhaps to avoid it becoming public knowledge), Gandhi deftly answered that he would do so 'as soon as I finish reading it.'[44] And, just as Justice Davar did in Tilak's case in 1908, Judge Broomfield allowed Gandhi to address the court before he was to be sentenced. In this statement, Gandhi delivered one of the greatest orations on the futility of the law on sedition:

> Section 124A under which I am happily charged is perhaps the *prince among the political sections of the Indian Penal Code designed to suppress the liberty of the citizen.* Affection cannot be manufactured or regulated by law. If one has no affection for a person or system one should be free to give the fullest expression to his disaffection, so long as he does not contemplate, promote or incite violence. . . . I know that some of the most loved of India's patriots have been convicted under it. I consider it a privilege, therefore, to be charged under that section.[45]

Gandhi then asked Judge Broomfield to inflict on him the severest punishment under the law:

> Non-violence implies voluntary submission to the penalty for non-co-operation with evil. I am here, therefore, to invite and submit cheerfully to the highest penalty that can be inflicted upon me for what in law is a deliberate crime and what appears to me to be the highest duty of a citizen. The only course to you, the Judge, is either to resign your post and thus dissociate yourself from evil, if you feel that the law you are called upon to administer is an evil and that in reality I am innocent; or to inflict on me the severest penalty if you believe that the system and the law you are assisting to administer are good for the people of this country and that my activity is therefore injurious to the public weal.[46]

Gandhi had decided to throw down the gauntlet, and in the face of it Judge Broomfield decided to perform and not abdicate his duty. Judge Broomfield sentenced Gandhi to imprisonment for six years (two years for each article in question), which Gandhi cheerfully accepted.[47]

Yet Judge Broomfield appeared to be a reluctant servant of the British government[48] and he felt the need to tell Gandhi that although it was his duty to sentence him, he fervently hoped that the British government would release him. If that were to happen, Judge Broomfield told Gandhi, 'no one will be better pleased than I.'[49] The publisher and printer of *Young India*, Shankarlal Banker, who was also tried for sedition along with Gandhi, was sentenced to a year in jail.[50]

As a parting statement and to show how 'honoured' he felt to be clubbed with nationalist leaders who had faced prosecution under Section 124A in the years gone by, Gandhi told Judge Broomfield, '[s]ince you have done me the honour of recalling the trial of . . . Tilak, I just want to say that I consider it to be the proudest privilege and honour to be associated with his name.'[51] Gandhi also thanked Judge Broomfield for performing what he saw as his duty and congratulated him by telling him, 'I could not have expected greater courtesy.'[52] Thus ended Gandhi's sedition trial in 1922.[53]

India in Bondage

Section 124A and the preservation of British sovereignty was also a theme in the *India in Bondage* case.[54] This was a rather unusual case.

Sutherland, an American, had authored a book titled *India in Bondage: Her Right to Freedom*, which was published in America. That book was printed in Calcutta by one Sajanikanta Das in 1928. The book spoke about the pitiable plight of India and advocated that it was high time that Britain conferred dominion status on India.[55]

In August 1929, the Governor-General ordered that all copies of this book must be seized. The order was issued under Section 99A of the Code of Criminal Procedure (1898), which authorized the Governor-General to seek the forfeiture of books which contained seditious material. Against the Governor's order, Das filed an application before the Calcutta High Court. Incidentally, Sutherland was not the first person to write on the manner in which Britain had drained India of its wealth and resources.

The 'Grand Old Man of India' and one of the founders of the Indian National Congress, Dadabhai Naoroji, had written extensively of how Britain had caused wanton economic destruction in India. In his landmark work, *Poverty and Un-British Rule in India*, published in 1901, Naoroji began by writing that although India had partially benefited from British rule, on the whole the manner in which the British governed India was 'destructive and despotic to the Indians and un-British and suicidal to Britain.'[56]

Naoroji painstakingly documented how 'every farthing of expenditure'[57] for British war efforts across the world were 'exacted from the Indian people. Britain has spent nothing.'[58] Naoroji was by no means alone in thinking along these lines. To support his thesis, Naoroji quoted from James Mill's *History of India*, in which Mill had said:

> It is an exhausting drain upon the resources of the country, the issue of which is replaced by no reflex; it is an extraction of the life blood from the veins of national industry which no subsequent introduction of nourishment is furnished to restore.[59]

This was the setting and the background in which the proceedings played out. In the High Court, Das's lawyer offered interesting arguments. It was argued that it was not 'sedition, if the "form," but not the "fact" of Government is brought into contempt.'[60] It was also argued that if Justice Strachey's formulation from *Tilak's* case was treated as the baseline, then '[i]t is an intellectual impossibility to criticise the Government in all suavity. Freedom includes freedom to think and speak.'[61] All of these contentions were rejected.

The High Court noted that the book in question contained passages which blamed the British for every ill that India suffered. It also contained prose which advocated that Britain must retain a connection with India, but that India's status must be that of an equal partner, such as in the relationship between Britain and Australia.⁶²

If the entire book were read as a whole, it did not make the government the object of hatred or enmity only, but advocated for change in the political equation between Britain and India. And this is how the book ought to have been read, because almost all the past cases on Section 124A had stressed on the fact that the seditious writing in question must be judged as a whole.⁶³

Here, however, the Calcutta High Court disavowed that approach. What weighed more with the High Court was the fact that large portions of the book in question had trenchantly criticized the ability of the British government to carry on its administration of India. The High Court paid more attention to those parts of the book which were critical of the British government in India to hold that such prose would undoubtedly excite disaffection against the British government, which in effect justified the forfeiture of all the printed copies of the book.⁶⁴

Mobilization

Mobilizing the peasantry in India was also treated as a challenge to the British government and an act of sedition. This was the theme in *Narayan Phadke's* case.⁶⁵ In 1939, the Bombay Tenancy Act and the Bombay Agriculture Debtors Relief Act were passed by the Bombay legislature, but were not brought into force.

With a view to impress upon the government to enact these two laws, Narayan Phadke launched a peasant movement in December 1939. He was prosecuted for sedition for some of the speeches he delivered in February–March 1940 and jailed for eight months with rigorous imprisonment.⁶⁶

What irked the Bombay High Court was that Phadke had in his speech portrayed the British government as one that only supported moneylenders and landlords. Phadke's speech was treated as seditious, now on a new ground: it was seditious for anyone to communicate the idea that the British government favoured one class of people over another. And suggesting that the British government harboured a preference for one class or group of people over another was tantamount to exciting disaffection against the British government.[67]

Blunting Sedition

At the time when the high courts in India were using Section 124A to punish those who questioned the sovereignty of the British government in India or its style of governance, there were also occasions when the courts moved to control the full reach of Section 124A.

The Morley–Minto Reforms was the moniker given to the Indian Councils Act of 1909. It was the brainchild of John Morley (the Secretary of State for India) and Lord Minto, the Governor-General of India. Gopal Krishna Gokhale, who was elected as the president of the Congress in 1906 and who led the 'moderate' section within the party, was instrumental in convincing John Morley to introduce some form of reform.[68]

The 1909 Act was passed by the British Parliament and was a measure to introduce reforms in lawmaking so as to provide Indians with greater representation in the Imperial Legislative Council, as well as in the councils in the various provinces. Although much of the power was still retained by the British administration, the reforms were only a small step towards allowing Indian representation in the legislature.[69]

Manmohan Ghose's Trial

In 1910, the Calcutta High Court handed down its decision in *Manmohan Ghose v. Emperor,* and here the High Court had to decide whether attacking the Morley–Minto Reforms ought to be treated as sedition.[70]

Ghose was the publisher of a newspaper, *Karmayogin*. In 1910, he was prosecuted for sedition for publishing, in December 1909, a letter by Aurobindo Ghose which trenchantly criticized the Morley–Minto Reforms. Manmohan Ghose's case reached the High Court because the trial court convicted him for sedition and sentenced him to six months of rigorous imprisonment.[71]

The High Court acquitted Ghose. Justice Holmwood and Justice Fletcher who heard the case adopted a stance to recalibrate Section 124A to allow the ventilation of grievances in strong language. Thus, when the Advocate General argued that the published letter in question doubted the motives behind the Morley–Minto Reforms and labelled them as lacking a 'genuine measure of constitutional progress,'[72] the High Court held that this was a legitimate expression of opinion, and that it was impossible to treat a political question about the motives of the Reform programme as an act of sedition.[73]

Indeed, the High Court broke new ground when it declared that terming legislation enacted by the British Parliament as 'monstrous and misbegotten' would not be sedition. As the High Court observed:

> The argument for the Crown is that the use of the words 'monstrous and misbegotten scheme,' as applied to the Reform Scheme hold the Government up to 'ridicule and vituperation.' But that does not appear to me to be

the natural consequences of these words. Doubtless the words are a strong condemnation of the Reform Scheme framed by the Government. The law, however, permits comments on actions of the Government provided they do not bring the Government into hatred or contempt or promote disloyalty. A statement that the Reform Scheme is monstrous and misbegotten, because it is not founded on democratic principles, is not by itself one that exceeds fair and reasonable comment.[74]

Indeed, the Advocate General had also pointed out that the letter in question had condemned the police and the judiciary, which were undoubtedly instrumentalities of the British government, as 'corrupt, unscrupulous, and partial.' The High Court, however, reasoned that the only grievance one could possibly have had to do with the choice of words.[75]

In fact, the article also contained statements exhorting the people to renew their pledge towards the swadeshi movement and withdraw support for any goods of foreign origin. Yet, this was viewed by the High Court as acceptable comment and treated as part of political speech and not as sedition.[76] As a result of this, Ghose was acquitted of the charge of sedition.

Tilak's Third Brush with Sedition

The issue of swaraj and self-governance once again made an appearance in Tilak's third case.[77] But this time Tilak was not prosecuted for sedition. Between May and June of 1916, Tilak had given a series of speeches on the issue of swaraj and Home Rule. These speeches were viewed as seditious, and therefore the magistrate, acting under Section 108 of the Code of Criminal Procedure (1898), asked Tilak to furnish a bond of good conduct.[78]

Tilak's case was heard by a Division Bench comprising Justices Batchelor and Shah, and in this case the Bombay High Court went in a different direction as compared to Tilak's previous encounters with sedition. Speaking to the people in Marathi about the slow pace of the Morley–Minto Reforms and advocating the cause for swaraj were not seditious subjects but, rather, they were legitimate political speeches.[79]

Remarkably, the High Court ruled that although Tilak may have used language which the court would not approve of, Tilak could only be guilty of 'bad taste or bad temper,' but it did not furnish any case for conviction under Section 124A.[80]

The High Court also made another remarkable observation. Tilak's speeches had been in Marathi, and in his speeches Tilak had proclaimed that the people of India were being kept in a position of 'slavery and servitude,' and that the British government in India was an 'alien Government looking mainly at its own interest.'[81]

However, the High Court ruled that these statements were part of an oration in which the general theme was on the nature of government that is suited for India and thus, taken together, the speeches were saved because they were *bona fide* political criticism.[82]

The High Court had essentially decided to take a broad and mature view of political critique. So much so that Tilak's accusations in his long speeches that the British had kept 'Indians in a position of slavery and servitude,' and that the British government was an 'alien government'[83] obsessed with self-preservation were all treated to be within the realm of 'fair political criticism.'[84]

Indeed, in the past, Tilak had been prosecuted for sedition for demanding swaraj. But remarkably now, Tilak's speeches in which he demanded swaraj were not seen through the lens of sedition but as a legitimate part of the political process which demanded political reform. Justice Batchelor who wrote the judgment for the Division Bench sided with Tilak:

> Now first, as to the general aim of the speaker, it is, I think reasonably clear that in contending for what he describes as *swarajya* his object is to attain for Indians an increased and gradually increasing share of political authority and to subject the administration of the country to the control of the people or peoples of India. I am of the opinion that the advocacy of such an object is not *per se* an infringement of the law, nor has the learned Advocate General contended otherwise.[85]

This was a remarkable conclusion. Going by the past cases, these very same words would have been treated as seditious in Tilak's sedition trial in 1897 and 1908. Indeed, in Tilak's first trial in 1897, Justice Strachey had taken a dim view of the people of India, labelling them an excitable lot because of which a much stricter standard had to be applied when judging political writings and speeches which were in the local languages.

Thus, the remotest suggestion that the British government was incompetent was treated as seditious. In 1919, however, the High Court took a broader view of the permissible limits of political speech and political mobilization advocating a new form of governance.

The Wounded Vanity of Governments

The most revolutionary reading of Section 124A occurred in 1942 in the *Niharendu Dutt Majumdar* case,[86] where the Federal Court cemented the position that Section 124A could only punish such speech and expression which led to the incitement of public disorder.

The Federal Court was created by the Government of India Act, 1935. It was designated as a court which was superior to all the high courts. Under the scheme of the 1935 Act, appeals from all high courts would have to be preferred to the Federal Court, and only thereafter could be taken further in appeal to the Privy Council.[87] Specifically, every court in India would be bound by the decision of the Federal Court (as well as of the Privy Council).[88]

This was in contrast to the previous system, where the decisions of the various high courts did not really have any precedential value when it came to courts located in other provinces. For the first time, the Federal Court was created as the apex judicial body in India, with the Federal Court's Chief Justice designated as the Chief Justice of India. As a result of this, its decisions were unencumbered by what had been declared as the law by the high courts in India. This would assume enormous importance when it came to the meaning of sedition.

Incidentally, the *Majumdar* case did not involve Section 124A of the IPC but the Defence of India Rules. Under Rule 34 of those Rules, one form of prejudicial acts prohibited were those which 'bring into hatred or contempt or excite disaffection' towards either the British Crown or the representatives of the British government in India. Majumdar had been convicted because he had fallen foul of Rule 34.[89] He had spoken at a public meeting in Calcutta, and what had irked the government was his assertion in the speech that the Governor of Bengal and the government establishment were complicit in inflaming communal disharmony.[90]

The decision of the Federal Court was handed down by a bench of three judges headed by Chief Justice Maurice Gwyer, who also authored the decision.[91] It is a decision that has been lauded by H.M. Seervai as a 'brilliant and masterly exposition of the law of sedition.'[92]

Unlike Chief Justice Petheram in the *Bose* case in 1891, the Federal Court did not have a tabula rasa before it when it came to the proper meaning of sedition. What it had was a long line of decisions which had taken a rather narrow view of what could be said and expressed against the British government in India.

Although there were a few cases which took a broader view of what constituted sedition, those cases were far and few between. So, the task which lay before the Federal Court was to devise a way to justify why the weight of past precedent, like the *Bose-Tilak-Prasad* cases, did not encumber the Federal Court's broader understanding of sedition.

What the Federal Court did was categorize all the past cases on sedition in India as creatures of their time, and not as cases whose decisions retained an enduring appeal:

> Hence many judicial decisions in particular cases which were no doubt correct at the time when they were given may well be inapplicable to the circumstances of today. The time is long past when the mere criticism of governments was sufficient to constitute sedition, for it is recognized that the right to utter honest and reasonable criticism is a source of strength to a community rather than a weakness.[93]

With this, the way was now clear for the Federal Court to narrow the field in which Section 124A could operate.

The 1940s were a time of great churning, and this was something that the Federal Court was mindful of. The most important nationalist movement which occurred was the launch of the Quit India Movement in August 1942, five years before India won independence. The effect of this movement was so strong that the British administration treated it as nothing short of the 'gravest threat to British rule in India since the revolt of 1857.'[94]

Cognizant of the weight of history and the winds of change which were blowing (although no specific instance was mentioned), Chief Justice Gwyer was forthright in recognizing that the 'time is long past when the mere criticism of governments was sufficient to constitute sedition.'[95]

The first move which Chief Justice Gwyer made for truncating the scope of Section 124A was to elevate the importance of speech as improving the political process. When it came to political speech, the Federal Court placed greater emphasis on the idea that it was well-nigh impossible to always speak of the government in favourable terms.[96]

Section 124A could not touch any speech or expression which criticized the government, even if it called for a transformation in the political system itself.[97] As the Federal Court declared:

> Criticism of an existing system of government is not excluded, nor even the expression of a desire for a different system altogether. The language of s. 124A of the Penal Code if read literally, even with the explanations attached to it, would suffice to make a surprising number of persons in this country guilty of sedition; but no one supposes that it is to be read in this literal sense.[98]

The second move which Chief Justice Gwyer made was to treat sedition as an offence only when some consequences ensued. For the Federal Court, what Section 124A really sought to preserve was public order. Seen in this light, the standard by which a court was to judge whether anything said or written was seditious was to see whether there existed a tendency to 'promote disorder, or incite others to do so.'[99]

To prevent abuse of power, the Federal Court was at pains to clarify that it would not lie within the power of the government to treat every single speech and expression against it as a threat to public order. In memorable prose, Chief Justice Gwyer sounded his note of caution thus:

> This [sedition] *is not made an offence in order to minister to the wounded vanity of Governments* but because where Government and the law cease to be obeyed because no respect is felt any longer for them, only anarchy can follow. Public disorder, or the reasonable anticipation or likelihood of public disorder, is thus the gist of the offence.[100]

The Federal Court had now substantially raised the bar for treating anything as sedition. Only such expressions which 'incite to disorder' or which are judged as having the 'intention or tendency,' to incite others to cause public disorder could be treated as sedition.[101] The old notions of speech resulting in loss of affection for the government and speech causing the people to dislike the State were no longer the guiding principles for launching prosecutions for sedition.[102]

What had now been achieved was a new and important balance between freedom of speech and public peace, and this new framework introduced a radical change. Sedition was no longer divorced from consequences. A person could no longer be punished merely for the words they used. It was no longer a crime to say something critical of the government or to question it or to flay it for its misdeeds. It became a crime of sedition only when a perceivable consequence ensued because of the seditious speech or expression.

There, however, remained one last knot to untie. What if a person used distasteful language to criticize the government? What if the speech or writing was not in measured tones but was an outburst containing the most vituperative and abusive language? What if the words used were such that the only conclusion that could be drawn was that the government would be made the object of hatred? The Federal Court untied this knot in the smoothest fashion.

It was impermissible to treat speech as seditious only because the language used was distasteful. 'Abusive language, even when used about a Government,' the Federal Court declared, 'is not necessarily seditious.'[103] What had to weigh with any court was not the choice of words but whether the speech in question incited people to cause public disorder. Sedition was a powerful tool in the hands of the government, and for that reason the Federal Court observed that 'even the violent expression of opinion' cannot always be treated as sedition.[104] Crassness of language and poor choice of words were not the guiding principles to launch a prosecution for sedition.

In one sense, the decision of the Federal Court hearkened back to the settled law in England on seditious libel. In the mid-nineteenth century, English law itself had enunciated the principle that political speech could only be punished when it reached the level of imminently causing destruction. In his *A History of the Criminal Law of England*, James Fitzjames Stephen wrote about the case of *R v. Collins* from the early 1840s.

A trial for seditious libel was launched against Collins, who, as part of an organization called General Convention, printed 'a placard which . . . described the police as a "bloodthirsty and unconstitutional force from London."'[105] In the trial, Judge Littledale drew a mature conclusion and decided that speech which is political in nature and is critical of state instrumentalities (here it was the police force) cannot routinely be made the subject matter of a seditious libel prosecution.

Only when the speech and writings in question reach the stage of causing demonstrable and imminent harm can the machinery of criminal law be set in motion; not a moment before that.[106] As Judge Littledale said to the jury:

> [I]f the object of it [the publication] were merely to show that the conduct of the police was improper, that would not be illegal, because every man *has a right to give every public matter* a candid, full, and free discussion. ...The people have a right to discuss any grievances that they have to complain of, but they must not do in a way to excite tumult.[107]

In large measure, there is an obvious parallel between the statement of English law on the crime of seditious libel and the meaning of sedition within the IPC. Perhaps what the Federal Court achieved in its decision was to synthesize the different strands of judicial thinking which had developed in India since the 1800s and present a coherent view on what sedition ought to truly mean.

In the specific case before it, the Federal Court acquitted Majumdar even though he used highly 'violent language'[108] in his speech, during which cries of 'shame', against the government, were heard from the audience.[109] Yet Chief Justice Gwyer could not bring himself to treat the speech as sedition.[110]

It is important to note that in this decision, the Federal Court made a significant value judgment, which none of the other decisions had ever made. Section 124A was not about an ordinary offence which had to be understood by its plain words. It affected something much more valuable: the freedom of speech and the freedom to engage in political speech. Courts had to be mindful of carefully balancing the preservation of public order with the 'freedom of speech and the right to criticise all matters of public interest.'[111] As the Federal Court declared:

> And in holding the scales evenly between Government and citizens they will be forgetful neither of the obligations of one towards the public at large nor of the individual and private rights of the other: for the preservation of order is a thing in which all citizens have an interest *no less than in the maintenance of freedom of speech and the right to criticise all matters of public interest.*[112]

Just before this decision was announced, the Privy Council (which in the order of things was superior to the Federal Court) had taken the view (in a case which arose from West Africa) that when it came to sedition, it was unnecessary to examine whether there had been any exhortation inciting violence.[113] Yet the Federal Court charted a different course for sedition in India.

This exceptional decision of the Federal Court, unfortunately, lasted for only about half a decade. It was overruled by the Privy Council in February 1947 in *Emperor v. Sadashiv Narayan Bhalerao*, which was an entirely different case altogether.[114]

In a sense, the *Majumdar* decision was destined to have a short-lived existence precisely because it was an outlier and incompatible with the general jurisprudential trend. Almost all the past cases on sedition had placed no importance on the consequences which followed the speech and expression in question.

Be that as it may, to say that the decision of the Privy Council in *Bhalerao*'s case was absurd would be an understatement. It was an intellectually dishonest judgment. In that decision, the Privy Council castigated the Federal Court's decision in the *Majumdar* case.

The Privy Council felt that the Federal Court was bound by the declaration of the law on sedition obtaining in Justice Strachey's instructions to the jury in Tilak's trial in 1897 in the Bombay High Court. Since it was bound by it, the Federal Court could not have disregarded it to declare that consequences mattered when it came to Section 124A.[115]

This was a patently wrong conclusion drawn by the Privy Council. By the terms of the Government of India Act, 1935, Section 212 expressly stipulated that the 'law declared by the Federal Court' will bind all the other courts in India, which obviously included the high courts.[116] In this scheme of the 1935 Act, it was the high courts which were subordinate to the Federal Court, and not the other way around.

The Federal Court was superior to the high courts, and the latter's decisions, that too from antiquity, could not possibly control the Federal Court in the 1940s. After all, the Federal Court was not some small causes court located in a remote town but sat at the apex of the Indian judicial system. It appears that the Privy Council was so obsessed with ensuring that Section 124A remained a means for implementing obedience that its decision did not contain even one reference to the new judicial scheme inaugurated by the 1935 Act.

Nonetheless, Chief Justice Gwyer's denouncement of sedition being marshalled against any and all forms of critical thinking and his ringing declaration that political speech deserves special protection would prove enormously important. For, when the tallest leaders of the freedom movement would begin the task of giving free India its Constitution, dealing with sedition and Section 124A would invigorate the deliberations of the Constituent Assembly and change the course of history.

4

The Many Lives of the Prince

———◆———

Such was the state of the law on sedition in India prior to independence that the greatest nationalist leaders, from Gandhi to Tilak, had been ensnared in it. Section 124A of the IPC had been nothing short of a sledgehammer with which the British government took aim at anyone who expressed the remotest form of dissent.

In his trial in 1922 before Judge Broomfield, Gandhi had proclaimed that it was highly improper to punish criticism of the British government in India when it was unaccompanied by direct calls to violence. In that trial, Gandhi had pejoratively called Section 124A 'the Prince'.

Perhaps taking a leaf out of Gandhi's oration during the trial, the Federal Court speaking through Chief Justice Maurice Gwyer, in 1942, moved to render Section 124A entirely inapplicable—even to the most virulent expressions of opinion against the government—so long as a call to cause public disorder was not given.

Section 124A was a catch-all provision which could be deployed to essentially infuse criminality into any sort of expression that spoke of the government in less than favourable terms. It was a provision which deliberately used an open-ended definition of disaffection. It assumed seditious intent in speeches and writings. It distanced itself from the actual consequences which followed any seditious act because convictions would have been harder to obtain.

Finally, it was a provision which made it literally impossible for any defence to be raised against a charge of sedition. All of these qualities which inhered in Section 124A were part of its grand design to make it improbable for anyone to escape its clutches, once they had spoken disaffectionately against the British government.

When the Constituent Assembly met in 1946 to begin its deliberations on the form that the fundamental right to freedom of speech and expression must take in the Indian Constitution, one of the greatest conundrums it faced was whether Section 124A should continue in free India. Intuitively, the answer would have been that it should not remain in force.

After all, why would those who had fought for independence decide to retain a law which was used to silence their voices during the freedom struggle? But intuition is not always the best guide when it comes to designing a constitution.

On the question of sedition, two paths were available to the Constituent Assembly. The first was to formulate a fundamental right to free speech which validated the law on sedition. This would effectively retain Section 124A in free India.

The other was to formulate the right to free speech expansively so as to constitutionally create a space for citizens to speak against the government in the most critical terms. In this formulation, Section 124A would die a natural death.

As we shall see, the Constituent Assembly was uncertain as to which path it must go down, and between 1946 and 1950 it kept wavering on the choice that it must make.

The Prince Buried

The Constituent Assembly met for the first time on 9 December 1946 in what is today the Central Hall of Parliament. This was the body which would give India its founding document. The Assembly had been created as a consequence of the recommendation of the Cabinet Mission, which by its statement of 16 May 1946 had proposed that it was best if 'a constitution can be settled by Indians for Indians.'[1]

The Cabinet Mission had recommended, in paragraph 18 of its statement, that the members constituting the Assembly must be elected on the basis of the recently concluded elections to the provincial legislatures, which had taken place in December 1945.[2]

The elections to the provincial legislatures had not been conducted according to the principle of universal adult franchise. The Sixth Schedule of the Government of India Act of 1935 contained a series of conditions for a person to be eligible to vote. For example, a person had to be a taxpayer. As a result of this, '28.5 per cent, of the total adult population' voted in the December 1946 elections.[3] The Cabinet Mission realized that although the Assembly members ought to be chosen in a manner to represent the entirety of the population, the only 'practicable course,' in 1946, was to draw the membership of the Assembly from those who had won in the provincial elections.[4]

A key proposal in the Cabinet Mission's statement was that once the members were elected to the Constituent Assembly, an Advisory Committee must be created to recommend a 'list of Fundamental Rights.'[5] Within a month of its convening, the Assembly began deliberating on constituting such an Advisory Committee. On 24 January 1947, G.B. Pant moved a resolution in the Assembly to nominate members to the Advisory Committee.[6] On that day itself, the Assembly voted on the resolution and constituted a fifty-member Advisory Committee.[7] A little over a month later, the Advisory Committee had its first meeting, at which Sardar Vallabhbhai Patel was elected the Committee's chairman.[8]

At its first meeting, the Advisory Committee decided that it would be best if the task of recommending a set of fundamental rights was delegated to a subcommittee, whose membership would be drawn from the Advisory Committee itself. That is how a ten-member Fundamental Rights Sub-Committee was constituted, comprising J.B. Kripalani, M.R. Masani, K.T. Shah, Rajkumari Amrit Kaur, Alladi Krishnaswami Ayyar, K.M. Munshi, Harnam Singh, Maulana Abul Kalam Azad, Dr B.R. Ambedkar and Jairamdas Daulatram.[9] On that day, the Advisory Committee also constituted subcommittees in respect of other matters, like the twenty-six member Minorities Sub-Committee.[10]

On the day it was constituted, the Fundamental Rights Sub-Committee had its first meeting, at which J.B. Kripalani was elected chairman.[11] At this meeting, the Sub-Committee embarked on a 'preliminary discussion' on how fundamental rights should be formulated in the new Constitution.[12]

Ayyar launched into a strident argument on why the Sub-Committee must follow the path of the US Constitution in enumerating enforceable fundamental rights. For him, the US

Constitution was the exemplar of a model constitution. '[I]t was no use,' believed Ayyar of 'laying down precepts which remained unenforceable or ineffective.'[13]

On the other hand, Munshi asked the Sub-Committee to consider whether fundamental rights must be enumerated only as model principles that need not be implemented. Although he personally believed that fundamental rights ought to be enforceable and that the people of India must have recourse to the constitutional courts to implement them. For this view of his, Munshi found support in Dr Ambedkar.[14]

It soon emerged that many in the Sub-Committee wanted to spend some time by themselves to formulate the ideal rights that must be deliberated upon by the Sub-Committee, as well as to carefully examine each other's proposals. To allow for this, it was decided that the Sub-Committee would adjourn for a month and resume its deliberations on 24 March 1947.[15]

In this short time span, several members such as Ayyar, Munshi, Harnam Singh and Dr Ambedkar drew up nuanced and carefully worked-out plans on how fundamental rights must be structured.[16] With these various proposals now in hand, the Sub-Committee met again on the appointed day in March 1947, to commence their deliberations. For more than a week, the Sub-Committee remained deep in discussion on the question of fundamental rights.[17]

The time given to the Sub-Committee members to prepare their own proposals proved fruitful. In fact, the Sub-Committee decided to use Munshi's memorandum on fundamental rights as its basic working draft.[18] Quite evidently, this decision considerably shortened the time the Sub-Committee spent on drawing up the fundamental rights. Otherwise, it would have had to draw up each fundamental right from scratch—an exercise that would have taken much more time.

On 3 April 1947, Kripalani presented the Sub-Committee's first report, along with a draft of the fundamental rights, to the Advisory Committee.[19] In this draft, the Sub-Committee recommended that the freedom of speech and expression would be subject to public order and morality, and that to say or express anything seditious would be an offence.[20]

After the report had been submitted, the Fundamental Rights Sub-Committee reconvened for two days in April 1947 in order to reconsider their recommendations.[21] This was occasioned by the fact that the Sub-Committee had not specified that the recommendations in their report had fetched dissent from certain members. Thus, a new report would be submitted, along with the points of dissent.[22]

On 16 April 1947, Kripalani presented this second report to the Advisory Committee, along with the draft of the rights as well as the dissent notes.[23] Here too, the freedom of speech and expression remained subject to, amongst other things, public order. Sedition was specifically enumerated as a curb on the freedom of speech and expression.[24] As a result of this, Section 124A would remain valid.

With this, the action now shifted to the Advisory Committee, which met on 21–22 April 1947 to discuss the recommendations of the Fundamental Rights Sub-Committee. During its deliberations, the Advisory Committee seemed relatively unconcerned with the fact that sedition was to remain a fetter on free speech. It was much more concerned with reconciling the freedom of speech with the need for curbing hate speech.[25]

The idea of sedition remaining a crime, and thus a restriction on the freedom of speech and expression, was confirmed by the Advisory Committee in its Interim Report on Fundamental Rights, which Patel submitted to the Constituent Assembly on 23 April 1947.[26] In the charter of 'Justiciable Fundamental Rights' which accompanied the Interim Report, Clause 8(a) dealt with the freedom of speech and expression.

Appended to this clause was a proviso which contained the list of restrictions on free speech, which included sedition. The litany of restrictions largely followed the recommendations of the Fundamental Rights Sub-Committee. The significant change made by the Advisory Committee was to make blasphemy yet another ground on which free speech could be curbed.[27]

With the Advisory Committee having made its recommendations, it was now time for the Constituent Assembly to debate and vote on the proposed rights. On 29 April 1947, Patel placed the Advisory Committee's Interim Report for debate in the Constituent Assembly.[28] The next day, the Assembly took up the freedom of speech and expression for debate. On that day, dramatic events unfolded.

Patel rose to address the Assembly, and when it came to free speech, suddenly and without forewarning, he announced that he would not throw his support behind the large number of restrictions recommended in the proviso appended to Clause 8(a).[29] With the command of authority, Patel told the Assembly, '*I do not* move the proviso to be found in the Report.'[30] With this one statement, the withdrawal of the whole host of restrictions occurred even before the Assembly could begin discussing the freedom of speech.

This radical move by Patel was by no means confined only to freedom of speech. For some of the other civil liberties which the Advisory Committee had recommended in Clause 8 of the charter of 'Justiciable Fundamental Rights' which accompanied its Interim Report, like the right to assemble peacefully without arms, and the right of citizens to form associations and unions, Patel refused to move the many restrictions which were appended in the provisos to each of these rights.[31]

In one fell swoop, Patel abandoned on the floor of the Assembly the restrictions proposed by the Advisory Committee on free speech, including sedition. This was a rare act of statesmanship, and Patel perhaps acted on a premonition which proved true—that to adopt a restriction-based approach to the freedom of speech and expression would be a bitter pill to swallow for the Assembly.

Patel was right. Soon after he told the Assembly that the many restrictions recommended by Advisory Committee for the freedom of speech and expression (which, apart from sedition, included obscenity, blasphemy and defamation) were no longer backed by him, and therefore the Assembly need not spend even a minute on them, a sense of calm prevailed. Many in the Assembly were ready to wage a long and arduous battle for removal of the whole panoply of restrictions on free speech recommended by the Advisory Committee.

In fact, on hearing Patel's announcement, one member, Somnath Lahiri, happily told the Assembly that with this, all his amendments seeking the removal of restrictions on free speech had 'become redundant.'[32] 'I am very glad, Sir, that these provisos against which I fought,' said Lahiri, 'have been done away with.'[33] Indeed, one of the amendments which Lahiri moved was to delete sedition as a restriction on free speech.[34] Which is why he told the Assembly that Patel's move had made this specific amendment of his 'unnecessary.'[35]

Patel won the day, and on 30 April 1947 the Assembly approved the freedom of speech and expression, without sedition being a restriction on this right.[36] In the final version of this fundamental right, all that the Assembly approved of was that the freedom of speech be subject to public order, morality, and a declared emergency.[37]

For now, at least, the Prince seemed to have been buried.

The Prince Exhumed

A fortnight after India attained Independence, the Constituent Assembly decided to change its approach to the drafting of the Constitution. To that end, a motion was moved in the Assembly to constitute a seven-member Drafting Committee. Alladi Krishnaswami Ayyar, N. Gopalaswami Ayyangar, Dr B.R. Ambedkar, K.M. Munshi, Saiyid Mohammad Saadulla, B.L. Mitter and D.P. Khaitan were nominated to be its members.[38] The Drafting Committee would be reconstituted twice thereafter. T.T. Krishnamachari was nominated as a member upon the passing away of D.P. Khaitan. And N. Madhava Rao was made a member to fill the vacancy left by B.L. Mitter.[39]

This Drafting Committee was to be the apex authority which would reduce all the decisions that the Assembly had taken since it first convened to articles in a Draft Constitution, which the Assembly could then scrutinize.[40] But B.G. Kher, a member from Bombay, wanted to innovate and modify the method for preparing the Draft Constitution.

He recommended that first, the Constitutional Advisor, Sir Benegal Narsing Rau, must prepare the initial draft of the Constitution which would represent the past decisions the Assembly had taken on several aspects of the Constitution.

Thereafter, the Drafting Committee could use Rau's Draft Constitution as a template to prepare its own version of the Constitution.[41]

Although there was some opposition to this two-tier approach to the preparation of the Draft Constitution,[42] Ayyar assured the Assembly that in preparing it, the Drafting Committee would ensure that the past decisions of the Assembly would be 'treated as binding,' and if any mistakes were discovered only then would the Assembly, 'review the decisions.'[43]

This statement of Ayyar's must be kept in mind for more than one reason. Ayyar was to be a member of the Drafting Committee and spoke from a position of authority, on the true role of the Drafting Committee. But above all, Ayyar's categorical assertion must be remembered because the Drafting Committee disregarded this very note of caution and brought back sedition as a curb on free speech, in open defiance of the Constituent Assembly's vote of 30 April 1947.

Eventually, the Assembly agreed with Kher's suggestion of a two-tier approach for preparing the Draft Constitution.[44] With this, the stage was set for B.N. Rau to prepare the first draft of the Constitution.

B.N. Rau was a prodigious and precocious talent.* A graduate of Cambridge, where his fellow peer was Jawaharlal Nehru, he joined the ranks of the Indian Civil Service in 1910 and had a meteoric rise. Although not trained as a lawyer, Rau was appointed as a judge of the Calcutta High Court in 1935. Later, he was called upon by the Viceroy to oversee the rehaul of the Indian legal system that had to take place in light of the Government of India

---

* In the interest of full disclosure, I must state here that I am related to B.N. Rau on my maternal side.

Act of 1935. For his skilful handling of that task, he was knighted in 1938.

When the Constituent Assembly was to be convened, Viceroy Wavell invited B.N. Rau to serve as the Constitutional Advisor. Rau was not a member of the Assembly, but his counsel was sought by members on different aspects of the Constitution.[45] So great was Rau's contribution that in his final speech to the Assembly, Dr Ambedkar reserved special praise for Rau's role in advising the Assembly:

> The credit that is given to me does not really belong to me. It belongs partly to Sir B.N. Rau, the Constitutional Adviser to the Constituent Assembly who prepared a rough draft of the Constitution for the consideration of the Drafting Committee.[46]

B.N. Rau was put on notice in August 1947 that he had to prepare the Draft Constitution, and he worked rapidly. Within a few months, the Draft Constitution was ready. In the Draft Constitution of October 1947 prepared by Rau, the freedom of speech and expression was contained in Clause 15(1)(a). By the main part of Clause 15, this right was subject only to restrictions aimed at preserving public order and morality.[47]

Unlike some members of the Drafting Committee—like Ayyar—who were enthused with the finesse with which the US Constitution enumerated fundamental rights, Rau modelled his version of the free speech right on the Irish Constitution. For good measure, he was careful to make a marginal noting of this next to the clause in his Draft Constitution.[48]

At any rate, this version of the free speech right was substantially the same as the version which the Assembly had approved on 30

April 1947. Even otherwise, this version of the right to free speech had deep echoes in history and was similar to the clause on free speech recommended in the Nehru Report of 1928, which was prepared by Motilal Nehru.[49] But a storm was to come when the freedom of speech and expression came to the attention of the Drafting Committee.

After it was constituted, the Drafting Committee had met for the first time on 30 August 1947. At that first meeting, all the members agreed to nominate Dr Ambedkar as the chairman of the Drafting Committee. After setting out a timeline for its activities, the Drafting Committee decided to reconvene once Rau's Draft Constitution was in their hands.[50]

On 27 October 1947, the Drafting Committee began its deliberations and set down to work on Rau's Draft Constitution.[51] Four days later, the Drafting Committee took up the freedom of speech and expression for discussion. On that day, this right underwent a dramatic transmogrification. In its new formulation which the Drafting Committee chose, the freedom of speech and expression was made subject to public order, health and morality.

In addition to this, the Drafting Committee also decided to reinstate sedition as a crime and as a curb on the freedom of speech.[52] The litany of restrictions which was appended as a new proviso to the clause on free speech virtually replicated the list of restrictions on free speech which had been proposed by the Advisory Committee in its Interim Report.[53]

Remarkably, the rehabilitation of sedition by the Drafting Committee occurred without so much as a proper discussion on the potential ramifications of the decision. Making sedition a crime, which essentially revived Section 124A, had far-reaching implications when it came to free speech in independent India. Yet none of these concerns seemed to have detained the Drafting

Committee for even a moment. All that is recorded in the transcript of the meeting is that the Drafting Committee took the decision to revise the right of free speech.⁵⁴ What made them *take* this decision is not known to us, for it is not recorded.

When the Drafting Committee met the next day, on 1 November, the list of restrictions on free speech were altered to empower the State to make laws on sedition which curbed free speech.⁵⁵ This new iteration of free speech empowered the State to enact laws, in the future, on the question of sedition.⁵⁶ No reference was made to the old laws but only to the power of the State to make laws prospectively. Momentarily, it appeared that Section 124A was not being validated. Unfortunately, here too the transcript of the meeting only records that a decision was taken to revise the free speech clause without a single reference to what occasioned this rehaul.⁵⁷

One member of the Drafting Committee, Alladi Krishnaswami Ayyar, was perturbed by the fact that the old law on sedition would not be valid in free India and thus sought to remedy this problem, so to speak, and suggested a change.

At the meeting of 4 November 1947, Ayyar recommended that the Drafting Committee must clearly specify that despite the freedom of speech and expression being recommended as a fundamental right, the continued existence of past laws, including sedition (under Section 124A) would not be thrown in jeopardy by the right to free speech in the new Constitution. The Drafting Committee ended up agreeing with this suggestion and voted to ensure that Section 124A would remain a fetter on the freedom of speech.⁵⁸

This was not only a conceptual change but a radical refashioning of the free speech right, because now Section 124A would once again be granted a new lease of life. The Prince, was exhumed and would haunt the citizens of the new republic.

What makes this development all the more alarming is that in its initial meetings, the Drafting Committee had decided to make the provision pertaining to the restrictions that could be imposed on the right to free speech prospective in nature. This meant that once the Constitution was finalized, a new law would have to be made to deal with sedition. However, with this intervention, Alladi Krishnaswami Ayyar made the clause pertaining to the restrictions on free speech Janus-faced.

The new Constitution would empower the State to make future laws to curb free speech as well as make the freedom of speech and expression wear Section 124A around its neck like an albatross. Far from unshackling free speech, this singular intervention of Ayyar's would end up shackling free speech in independent India. At all its subsequent meetings, the Drafting Committee retained sedition as a curb on free speech.

On 21 February 1948, the Drafting Committee submitted the first version of the Draft Constitution to Dr Rajendra Prasad, the president of the Constituent Assembly.[59] After having done so, the Drafting Committee worked on the Draft Constitution once again to respond to the multitude of comments which had been received on the first version of the Draft Constitution. That process took about eight months, and on 26 October 1948 Dr Ambedkar submitted the revised version of the Draft Constitution to Dr Rajendra Prasad.[60] It was this Draft Constitution which Dr Ambedkar introduced in the Constituent Assembly on 4 November 1948.[61]

In the Draft Constitution, the fundamental right to the freedom of speech and expression was enumerated in draft Article 13(1) (a). In draft Article 13(2), it was specified that this right would not affect any law (whether already in existence, as well as any future law) which dealt with libel, slander, defamation, *sedition*, decency, morality, or with issues which undermine the security of or tends to overthrow the State.[62]

Interestingly, in draft Article 13(2), 'public order' was not a ground for restricting free speech, although 'sedition' still remained a restriction, and indeed a crime. As we shall see, the omission of 'public order' in the Constitution, as an enumerated ground to limit free speech would have explosive consequences in 1950–1951.

After surveying the deliberations of the Drafting Committee, it is natural to wonder as to what led the Drafting Committee to reinstate sedition as a curb on the freedom of speech, especially when in April 1947, the Constituent Assembly had voted on this fundamental right without sedition being a restriction. More intriguingly, there is an inherent contradiction in Ayyar suggesting that sedition should be reintroduced as a curb on free speech (along with other restrictions such as defamation).

The contradiction is on account of the fact that Ayyar had unequivocally told the Constituent Assembly on 29 August 1947 that the Drafting Committee was bound by all the past decisions that the Assembly had taken. This would obviously include the Assembly's vote of 30 April 1947 approving the freedom of speech without sedition as a curb on it. Evidently, Ayyar's counsel to the Assembly was discarded by him in the Drafting Committee.

The rehabilitation of Section 124A through the means of the new Constitution was entirely irreconcilable with the principal purpose for which the Drafting Committee had been constituted— to reduce *the past decisions* of the Assembly into articles in a Draft Constitution. No one emphasized the importance of this function more than Ayyar himself. He had, on 29 August 1947, during the debates on the motion to constitute the Drafting Committee, emphatically said:

> Sir, on a matter like this it is as well we are sure as to what exactly the import of the resolution is. One thing must be made quite clear, namely, that *in regard to the decisions already reached, they will be treated as binding*, though *if errors are discovered* or *unforeseen difficulties arise*, it will always be open to the House to review the decisions.[63]

Indeed, during this speech of his, Ayyar had specifically referred to the decisions that the Assembly had taken on fundamental rights in April 1947. He was clear that so far as these past decisions were concerned, 'the scope of review at a later stage must naturally be limited.'[64] In the context of free speech, this can only be taken to mean that the decision of the Assembly to narrowly tailor the list of restrictions on this right ought not to have been disturbed this lightly by the Drafting Committee.

Had the Drafting Committee remained true to Ayyar's counsel, it would have implemented the Constituent Assembly's decision of 30 April 1947 which adopted the free speech clause without sedition as a curb on it. Yet the Drafting Committee went along a different direction, and rather than respecting this past decision, the Drafting Committee reinstated almost all the curbs on free speech which the Assembly had categorically voted against.

Unfortunately, the transcripts of the Drafting Committee meetings do not reveal any concrete discussions being had on why sedition as contained in Section 124A ought to remain a crime in free India. All that the transcripts record is that a new version of the free speech right was formulated, with sedition as a restriction on this right. From the official records it appears that the Drafting Committee seemed much more concerned with structuring the list of restrictions that could be imposed on the freedom of speech. Almost no time was spent in discussing whether it was proper to retain sedition in the Constitution.

Furthermore, nothing in the transcripts of the Drafting Committee's deliberations even momentarily suggests that the Assembly had made an error when it approved the free speech right back in April 1947 which had to now be corrected by the Drafting Committee. If no error was found in that decision, then according to Ayyar's own counsel, the Drafting Committee could not have undone that decision in the Draft Constitution.

The only possible reason for this volte face to have occurred is that perhaps several members of the Drafting Committee, like Alladi Krishnaswami Ayyar, Dr B.R. Ambedkar and K.M. Munshi had also been members of the Advisory Committee as well as the Fundamental Rights Sub-Committee. On both these committees, they had all voted in favour of retaining sedition. It was Patel alone who was responsible for discarding sedition as a curb on the freedom of speech. The abandonment of sedition as well as the other curbs on free speech was done extempore by Patel on the floor of the Assembly on 30 April 1947.

Now, in the Drafting Committee, a second chance at reinstating sedition as a crime had presented itself and, quite evidently, this opportunity was fully seized upon. It is no wonder that the language chosen to structure the restrictions on the freedom of speech in the Draft Constitution so closely mirrored the language which was used by the Fundamental Rights Sub-Committee as well as by the Advisory Committee in formulating the curbs on free speech in their respective reports.

The Architecture of Constitutional Reason

In discussing the specifics of the freedom of speech and expression, the deliberations of the Drafting Committee seemed to focus almost exclusively on fine-tuning the kinds of restrictions that should be imposed on free speech. The entire agenda was concerned with only one thing: how the restrictions on free speech should be worded. There was almost no discussion of the fundamental importance of free speech and whether a more guarded approach ought to be adopted with respect to the curbs that can be imposed on it.

Moreover, there was hardly any discussion on the fact that certain forms of speech deserve a special level of protection (like political speech), and other forms of speech like obscenity and defamation require a different form of regulation.

It was Dr Ambedkar, as chairman of the Drafting Committee, who realized that abridging civil rights, including the freedom of speech, with a plethora of restrictions would be a bitter a pill to swallow for the Constituent Assembly. When the proposals of the Drafting Committee contained in the Draft Constitution were presented to the public, the chapter on fundamental rights had generated enormous criticism. The criticism was that the Drafting Committee had prepared a Constitution which told you when you could not exercise your rights.[65]

So, when Dr Ambedkar introduced the Drafting Committee's Draft Constitution in the Constituent Assembly on 4 November 1948, he decided to meet this criticism head on and spent a good deal of time justifying exactly why the Drafting Committee had spent so much time in formulating extensive restrictions for civil rights. To make his case, he focused on the freedom of speech.[66]

Dr Ambedkar acknowledged that of all the features of the Draft Constitution, the chapter on fundamental rights was the 'the most criticized part.'[67] As he saw it, critics were worried that civil rights (enumerated in draft Article 13) were 'riddled with so many exceptions that the exceptions have eaten up the rights altogether.'[68] Critics also viewed civil rights, in Dr Ambedkar's opinion, 'as a kind of deception.'[69]

The root cause for this criticism, according to Dr Ambedkar, was this: the critics looked to the US Constitution, in which many of the fundamental rights stipulated that no law could be made to truncate those rights.[70] As Dr Ambedkar put it, the critics viewed the US Constitution as guaranteeing rights which 'are real because they are not subjected to limitations or exceptions.'[71]

Dr Ambedkar laid out all these points of criticism not because he accepted them but because he wanted to disabuse the Constituent Assembly of any wrong notions they may harbour about fundamental rights being unconditional. 'I am sorry to say that the whole of the criticism about fundamental rights,' Dr Ambedkar said, 'is based upon a misconception.'[72]

When it came to the earlier civil rights, the constitution which proved most useful as a model worthy of emulation was the US Constitution. This was because the US Constitution created a paradigm to make fundamental rights enforceable and justiciable.[73] But, Dr Ambedkar told the Assembly, the US Constitution was filled with tension and gave rise to immense difficulties in its actual implementation.

The Bill of Rights made grand declarations, as in the 1st Amendment to the US Constitution, which declared that the US Congress could never make a law abridging the freedom of speech. This absolute declaration, said Dr Ambedkar, could not possibly mean that the free speech right was absolute and unconditional. Could a person exercising the freedom of speech stoke violence or cause public disorder? The US Constitution offered no guidance to lawmakers as to the way the freedom of speech could be regulated.[74]

Dr Ambedkar told the Assembly that this was the tension which afflicted the US Constitution, and to resolve it the US Supreme Court developed what is called the doctrine of police powers. According to this principle, the US Supreme Court incrementally and over a period of time identified certain areas which were not off limits when it came to governmental regulation of the freedom of speech. Simply stated, the State could police some aspects of free speech for a public order purpose.[75]

In the exercise of its police powers, states could regulate and even prohibit certain kinds of speech and expression. By using the police powers doctrine, the US Supreme Court crafted a constitutional scheme in which the freedom of speech could be regulated by law, despite the absolute declaration of the 1st Amendment to the US Constitution to the contrary.[76]

Drawing the Assembly's attention to a 1925 decision of the US Supreme Court which stated this point of constitutional law, Dr Ambedkar advised the Assembly that in the scheme of the US Constitution, regulation of speech which 'corrupt public morals, incite to crime or disturb the public peace' were not deemed unconstitutional.[77] Dr Ambedkar hoped to convince the Assembly that the attainment of civil peace and orderly progress of society was the foundation for regulating all civil rights, including free speech.[78]

From here, Dr Ambedkar attempted to turn the tables on the critics. For the Drafting Committee, the creation and implementation of the police powers doctrine in the US was a cautionary tale, because this was a doctrine which was not the most precise. The courts and the legislature would be locked in a battle of trial and error. The legislature would make a law to regulate free speech and would have to wait to be told by the US Supreme Court whether the law was a legitimate exercise of the State's police powers.[79]

To avoid this trial-and-error method from taking root in India, the Drafting Committee had decided that this resort to the doctrine of police powers was best avoided. Dr Ambedkar told the Assembly that it was better, and practically more feasible, if the Constitution identified the specific grounds on which the freedom of speech and expression could be curbed. This would clarify both to the State as well as to the courts the precise circumstances under which the freedom of speech can be regulated.[80] As Dr Ambedkar saw it:

> What the Draft Constitution has done is that instead of formulating fundamental rights in absolute terms and depending upon our Supreme Court to come to the rescue of Parliament by inventing the doctrine of police power, it permits the State directly to impose limitations upon the fundamental rights.[81]

Many in the Assembly did find Dr Ambedkar's explanation for the litany of restrictions on free speech a bitter pill to swallow. K.T. Shah, Dr Ambedkar's colleague from the Advisory Committee, remarked that civil rights were being overrun with 'exceptions.'[82] Arun Chandra Guha, a member from West Bengal, thought that Dr Ambedkar had spurred a 'metaphysical debate' on fundamental rights.[83] Guha believed that although fundamental rights cannot be absolute, it was an oddity for fundamental rights to be immediately 'negatived by putting some provisos and some subsidiary clauses.'[84]

K. Santhanam, a member from Madras, expressed the fear that if rights were to be subject to such a long line of restrictions, it might be better to do away with fundamental rights altogether.[85] In a somewhat similar vein, Muhammad Ismail Sahib, also a member from Madras, believed that the numerous exceptions to the fundamental rights demonstrated that the exceptions 'have actually eaten up the rights.'[86]

Likewise, Begum Aizaz Rasul, a member from the United Provinces, believed that the manner in which the Drafting Committee had subordinated civil rights to a whole host of restrictions was highly improper. Such an approach only demonstrated that civil rights would not act as a bulwark against State action. On the contrary, they would empower the State to take away these precious liberty rights.[87]

Alladi Krishnaswami Ayyar thought these attacks on the Draft Constitution were unjustified. Echoing Dr Ambedkar, Ayyar told the Assembly that it was wisest for the Drafting Committee to enumerate the specific grounds on which fundamental rights could be truncated. If that were not done, the Constitution would inaugurate a regime where it would be the courts which would, through the medium of 'judicial legislations,' decide when and how the State could curb fundamental rights.[88]

Ayyar's speech made it clear to the Assembly that so far as the Drafting Committee was concerned, it was not going to withdraw its support for the manner in which the Draft Constitution dealt with civil rights, including the freedom of speech. But when the freedom of speech was taken up for consideration by the Assembly, things moved in an entirely different direction.

The Re-burial of the Prince

The debates on Dr Ambedkar's motion of 4 November 1948 placing the Draft Constitution for debate carried on till 9 November 1948.[89] On 15 November 1948, the Constituent Assembly formally began the clause-wise discussion of the Draft Constitution.[90] Sixteen days later, on 1 December 1948, the Constituent Assembly took up for discussion the clause on the freedom of speech and expression in the Draft Constitution. With the Drafting Committee having thrown its weight behind sedition and Section 124A of the IPC, the battle lines were clearly drawn in the Assembly between those who hoped to retain sedition in independent India and those who wanted to ensure its certain death.

As soon as the debates began, Damodar Swarup Seth, a member from the United Provinces, fired the first volley. Accusing the Drafting Committee of having 'clumsily drafted' the freedom of speech and expression, he told the Assembly that 'citizens will have no means of getting a sedition law invalidated, however flagrantly such a law may violate their civil rights.'[91]

Another member, H.V. Kamath, was shocked by the Drafting Committee's dereliction of duty. In April 1947, the Assembly had voted not to accept sedition and several other restrictions as curbs on free speech. That decision was now disregarded, because in recommending sedition as a restriction in draft Article 13, the Drafting Committee had ignored the unanimous past decision of the Assembly to do away with the crime of sedition forever.[92] As Kamath told the Assembly:

[W]e have the Report of the Fundamental Rights Sub-Committee presided over by the Honourable Sardar Patel, and later on the same report was discussed in the

Assembly and modifications were made in that, and the elaborate provisos which appeared in the original report of the Fundamental Rights Committee do not find a place in the resolution on the report which was adopted by the Constituent Assembly. This perhaps needs an explanation from Dr. Ambedkar.[93]

Recognizing that it was the presence of the word 'sedition' which was the cause of much controversy, K.M. Munshi, moved an amendment motion to delete 'sedition' from the list of restrictions on the freedom of speech.[94] Munshi was no stranger to the law of sedition. In fact, he was an advocate of repute in the Bombay High Court and had appeared in cases which involved Section 124A.[95] But although the sponsor of this progressive amendment motion, there was a dissonance in Munshi's stance.

When the Drafting Committee had reinstated sedition as a crime and a curb on free speech, Munshi was very much in attendance at those meetings but had not recorded any dissent against this move. Now, however, in the Constituent Assembly, Munshi had seemingly had a change of heart and wanted to get rid of sedition from the Constitution as well as from free India.

Importantly, Munshi only wanted to delete the word 'sedition' as a restriction on the freedom of speech and expression to ensure that Section 124A was forever buried. Munshi told the Constituent Assembly that one thing was clear: no one desired that Section 124A should remain on the statute book in free India. It was a pernicious provision which had been used to crush any criticism against the colonial government.

India was adopting the parliamentary form of democracy, and an essential tenet of democracy was the ability of its citizens to openly air their grievances against the government.[96] As he told the Assembly, the 'advocacy of the replacement of one Government by another,' is a shining hallmark of the Indian democratic experiment.[97]

Though Munshi wanted Section 124A done away with, he did offer a caveat. He was in favour of only such a law which punished speech and expression which reached the level of 'incitement which would undermine the security or order on which civilized life is based, or which is calculated to overthrow the State.'[98]

For this reason, Munshi told the Assembly that in draft Article 13(2), he wished for 'sedition' to be deleted and replaced with 'a much better phraseology, viz., "which undermines the security of, or tends to overthrow, the State."'[99] In making this argument, Munshi recalled the decision of the Federal Court in the *Majumdar* case, where Chief Justice Gwyer had observed that speech becomes the crime of sedition only when direct incitement to disturb public order is established.[100]

However, Munshi's formulation of what constituted sedition went much further than the standard laid down by the Federal Court. In the *Majumdar* case, the Federal Court had linked sedition with public order to say that Section 124A could punish only such speech and expression which led to the breakdown of public order.

In Munshi's estimation, however, it would be sedition only when the incitement in question threatened the very security or foundation of the State. Short of that, it would be an abstruse conception to penalize citizens in a democracy for airing their views, no matter how unacceptable they may be to the government of the day.[101]

This was an important advance made by Munshi, which was entirely his own. To make his intentions abundantly clear, Munshi proclaimed that if 'sedition' was not deleted, an 'erroneous impression would be created that we want to perpetuate [Section] 124-A of the IPC or its meaning which was considered good law in earlier days.'[102]

Essentially then, through Munshi's amendment motion the *Bose–Tilak–Prasad* triumvirate of cases which had been followed in many of the later high court decisions in the 1900s were rendered bad law. Munshi's efforts at getting rid of sedition came in for praise by Pandit Thakur Dass Bhargava, who lauded Munshi's initiative of ensuring that Section 124A would no longer be a valid law in free India.[103]

When the debates on the freedom of speech resumed on 2 December 1948, Seth Govind Das, a member from the Central Provinces, also praised Munshi's efforts to get rid of sedition from the Constitution. For Das, the battle with sedition was not only a constitutional one but a deeply personal one. As he told the Assembly, his great-grandfather was given a 'gold waist-band inlaid with diamonds' for assisting the British regime in quelling the Revolt of 1857.[104]

Sometime in 1930, Das had given a speech in which he said that he was so embarrassed and ashamed that his family had received such an extravagant gift for siding with the British that he 'wanted to have engraved on it that the sin committed by my great-grandfather in helping to keep such a government in existence had been expiated by the great-grandson by seeking to uproot it.'[105] For this speech, instead of receiving another gold waistband inlaid with diamonds from the British government, he was convicted for sedition and awarded a two-year sentence of rigorous imprisonment.[106]

Many others also welcomed the deletion of sedition. Rohini Kumar Chaudhari was happy that sedition was being gotten rid of. In fact, Chaudhari castigated Section 124A by holding it 'responsible for a lot of misery in this country' and blaming it for having 'delayed for a considerable time the achievement of our independence.'[107] T.T. Krishnamachari also held Section 124A to be that one provision of law which had earned the ire of the whole of India. As he said in the Assembly:

> Sir, in this country we resent even the mention of the word 'sedition' because all through the long period of our political agitation that word 'sedition' has been used against our leaders, and in the abhorrence of that word we are not by any means unique. ...That kind of abhorrence to this word seems to have been more or less universal even from people who did not have to suffer as much from the import and content of that word as we did.[108]

With so many in the Constituent Assembly supporting Munshi in his fight to have sedition deleted from the Constitution, Dr Ambedkar sensed that it would be wisest to accept Munshi's amendment motion. The tide had now turned against sedition and the last days of Section 124A were near.

As the debates on the freedom of speech neared their end on 2 December 1948, Dr Ambedkar told the Assembly that he was willing to accept Munshi's amendment motion which sought the deletion of sedition.[109] Now, none other than the chairman of the Drafting Committee wanted to bury Section 124A—the Prince.

On that day Munshi's views prevailed, with the Assembly voting to delete sedition as a restriction on the freedom of speech and expression.[110] Munshi's successful intervention on sedition went undisturbed, and in the final Constitution which the Constituent Assembly approved on 26 November 1949, sedition was not a ground on which the freedom of speech and expression could be restricted.

The Constitution came to life on 26 January 1950. The charter of fundamental rights was contained in Part III of the Constitution. In that, Article 19 contained seven civil rights. The freedom of speech and expression was enumerated in Article 19(1)(a), with Article 19(2) containing the grounds on which restrictions could be imposed on that freedom.

Consistent with Munshi's suggestion, a law could impose curbs on free speech only in respect of, among others, such speech which undermined the security of the State or tended to overthrow it. In the newly inaugurated republic, the fundamental right to freedom of speech and expression read thus:

> 19.(1) All citizens shall have the right—
>
> to freedom of speech and expression;
>
> (2) Nothing in sub–clause (a) of clause (1) shall affect the operation of any existing law in so far as it relates to, or prevent the State from making any law relating to, libel, slander, defamation, contempt of court or any matter which offends against decency or morality or which undermines the security of, or tends to overthrow, the State.

With the new Constitution, sedition as well as Section 124A had been given a fitting burial, and the importance of this progressive stride was recognized as soon as the Constitution took in its first few breaths.

5

Thunder and Lightning

---·---

The Rumblings Begin

During the debates in the Constituent Assembly on 2 December 1948, K. Hanumanthaiya, a member from Mysore, had sounded an ominous note of caution. He had warned that looking at the manner in which the fundamental rights had been structured (with each right being accompanied by a litany of restrictions) it was but inevitable that the Supreme Court would become the new battleground for fundamental rights.[1] Hanumanthaiya was right and his prediction came true quickly. Before the ink on the Constitution could even dry, the Supreme Court quickly became the theatre for the fight to save the freedom of speech.

On 26 May 1950, exactly four months after the Constitution had come into force, the Supreme Court handed down two important decisions on the freedom of speech and seemingly sealed the fate of sedition. The first decision came in *Romesh Thappar v. State of Madras*,[2] and the other in *Brij Bhushan v. The State of Delhi*.[3]

Both these cases were heard by a Constitution Bench of six justices comprising Chief Justice of India Hiralal Kania and Justices Saiyid Fazl Ali, Patanjali Sastri, Meher Chand Mahajan, Bijan Kumar Mukherjea and Sudhir Ranjan Das. In both the cases, Justice Sastri authored the judgment for the majority, and in both Justice Fazl Ali dissented. Incidentally, except for Justice Fazl Ali, all the others went on to serve as Chief Justice of India between 1951 and 1956.

Romesh Thappar[4] and Brij Bhushan were not of the same ilk. Thappar wrote against government action which was aimed at those who aligned themselves with communism. Bhushan was the publisher of *Organiser*, a paper of the Rashtriya Swayamsevak Sangh (RSS). Although ideologically apart, what united them in the Supreme Court was the battle to stave off governmental efforts which interfered with the publication of their respective journals.[5] Thappar published the weekly *Cross Roads* in Bombay which, shortly after the Constitution came into force, carried articles which were critical of governmental efforts aimed at suppressing the activities of those who were inspired by the communist ideology.[6]

In March 1950, the Madras government issued an order prohibiting the sale and circulation of *Cross Roads* in the state of Madras. To ban the sale of *Cross Roads*, the Governor-General of Madras invoked powers under Section 9(1-A) of the Madras Maintenance of Public Order Act, 1949. That provision authorized the government to issue injunctive orders with a view to safeguard public order and public safety. Thappar challenged the constitutional validity of Section 9(1-A) directly in the Supreme Court by invoking Article 32 of the Constitution.[7]

That Section 9(1-A) would fall was really a foregone conclusion. As the Constitution stood in 1950, public order and public safety were not enumerated as grounds on which the freedom of speech could be restricted. Thappar's right to have *Cross Roads* made available in Madras had been barred on the ground of preserving public order. Since the Constitution did not authorize any restriction based on public order, the ban order as well as the law which led to the ban order were constitutionally unsustainable.

At the outset, the Supreme Court rejected the objection raised by the Advocate General of Madras that Thappar could not have approached the Supreme Court directly.[8] Under the scheme of the Constitution, it was a fundamental right under Article 32 to move the Supreme Court itself for the implementation of fundamental rights. A mechanism for enforcing fundamental rights had been considered essential from the very beginning, or else fundamental rights would have been nothing but a constitutional homily.

Since the emphasis lay on the enforcement of fundamental rights, the Constitution had specifically ensured that none other than the highest court of the land had to throw open its doors to any citizen who complained that the State denied them the full enjoyment of their fundamental rights.[9]

Article 32 is often considered one of the most important rights. At the time the Constituent Assembly debated this article, Dr Ambedkar had remarked on its importance thus:

> If I was asked to name any particular article in this Constitution as the most important—an article without which this Constitution would be a nullity—I could not refer to any other article except this one. It is the very soul

of the Constitution and the very heart of it and I am glad
that the House has realised its importance.[10]

The high importance of Article 32 was not lost on the Supreme Court. 'This Court,' Justice Patanjali Sastri declared, 'is thus constituted the protector and guarantor of fundamental rights.' Once the Court is invited to decide whether a measure violates fundamental rights, it cannot 'refuse to entertain applications seeking protection against infringement of rights.'[11] To this day, this declaration remains an enduring testament to the scheme that the Constitution inaugurated, where any citizen from anywhere in India could directly knock on the doors of the Supreme Court when their fundamental rights were in jeopardy.

Justice Sastri then moved to carve out a constitutional space to recognize not only the substance of the free speech right but also the attendant rights which are essential for people to freely express themselves. Justice Sastri declared that Article 19 not only guarantees the core right to speak about or express one's thoughts and opinions, but also guarantees concomitant rights to ensure that one's message can reach a wider audience.

After all, what use is a free speech right if the medium of expressing it is itself made unavailable or banned. Thus, if the case involved the freedom of the press, then the right to have one's newspaper in free circulation became as important as the fundamental right to free speech and expression itself. Which is why a restriction on circulation was to be viewed most seriously, because it directly led to a restriction on the freedom of speech itself.[12]

The *Thappar* case essentially turned on whether a restriction imposed by a law on free speech, claiming that the interest of public safety and public order justified it, was protected by Article 19(2).

Here the Supreme Court found that the Constitution recognized restrictions to be imposed on matters which undermined the security of the State (the other grounds for imposing restrictions such as defamation were not in dispute, for the restriction was not justified under them). However, the Court declared, public order or public safety, which signified 'security of the public or their freedoms from danger,'[13] was not an enumerated ground to curb free speech.

Although it was true that matters that involved the security of the State would inevitably involve matters of public order, the converse was not true. A case of public disorder would not necessarily jeopardize the stability of the State. The only sort of speech that could be curbed was those which truly threatened the foundations of the State leading to violent instability, or where the security of the State would be in dire jeopardy. Short of that, the Constitution disallowed any restriction to be imposed on the freedom of speech by simply invoking a public order interest.[14]

The statutory provision under challenge—Section 9(1-A) of the Madras Maintenance of Public Order Act, 1949—dealt only with 'public order'. It did not deal with any matter affecting State security. In light of this, the Supreme Court declared this provision of the 1949 law unconstitutional. 'Public order' was not expressly mentioned in the text of Article 19(2), and thus the State could not invoke the preservation of public order interest to impose a ban on the expression of opinions.[15]

In the *Thappar* case, the Supreme Court also commented that the law on sedition contained in Section 124A of the IPC no longer survived under the new Constitution. The Constituent Assembly had taken the decision that when the Constitution came into force, all laws which existed in India prior to 1950 would automatically continue in free India. There was to be no break in continuity.

This scheme was set forth in Article 372(1)[16] as well as in Article 366(10).[17] The only laws which the Constitution itself repealed were the Indian Independence Act of 1947 and the Government of India Act of 1935.[18] Nevertheless, all pre-constitutional laws had to measure up to the fundamental rights enumerated in Part III of the Constitution. Their continued existence was contingent on their complying with the fundamental rights.

In Part III of the Constitution, Article 13(1) stipulated that all colonial-era laws which were not compliant with fundamental rights would be void.[19] This meant that such pre-constitutional laws which irreconcilably collided with the fundamental rights would be bereft of legality. They would be constitutionally invalid. But the paradox was that such laws would continue to operate till the time a court declared them unconstitutional.

In Article 19(2), sedition was not a ground on which free speech could be curbed. As a result of this, Section 124A was constitutionally invalid because it was not protected by Article 19(2). However, Section 124A had not been legislatively repealed, and therefore it had to be declared unconstitutional for violating the freedom of speech and expression. Otherwise, it would continue to operate, despite being unconstitutional. Fortunately, the Supreme Court rose to the occasion and Justice Sastri willingly took up the task to make the ringing declaration that Section 124A was unconstitutional, rather than waiting for Parliament to repeal the law.

The Constituent Assembly had consciously expunged 'sedition' from the list of restrictions which could be imposed on the freedom of speech. The Assembly had decided that speech affecting the national interest could be restricted only when it undermined the security of the State or where it tended to overthrow the State. Nothing more and nothing less. This decision of the Assembly, in Justice Sastri's opinion, effectively sealed the fate of Section 124A:

> Deletion of the word 'sedition' from the draft Article 13(2), therefore, shows that *criticism of Government exciting disaffection or bad feelings towards it is not to be regarded as a justifying ground for restricting the freedom of expression and of the press*, unless it is such as to undermine the security of or tend to overthrow the State.[20]

Very clearly, nothing in Section 124A even remotely suggested that it related to any matter which pertained to the security of the State. It only pertained to such speech and expression which excited disaffection against the State. Disaffection for the government had nothing to do with the security of the State.

As Justice Sastri noted, 'narrow and stringent limits'[21] have been set out in the Constitution as to when the freedom of speech can be abridged. This meant that if the law had no connection to the grounds mentioned in Article 19(2), then it could not survive for even a moment longer. As soon as it was clear that Section 124A had no connection with any of the enumerated grounds in Article 19(2), the Constitution offered no protection to the law of sedition contained in the Indian Penal Code.[22]

An important value-based judgment informed the Supreme Court's decision in declaring Section 124A unconstitutional. One look at the mass of cases which Section 124A generated from the last decade of the nineteenth century till the 1940s made it clear that the law's victim was any person who discussed governmental affairs in critical terms. Although many of these past decisions contained paeans to the moderation which inhered in the language of Section 124A and the balance it struck in allowing people to ventilate their grievances, the fact of the matter was that the balance was observed in the breach. Indeed, the vagueness which haunted Section 124A was chiefly responsible for a multiplicity of conflicting judgments.

Now that the Indian Constitution had inaugurated an era of representative democracy, it was paramount to closely guard the space in which citizens could engage in political activity. Exciting disaffection could not be a crime. Rather, freedom to engage in political speech and to speak up against the State was a hallmark of the new Constitution, and it was this which led Justice Sastri to declare in ringing terms:

> Thus, very narrow and stringent limits have been set to permissible legislative abridgement of the right of free speech and expression, and this was doubtless due to the realisation that freedom of speech and of the press lay at the foundation of all democratic organisations, *for without free political discussion no public education, so essential for the proper functioning of the processes of popular Government, is possible.*[23]

There was one last paradox which the Supreme Court decided to resolve. What if there was a law of which only a part was relatable to Article 19(2) but the other portions were not? For instance, what was the constitutional status of a law which sought to curb speech on the ground of both security of the State as well as public order? The former was recognized as a ground to curb free speech, but the latter was not.

Here, the Supreme Court ruled that even if part of the law curbed speech on a ground not found in Article 19(2), then the whole law had to be struck down for violating the freedom of speech. This was because such a law restricted the freedom of speech on a ground not recognized by the Constitution. Once it appeared that a law strayed into forbidden constitutional territory by restricting free speech on grounds not authorized by the Constitution, then the law had to be banished.

Such a law could not be rehabilitated by the judiciary donning the hat of a legislator and rewording the law in order to somehow make it consistent with the Constitution.[24] 'So long as the possibility of its being applied for purposes not sanctioned by the Constitution cannot be ruled out,' declared Justice Sastri 'it must be held to be wholly unconstitutional and void.'[25]

Justice Sastri had struck a fatal blow to Section 124A, and if any doubts lingered as to whether in free India sedition remained a crime, they were swiftly and emphatically put to rest. Indeed, a month after the decision in the *Thappar* case, Sardar Patel penned a letter to Jawaharlal Nehru in which he noted that after this judgment, 'criticism of the government, creating disaffection or bad feelings towards it was not to be regarded as a justifying ground for restricting the freedom of the press unless it was such *as to undermine the security of the state*.'[26]

The law involved in the *Brij Bhushan* case too was declared unconstitutional. Here, Section 7(1)(c) of the East Punjab Safety Act of 1949 was under challenge, because acting under it the Chief Commissioner of Delhi had required that before any issue of the *Organiser* was printed, a copy was to be deposited with the Chief Commissioner for scrutiny. This was essentially a case of prior restraint, where the government would decide whether something was worthy of publication.[27]

The problem with Section 7(1)(c) of the East Punjab Safety Act of 1949 was that it authorized the State to interfere with the freedom of speech in order to protect and preserve public order.

Effectively, this law suffered from the same problem which the law in the *Thappar* case had.

The majority, speaking through Justice Sastri, applied their decision in the *Thappar* case and concluded that Section 7(1)(c) of the East Punjab Safety Act of 1949 was unconstitutional, for this law allowed restrictions to be imposed on the press on the ground of public order. Public order was not enumerated as a ground to restrict free speech in Article 19(2), and in *Thappar* the Court had made it clear that any law which claimed to restrict the freedom of speech and expression on the grounds of public order was per se unconstitutional. For this reason, the law in the *Bhushan* case did not create any special difficulties for the Supreme Court.[28]

One judge, Justice Fazl Ali, disagreed.[29] He could not bring himself to agree with the majority's formulation because he believed that public order, public tranquillity and the security of the State were inextricably intertwined. They essentially meant the same thing. As he saw it, it was impossible to keep the State secure without maintaining public order. To introduce any distinction between these concepts would only be possible by straining logic.[30] Justice Fazl Ali also chided the majority's decision (in the *Thappar* case) for declaring Section 124A unconstitutional.[31]

Justice Fazl Ali seemed to think that once it was agreed that the preservation of public order inhered in the preservation of the security of the State, then sedition had to be a crime, because in essence it would result in destabilizing the State, which inevitably harmed public order. What affected the security of the State, reasoned Justice Fazl Ali, essentially implicated public order and public safety.[32] This led him to declare, 'it is difficult to hold that public disorder or public tranquility are not matters which undermine the security of the State.'[33] However, in adopting this line of thinking, Justice Fazl Ali was in error.

While designing Article 19 as a whole, the Constituent Assembly had consciously decided when the preservation of 'public order' could be a ground to restrict civil rights. For example, the right to assemble peacefully without arms guaranteed by Article 19(1)(b) and the right to form associations and unions guaranteed by Article 19(1)(c) had corresponding provisions—Articles 19(3) and 19(4), respectively—by which restrictions could be imposed on these rights. One of the specifically enumerated grounds on which restrictions could be imposed was 'public order.'

Article 19 contained other civil rights as well, such as the right to move freely throughout India guaranteed by Article 19(1)(d), the right to settle and live anywhere in India guaranteed by Article 19(1)(e), the right to property guaranteed by Article 19(1)(f)[34] and the right to decide one's choice of occupation, trade and business guaranteed by Article 19(1)(g). The corresponding provision under which restrictions could be imposed—Articles 19(5) and 19(6), respectively—included the specific ground of 'general public interest.'

As we saw, during the debates in the Constituent Assembly, amendments had been moved to include 'public order' as a ground to restrict the freedom of speech, but they had not fructified into an enumerated ground of restriction in Article 19(2). The Assembly had categorically voted not to include public order as a restriction on the freedom of speech and expression.[35]

Taking all this together, it was clear in 1950 that 'public order' could not be used by the State as a ruse to curb the freedom of speech. This schema of Article 19 is of telling importance, for it shows that in 1950, under Article 19(2), neither general public interest nor public order could be deployed to restrict the freedom of speech. It was to this schema of Article 19 on which Justice Patanjali Sastri had placed a very high premium when holding that 'public order' could not possibly be read into Article 19(2).[36]

Justice Fazl Ali was right in thinking that public order is a legitimate ground to restrict free speech. Yet its absence as an enumerated ground in Article 19(2) was a deliberate decision of the Constituent Assembly. To therefore read 'public order' into the ground of 'security of the State' would undo the carefully calibrated approach adopted by the Constituent Assembly of enumerating specific and limited grounds on which the freedom of speech could be restricted.

The duumvirate of the *Thappar–Bhushan* cases and its expansive embrace of the freedom of speech soon began to take root. In September 1950, the Gujarat High Court invalidated a pre-censorship order (similar to the one in the *Bhushan* case) issued by the Chief Secretary of the Saurashtra government against a publisher in the city of Rajkot. The High Court found that the law under which it was issued had no connection with any enumerated ground in Article 19(2).[37]

In the same month in the case of *Amar Nath Bali*,[38] the Punjab and Haryana High Court invalidated a forfeiture order issued under the Press (Emergency Powers) Act of 1931 by the Chief Commissioner of Delhi. The book in question authored by Bali, *Now It Can be Told*, chronicled the violent aftermath of Partition and the carnage caused by the ensuing communal riots. The forfeiture order was declared bad in law because the Chief Commissioner of Delhi had exercised powers under a provision of the 1931 Act, which could not be sustained under Article 19(2).

Tara Singh and Sedition

In November 1950, Section 124A suffered a second blow when the Punjab and Haryana High Court reaffirmed that Section 124A was a dead law.

Master Tara Singh was a leading member of the Indian nationalist movement and an important figure in the Sikh community. He was one of the most notable proponents of the demand for a separate Punjabi state—a demand which was accepted in 1966.[39] But in 1950, Master Tara Singh had a brush with Section 124A, and he demanded that the Punjab and Haryana High Court strike it down.[40]

None other than M.C. Setalvad, the Attorney General for India, appeared for the state. Setalvad tried to convince the High Court that Section 124A of the IPC was perfectly constitutional because it pertained to the security of the State and also to matters relating to the overthrow of the State. He argued that even otherwise, the observations of the Supreme Court on Section 124A in the *Thappar* case were only incidental remarks and did not affect its constitutional validity.

The High Court thought otherwise. Chief Justice Weston, who wrote the judgment, declared that by its very nature Section 124A punished any attempt to excite disaffection against the government. It was plausible to imagine that such attempts may have no effect either on the security of the State, nor would they result in the overthrow of the State. Even though there may be some instances in which the State's security might be affected, the sheer possibility of such an occasion arising in a particular situation did not justify prohibiting all forms of political speech directed against the government.[41]

Like the Supreme Court's decision in the *Thappar* case, the High Court too reasoned that Section 124A did not deal exclusively with matters concerning the security of the State. This rendered it unconstitutional. The High Court clearly declared that if it were within the realm of likelihood that Section 124A could be used for purposes 'not sanctioned by the constitution,' then it ought to be struck down for violating the freedom of speech and expression.[42]

The Last Straw

In the days following the enactment of the Constitution, the *Thappar–Bhushan* duumvirate of cases played an outsized role in the progressive manner in which the freedom of speech and expression was to be understood. These two cases had set the tone for a more expansive embrace of the liberty to express oneself. Not everyone, however, was convinced that India could afford such an expansive conception of free speech.

A few months before the decision in the *Tara Singh* case was announced, the Patna High Court in September 1950 handed down a decision which set the judiciary on a collision course with Parliament. The net result would be that Article 19(2) would undergo a dramatic transformation in 1951.[43]

Shailabala Devi was the keeper of the Bharati Press in the town of Purulia in Bihar. In September 1949, she was required to deposit a princely sum of Rs 2,000 as security with the Deputy Commissioner. This demand was made under the Press (Emergency Powers) Act, 1931, a colonial-era law which authorized the government to ask printers and publishers to make a security deposit, when it appeared that they had published some material which contravened the Act.

The occasion for demanding that Shailabala Devi deposit Rs 2,000 was that her printing press had published *Sangram*, a pamphlet in Bengali, which contained long rambling prose giving a call to mass violence.[44] Below is a sample of what was published:

> Oh, thou the people with the burning pain of thine heart burn the heart of the oppressive high handed oppressor. Let all wrongs, all highhandedness, all oppressions, all tyrannies be burnt in the flame.[45]

The 1931 Act allowed the government to demand that a security amount be deposited by the keeper of a printing press, if it appeared to the government that such a press published material which violated Section 4 of the Act. In Shailabala Devi's case, the government concluded that the publication of *Sangram* violated Section 4(1)(a) of the Act, a provision which disallowed anything to be published which incited or encouraged others to commit offences such as murder, or any other act involving violence. Hence, the government demanded that she deposit a security amount.

The constitutional question which the Patna High Court had to decide was whether a restriction on writings which advocated violence of any kind could be sustained under Article 19(2). A three-judge bench of the Patna High Court heard the case and concluded that Section 4(1)(a) of the 1931 Act was unconstitutional.[46]

Justice Sarjoo Prasad's majority opinion reasoned that the only possible ground in Article 19(2) under which Section 4(1)(a) could be sustained was the security of the State or matters relating to the overthrow of the State. None of the other enumerated restrictions (such as libel and morality) in Article 19(2) had anything to do with Section 4(1)(a).

Justice Prasad held that giving a call, for instance, to carry out political assassinations, would implicate matters of State security. Nonetheless, the High Court declared that Section 4(1)(a) did not deal exclusively with matters of State security or matters affecting activities designed to overthrow the State. It was too broadly worded. Faced with this reality, it was impossible to uphold the law in question, even if it was shown that the intent behind the law was to preserve 'public order.'[47]

Once it appeared to the courts that the law dealt with an interest not contemplated in Article 19(2) (a reference to public order), it was impossible to save Section 4(1)(a) by refashioning it to apply only in instances where State security was involved. The High Court did not deem it fit to reword and reconstitute Section 4(1)(a) in order to bring it within the four corners of Article 19(2).[48]

Although this was his ruling, Justice Prasad was deeply unhappy with it.[49] As we saw, the judgments of the Supreme Court in the *Thappar-Bhushan* cases required a very strict analysis of the law. The moment it appeared that the law dealt with matters not enumerated in Article 19(2), the entire law had to fall, even though some part of it dealt with the enumerated grounds in Article 19(2).

It was this declaration by the Supreme Court, Justice Prasad observed, which had forced his hand and 'constrained'[50] him to declare the law unconstitutional.[51] However, before concluding his judgment, Justice Prasad sounded an ominous note about the perils of an expansive conception of freedom of speech:

> I am compelled to observe that from the above discussions of the Supreme Court judgments, it follows logically that if a person were to go on inciting murder or other cognizable offences either through the press or by word of mouth, he would be free to do so with impunity inasmuch as he would claim privilege of exercising his fundamental right of freedom of speech and expression. Any legislation which seeks or would seek to curb this right...would have

to be declared void. This would be so, because such speech or expression would fall neither under libel nor slander nor defamation nor contempt of court nor any matter which offends against decency or morality or which undermines the security of or tends to overthrow the State.[52]

Justice Prasad also added:

> I cannot with equanimity contemplate such an anomalous situation but the conclusion appears to be unavoidable on the authority of the Supreme Court judgments with which we are bound.[53]

Since the advent of the Constitution, the Supreme Court and the high courts had been knocking down laws curbing the freedom of speech and expression, one after the next. Justice Prasad's observations and his plaintive cry for reforming the free speech right was the proverbial last straw which broke Parliament's back.

In 1951, Parliament would begin to introspect to find a solution to balance out the freedom of speech and Article 19(2). This introspection would controversially result not only in the exhumation of the Prince in the IPC (Section 124A) but also result in his anointment as King.

6

The Prince Is Dead, Long Live the King

Sedition and the First Amendment

ON 20 JANUARY 1962, SIX DAYS BEFORE INDIA'S TWELFTH ANNIVERSARY as a republic, the Supreme Court turned the clock back on the meaning of freedom and anointed the Prince—Section 124A of the IPC—as King.

In *Kedar Nath Singh v. State of Bihar*,[1] a Constitution Bench of the Supreme Court, comprising five justices and headed by Chief Justice of India B.P. Sinha, declared that Section 124A was constitutional and, therefore, a valid law. It was Chief Justice Sinha who authored the judgment for a unanimous Constitution Bench.

In the town of Begusarai in Bihar, Kedar Nath Singh, a firebrand orator, was prosecuted for sedition. In addressing a gathering of farmers, he had taken aim at everyone—from the government to the police. For his vituperative speeches, he was convicted for sedition and sentenced to a year's imprisonment. When the case reached the Supreme Court, he challenged the constitutional validity of Section 124A, and a Constitution Bench of five justices was formed to hear his plea against sedition.[2]

Since 1962, this decision has remained undisturbed. But in 2021, a slew of petitions were filed in the Supreme Court, which questioned the constitutional validity of Section 124A. On 11 May 2022, the Supreme Court suspended the operation of Section 124A, pending a final decision on the validity of sedition. For the time being, the Supreme Court has injuncted the police from filing any fresh cases under Section 124A and has directed that none of the court cases concerning sedition should proceed further. Clearly, the Supreme Court found some merit in the argument that Section 124A was problematic which raised some constitutional concerns.

Yet, the reality is that the sedition law still remains on the statute books. Its temporary suspension is only a partial relief. In light of this, it becomes all the more important to examine why Section 124A is fundamentally incompatible with the Constitution.

This chapter examines the *Kedar Nath Singh* case in the context of the First Amendment to the Indian Constitution. A large part of the decision in this case was based on the idea that First Amendment gave sedition a new lease of life in free India. The Court concluded that with 'public order' added to Article 19(2), Section 124A was validated.

The belief that the First Amendment validated sedition is flawed. For too long now, the dominant narrative has been that sedition and Section 124A were purposely revived by the First Amendment to the Constitution that Parliament passed in June 1951. This is simply not true. Section 124A has been a dead letter since 1950 and was never brought back to life by the First Amendment to the Indian Constitution.

Schema of the First Amendment

In the summer of 1951, the Constituent Assembly, which became the provisional Parliament of India on 26 January 1950, was deep in discussion over the Representation of the People Act. This was the provisional Parliament's act of active lawmaking to lay down the conditions and requirements for conducting elections in free India. Amidst the deliberations, on the morning of 12 May 1951, at exactly one minute past half past nine, Prime Minister Nehru rose to make an intervention. He moved a bill—the Constitution (First Amendment) Bill—to alter parts of the newly framed Constitution.[3]

On 16 May 1951, the debates on the First Amendment began in earnest,[4] and two days later Parliament decided to refer the First Amendment Bill to a Select Committee.[5] On 25 May 1951, the Select Committee submitted its report,[6] which Nehru placed before Parliament on the same day.[7] Four days later, discussions on the First Amendment Bill and the Select Committee's report resumed, which carried on till 2 June 1951. The final version of the First Amendment Bill was approved and passed by Parliament on 2 June 1951, and it became law on 18 June 1951 when it was published in the Gazette of India, after receiving presidential assent. It was officially titled 'The Constitution [First Amendment] Act, 1951.'[8]

In the First Amendment Bill, the proposed changes to the freedom of speech took centre stage. Section 3(1)(a) of the First Amendment Bill introduced a brand-new Article 19(2), by which the freedom of speech could be curbed on three new grounds—'public order,' 'friendly relations with foreign states,' and 'incitement to an offence.'[9]

Public order was introduced as a new ground in Article 19(2) to give effect to Justice Fazl Ali's dissenting judgment in the *Thappar–Bhushan* cases.[10] With this, the entire gamut of laws pertaining to public order, public safety and public tranquillity, including laws by which the freedom of the press could be curbed, would now be valid.

Incitement to an offence was introduced as a ground to specifically neutralize the Patna High Court's decision in the *Shailabala Devi* case.[11] And 'friendly relations with foreign states' was introduced to ensure that speech which bordered on war-mongering could be curbed.[12]

Further, the First Amendment proposed to delete 'slander' and 'libel' in Article 19(2), since they fell within the head of 'defamation,' which anyway was an enumerated restriction in the original Article 19(2).[13]

Although these proposed amendments were eventually approved, Parliament ensured that the State would not have unlimited powers in restricting the freedom of speech and expression. When the First Amendment Bill went to the Select Committee, it was decided that the power of the State to curb free speech must have limits. This was achieved by introducing, in Article 19(2), the phrase 'reasonable restrictions'[14]—a proposal which Parliament approved.

The new Article 19(2) had several implications. As a primary matter, if a law affecting the freedom of speech which pre-dated the Constitution could now trace its roots to the new grounds enumerated in Article 19(2), the law would be saved from unconstitutionality. There were many colonial-era laws that had not yet come under the judicial scanner and hence had not been declared unconstitutional, for violating the freedom of speech.

The new Article 19(2) hoped to save such laws before they were declared constitutionally invalid by a judicial decision.

In Parliament, the law minister, Dr B.R. Ambedkar, took the example of the Foreign Relations Act of 1932, which could potentially be invalidated because 'friendly relations with foreign states' had not been enumerated in the original Article 19(2), as a ground on which free speech could be restricted. The State could not make a law curbing the right of a citizen to criticize countries which were friendly with India. If the State did try to curb such speech, the law would have likely been invalidated, because none of the grounds enumerated in the original Article 19(2) could have helped to sustain the 1932 Act.

It was to avoid this eventuality in respect of this as well as of other laws dealing with, for instance, public order, that motivated the restructuring of Article 19(2).[15] 'I do not think it requires an astrologer to predict,' Dr Ambedkar said, 'that when that question comes before the judiciary, they will follow the same line of interpretation.'[16]

In short, such laws had to be saved—by resort to constitutional amendments—before they were declared unconstitutional by the judicial branch. For his part, however, Nehru believed that the 1932 Act was well past its expiry date since the purposes for which it was enacted no longer existed and the country which it spoke of (Nepal) already had friendly relations with India.[17]

The enumeration of new grounds in Article 19(2) also empowered the State to make new laws to curb the freedom of speech and expression for preserving 'public order'—something that could not have been done under the original Article 19(2). In this sense, the new Article 19(2) was anticipatory in nature. This was the second important purpose that the new Article 19(2) served.

Finally, the First Amendment also sought to retrospectively validate those laws which had been struck down for violating the freedom of speech in the 1950s. In this sense, the new Article 19(2) was also retrospective in nature.

The First Amendment declared that the new Article 19(2) would be deemed to have been the only Article 19(2) the Constitution had ever known. In other words, the new Article 19(2) was deemed to have always been a part of the Constitution—that is, from 26 January 1950. Section 3 of the First Amendment which introduced the new Article 19(2), announced in no uncertain terms that the new Article 19(2) 'shall always be deemed to have been enacted in the following form.' Effectively, the original Article 19(2) which was approved by the Constituent Assembly in 1950 was effaced—as if it had never existed.

To further clarify exactly how Article 19(2) would be retrospective, the First Amendment contained a separate clause which dealt with the revival of those laws which had been struck down in the 1950s, for violating the freedom of speech, as in the *Thappar–Bhushan* cases. This 'savings clause,' as it was known, was enumerated in Section 3(2) of the First Amendment Bill and was to be a new article which would seemingly be placed after Article 19(6) in the Constitution. Section 3(2) read:

> No law in force in the territory of India immediately before the commencement of the Constitution which is consistent with the provisions of article 19 of the Constitution as amended by sub-section (1) of this section shall be deemed to be void, or ever have become void, on the ground only that, being a law which takes away or abridges the right conferred by sub-clause (a) of clause

(1) of the said article, its operation was not saved by sub-clause (2) of that article as originally enacted.[18]

What the First Amendment did was this: if a law was struck down on the ground that it could not be traced to any enumerated restriction in the original Article 19(2), and if after the First Amendment the same law could now be in conformity with the newly enumerated restrictions (for instance, public order), such a law would revive. There legislature need not re-enact such a law. But there was an important stipulation. In order for these dead laws to revive, they had to satisfy all the requirements of the new Article 19(2). This meant that such laws would have to also measure up to the standard of being reasonable restrictions on the freedom of speech.

As we shall see, Section 124A does not fulfil the requirements of Article 19(2), and, cannot be classified as a reasonable restriction on the fundamental right to free speech. In Parliament, none other than Nehru would make a passionate case for why sedition no longer survived, even after the First Amendment. However, this proposed Section 3(2) of the First Amendment Bill has a rather mysterious life. Although it was passed by Parliament, it never actually entered the Constitution. And to this day it remains absent from the text of the Constitution.

In addition to the freedom of speech, other fundamental rights as well as other parts of the Constitution also underwent changes, like the inclusion of a new fundamental right pertaining to reservation for backward classes. But, above all, the proposed amendments in the First Amendment Bill regarding property rights were the most far-reaching and proved to be as controversial as the amendments to Article 19.

It had been the resolve of the Congress Party to ensure that in free India, equality in the realm of landholding and agrarian reform was achieved, with a special focus on completely dismantling the zamindari system of landholding.[19] In Part III of the Constitution, Article 31 inaugurated a scheme under which property could be acquired by the State upon the payment of compensation. But the implementation of Article 31 proved deeply problematic.[20]

Soon after the Constitution came into force, land reform laws were challenged in the high courts. The Patna High Court, in the *Kameshwar Singh* case, declared the Bihar Land Reform Act, 1950 unconstitutional.[21] This decision set off alarm bells in the government, because the government feared that if land reform laws could not be sustained under the Constitution, a vital promise of the Congress government would remain unfulfilled. 'If there is one thing to which we as a party have been committed in the past generation or so,' Nehru said in Parliament when introducing the First Amendment, 'it is the agrarian reform and the abolition of the zamindari system.'[22]

To ensure that laws relating to land reform and acquisition of property would not be rendered vulnerable in future, the First Amendment Bill introduced two new articles. By Section 4 of the First Amendment Bill, a new Article 31A was introduced, which declared that any law by which the State sought the acquisition of any estate or any right in an estate could not be declared unconstitutional by any court, even if a fundamental right was violated.[23] But what of the laws, such as the Bihar law, which had been declared unconstitutional? How were they to be saved?

The answer was a new Article 31B and a companion schedule, the Ninth Schedule. The idea for creating a special schedule which granted blanket protection to laws from any form of judicial review originated in a suggestion made by V.K. Thiruvenkatachari, the

Advocate General of Madras. He, in a letter of 14 March 1951, recommended to K.V.K. Sundaram, the Law Secretary, that a new schedule should be created that must include laws which can never be rendered unconstitutional, even if they violated a provision of the Constitution.[24]

Section 5 of the First Amendment Bill introduced Article 31B,[25] and Section 14 introduced a new Ninth Schedule in the Constitution.[26] This new article served two purposes. If a law was placed in the Ninth Schedule, it could never be called into question for violating fundamental rights. Further, if any law had been declared unconstitutional by any court (whether a high court or the Supreme Court), then Article 31B empowered Parliament to place that law in the Ninth Schedule. Once that was done, the law would revive, as if it had never been invalidated.

The moment any law which violated fundamental rights, including a law that had previously been declared unconstitutional, was placed in the Ninth Schedule, then no court—not even the Supreme Court—could call it into question. The First Amendment Bill proposed that eleven land reform laws must be placed in the Ninth Schedule.[27] Eventually, when the First Amendment was passed by Parliament in June 1951, thirteen such laws were placed in the Ninth Schedule.

Under current constitutional doctrine, the high courts and the Supreme Court are invested with the power to declare a law unconstitutional. Articles 13(1) and 13(2) of the Constitution ordain that once a law is declared unconstitutional, that law is rendered void, which means that it no longer possesses any legally binding force.[28] When this declaration is made by the courts, the only way in which the law in question can then be revived is by the legislature curing the law of its constitutional ailments and reworking the offending parts so that the law is brought in conformity with the Constitution. Until this is done, a law declared void remains in suspended animation.[29]

In the First Amendment, provisions such as Article 31B hoped to avoid this long-drawn procedure of the legislature correcting the laws and bringing them in line with the Constitution. It simply deemed these laws valid once they were put in the Ninth Schedule, even though they affected fundamental rights in a deleterious manner.

Articles 31A and 31B were introduced even though the Supreme Court was yet to make a declaration on whether the land reform laws, particularly the Bihar Land Reform Act, were constitutional. Incidentally, the very first law added to the Ninth Schedule by the First Amendment was the Bihar Land Reform Act. By contrast, the amendments to Article 19 were made after the Supreme Court had arrived at a decision in the *Thappar–Bhushan* cases.

That was why when the Supreme Court heard the *Kameshwar Singh* case in 1952 it remarked that the First Amendment had rendered any decision by the Supreme Court on the validity of the Bihar Land Reforms Act redundant, so far as fundamental rights were concerned.[30] Article 31B created an impenetrable shield for laws which Parliament decided to house in the Ninth Schedule.[31]

The First Amendment on the Floor of Parliament

Nehru had introduced the First Amendment Bill on 12 May 1951, and four days later Parliament commenced its deliberations over these proposals. On that day, Nehru delivered a long speech in defence of the First Amendment, particularly of the changes being made to Article 19. Nehru was forthright in admitting that a series of judicial decisions had led to the realization that when it came to the Constitution, the Constituent Assembly may have made 'errors in drafting.'[32] And now that these errors had been brought to light, it became the bounden duty of Parliament to correct them in its constituent capacity.[33]

Nehru believed that of all the proposals the First Amendment Bill contained, the amendment of Article 19 and the amendments on property rights were the most important and far-reaching.[34] Cries of 'shame' against the press were heard from members in Parliament, when Nehru castigated a section of the press for 'poisoning the mind of the younger generation, degrading their mental integrity and moral standards.'[35] The entire issue thus became one of amending Article 19 to protect impressionable minds from the 'untruth' and 'falsehood' that was routinely published.[36]

A large part of Nehru's speech focused on how the press in India had lost its way and had ended up becoming a caricature of itself. As he put it, the conduct of the press raised not only a constitutional problem, but also 'a moral problem.' 'From the way untruth is bandied about and falsehood thrown about,' Nehru said in Parliament, 'it has become quite impossible to distinguish what is true and what is false.'[37]

Many events influenced the proposals in the First Amendment, but uppermost amongst them was Justice Sarjoo Prasad's observations in the *Shailabala Devi* case—that the Constitution did not bar the incitement of crime. Nehru told Parliament that if one could stoke violence and criminal behaviour and take shelter under the freedom of speech, that would be an 'extraordinary state of affairs.'[38]

Moreover, judicial decisions had made it difficult to sustain a law which curbed freedom of speech to preserve public order. As we saw, the *Thappar–Bhushan* decisions had held that 'public order' could not become the basis for restricting free speech since it was not an enumerated restriction in the original Article 19(2). On this score, Nehru told Parliament that by introducing 'public order' in Article 19(2), Parliament would now be empowered to deal with emergent situations.[39]

S.P. Mookerjee was the first person to reply, and what troubled him was the introduction of public order as a restriction in Article 19(2). Mookerjee argued that this amendment was unnecessary. Instead, he seemed to think that the executive was already armed with powers under the Preventive Detention Act (passed in 1950), and it was this law which had to be used to detain any person who potentially threatened public order and tranquillity.[40]

This was a problematic solution. Preventive detention is one of the most serious limitations that can be imposed on a person's liberty, because when persons are preventively detained, they are detained without having committed a crime. They can be detained on the mere suspicion that they may potentially commit a crime or pose some sort of threat to law and order.

Preventive detention does not require a trial or the marshalling of evidence for convicting a person. It is a mechanism to detain a person without a charge and without a trial. To propose that people ought to be detained indefinitely on the suspicion that they are a threat to public order because of what they express was to suggest a far more pernicious method of curbing a person's liberty than a law which curbs only the freedom of speech on a matter affecting public order. Pandit Thakur Dass Bhargava who spoke after Mookerjee highlighted all these problems and advised Parliament that going down the route of preventive detention in respect of the freedom of speech was not the best course of action.[41]

Bhargava vociferously opposed the First Amendment Bill in bringing back sedition. 'I am stunned,' Bhargava exclaimed in Parliament, referring to the prospect of the First Amendment once again installing Section 124A as a valid law.[42] Bhargava spent a large part of his speech praising the Constituent Assembly's decision of getting rid of sedition as a curb on free speech, because sedition in India had had a particularly odious history.[43] Now that India had made this advance, Bhargava wondered, why must the First Amendment attempt to 'see that those very laws which were obnoxious and were never liked by us are revived.'[44]

The law minister, Dr Ambedkar, addressed Parliament on 18 May 1951 to present a robust defence of the First Amendment. Dr Ambedkar told Parliament that with many laws struck down for violating the freedom of speech between 1950 and 1951, several options were available for reviving these laws that the country needed. Rather than letting these laws lapse or waiting for the legislatures to re-enact them, it was decided that in the First Amendment Bill a separate provision should declare these laws retrospectively valid—as if they had never been invalidated.

However, there was an important caveat to this: the laws that had been struck down (which would include Section 124A) would be revived only on one condition—that they measured up to the standards stipulated in the new Article 19(2).[45] If it was proved that despite the First Amendment, these past laws that had been invalidated could not be rescued by the new Article 19(2), then the law would continue to remain unconstitutional.[46] As Dr Ambedkar said in Parliament:

> The Bill says: let the laws which have been declared by the Supreme Court and the High Courts to be null and void

be deemed to be alive but subject to one proviso and that proviso is that they shall not be alive in their original body and flesh but they shall be alive only in such degree and in such manner as is consistent with the amended article 19. That is the position now.[47]

This novel solution for reviving these dead laws was born out of administrative convenience. Dr Ambedkar told Parliament in no uncertain terms that it was wishful thinking to wait for the legislatures to go back to the drawing board and redraft the laws which had been struck down. The better and quicker option was to retrospectively validate these laws through an amendment to the Constitution.[48] Nonetheless, questions still loomed as to whether this was the correct process. When Dr Ambedkar was pointedly asked by Shiv Charan Lal whether it was constitutionally proper for Parliament to validate all these laws through the means of a constitutional amendment, Dr Ambedkar simply replied, 'Oh yes; undoubtedly.'[49]

Administrative convenience also influenced the framing of Article 31B and the Ninth Schedule. Dr Ambedkar recognized that the process of amending the Constitution to validate laws and rescuing them from judicial review was an 'unusual procedure.'[50] But it was too much to ask of the Union Government to vet every state law on land reform and redraft it to bring it in line with the Constitution. The easier and more feasible option was to place land reform laws enacted by different states in the Ninth Schedule.[51]

This was, after all, the first ever amendment being made to the Constitution and there was no precedent for what could or could not be done by Parliament in its constituent capacity. It was only in 1973 that Parliament was told by a bench of thirteen justices of the Supreme Court in the *Kesavananda Bharati* case—the largest bench ever constituted to hear a case in the history of India—that Parliament could not use its amending powers to tinker with the basic structure of the Constitution.[52]

There was a noticeable difference in the way the government treated laws affecting land reform laws and free speech. When it came to land reform laws, Article 31B made a blanket declaration: even if the law was invalidated by the courts, once it was housed in the Ninth Schedule the law would stand revived even though it offended fundamental rights and had been struck down on that score.

This blanket protection was not granted to the laws curbing free speech which were struck down between 1950 and 1951. On the other hand, the laws affecting free speech would be revived only on the condition that they complied with the new Article 19(2). Otherwise, they would continue to remain unconstitutional.

More tellingly, in the First Amendment Bill, only land reform laws were proposed to be placed in the Ninth Schedule and not a single law which had been invalidated for violating the freedom of speech, including Section 124A, was to be placed in the Ninth Schedule. The debates on the new Article 19(2) were rocked by bitter rancour, particularly because many members did not want the laws which had been the bane of their existence during the freedom struggle to once again take root in free India. That was perhaps the reason why Dr Ambedkar hoped to win the confidence of the House by stating that laws affecting free speech would be revived, but only conditionally.[53]

Dr Ambedkar, however, was not able to allay everyone's fears. J.P. Srivastava decried the retrospective validation of laws as 'extremely reprehensible,'[54] while P.D. Himatsingka termed the First Amendment as more in the nature of a 'validating measure than a mere enabling one.'[55] To reassure members, Nehru intervened in the debates on 18 May 1951. He too told Parliament that the validation measure in respect of the freedom of speech and expression was a conditional measure.

Under it, laws which had been struck down for violating the freedom of speech would not rise up immediately like a phoenix from its ashes. Rather, they could only revive so long as they remained consistent with the new Article 19(2). Hence, it was possible for these laws to remain unconstitutional, despite the First Amendment.[56]

A Mysterious Disappearance

With Nehru's assurance, Parliament referred the First Amendment Bill to the Select Committee. To the government's credit, the greatest and harshest critics of the First Amendment Bill, including S.P. Mookerjee and H.N. Kunzru, were nominated to the Select Committee. This itself is an enduring testament to the power of collaborative lawmaking amongst legislative members who fundamentally disagree on important constitutional issues.

As we saw, the First Amendment contained a separate provision in Section 3(2), which announced that all laws affecting free speech which had been struck down would be revived if they could now trace their roots to the new Article 19(2). Section 3(2) received close scrutiny in the Select Committee. But this provision has a remarkable story, which only begins after the First Amendment was approved by Parliament.

Of the twenty-one members of the Select Committee, which included Nehru, Dr Ambedkar as well as the Home Minister, C. Rajagopalachari (who also served as India's last Governor-General), six members dissented with the recommendations of the Select Committee. The majority of the Select Committee put their seal of approval on Section 3(2) in the First Amendment Bill, but not the dissentients.

Kunzru, in discussing Section 124A, thought that it was a retrograde law and a fossil of a time that had thankfully gone by, which was why it ought not be revived at all.[57] Another dissenter, Naziruddin Ahmed, thought Section 3(2) of the First Amendment Bill to be a 'dangerous provision' because 'dead laws' would be brought back to life.[58]

Ultimately, Parliament decided to approve Section 3(2) of the First Amendment Bill and gave it its vote of approval on 1 June 1951.[59] But here things take a mysterious turn.

In the text of the First Amendment, which was published in the Gazette of India, Section 3(2) was present, but for unstated reasons it never found a place in the Constitution. This is a mystery for which there is no adequate explanation.

At any rate, Section 3(2) was strangely worded. In the First Amendment Bill, each section commenced with a heading announcing which article of the Constitution was being amended. If a new article was being introduced, then that particular clause in the First Amendment made a declaration to that effect and mentioned its numbering in the Constitution. For instance, Section 5 of the First Amendment, which introduced Article 31B, began with the heading 'Insertion of a new article 31B.'

This was true for other sections in the First Amendment too, and one could tell which section added which new article to the Constitution. But in the text of the First Amendment, Section 3(2) had no heading. Nothing indicated which article in the Constitution Section 3(2) was to become, and nothing suggested whether it was to be added to Article 19(2) or not. In short, we do not know what article number was to be given to Section 3(2) in the Constitution.

More than a decade and a half after the passage of the First Amendment, the mysterious disappearance of Section 3(2) caught the attention of the Supreme Court.

In 1967, eleven justices of the Supreme Court (which at that time was the largest bench of judges that had ever assembled) announced their decision in the *Golak Nath* case.[60] Here, the Supreme Court was mainly concerned with Parliament's power to amend the Constitution. One judge, Justice Hidayatullah,[61] in his separate judgment commented on the mystery surrounding the disappearance of Section 3(2) of the First Amendment. This is what Justice Hidayatullah observed:

> This sub-section [Section 3(2)] *was not included* in the Constitution. *That device was followed in respect of certain State statutes dealing with property rights by including them in a new Schedule.* It did not then occur to Parliament that the laws could be placed under a special umbrella of constitutional protection. Perhaps it was not considered necessary because Article 19(2) was retrospectively changed, and the enactment of this sub-section was an ordinary legislative action. If the amendment had failed, the second sub-section of Section 3 would not have availed at all.[62]

Even the Supreme Court confirms the theory which has been advanced here, that Section 3(2) of the First Amendment never actually entered the text of the Constitution. Justice Hidayatullah suggested that this particular provision was probably kept out since it only clarified what was always the meaning of the First

Amendment with regard to the fundamental right to free speech: that the new Article 19(2) would be the basis for validation of the laws which had been felled by the courts between 1950 and 1951, and therefore there was no need to restate that same principle in another provision.

Nehru's Intervention

In *Kedar Nath Singh*, the Supreme Court reasoned that Section 124A was a valid law because it pertained to the preservation of public order. With 'public order' becoming part of Article 19(2), the logic ran, sedition was saved from unconstitutionality, given that Article 19(2) had retrospective effect. In the judgment, several pages were devoted to drawing a strong connect between Section 124A and how it was in the interest of public order.

What appears to have animated the Supreme Court's reasoning was the decision of the Federal Court in the *Niharendu Dutt Majumdar* case. As we saw, the Federal Court had ruled that Section 124A was applicable to those situations when, as a result of the speech in question, public order was threatened. This strand of reasoning was picked up by the Supreme Court to declare that Section 124A was, therefore, in the interest of public order.

As a result, the Supreme Court held that the introduction of 'public order' as an enumerated ground in Article 19(2) by the First Amendment revived Section 124A.[63] Although an appealing proposition in itself, the First Amendment to the Constitution introduced a fundamental change in what 'public order' meant when it came to restrictions on free speech. This paradigm decisively rejected drawing of any link between public order and Section 124A.

The amendments to Article 19(2) were not intended to enumerate a new ground of restriction by which Section 124A was to be saved. Moreover, when the ground of 'public order' was enumerated in the new Article 19(2), Section 124A continued to remain unconstitutional because 'public order' could not sustain it. This is because 'public order' relates only to matters affecting public tranquillity and community interests. In other words, it relates to matters which are local in nature. That is how the Supreme Court had defined 'public order' in the *Romesh Thappar* case.

As the Constitution saw it in 1950, sedition could only be a crime when it pertained to speech and expression which directly harmed State security and the foundations of the State. For the purposes of the Constitution, public order and sedition relate to entirely different sets of circumstances, for sedition has nothing to do with public order.

During the debates in Parliament, it had appeared to many that the First Amendment would create new grounds on which to breathe life into Section 124A. Nehru sought to dispel those concerns. Speaking in Parliament on 18 May 1951, Nehru proclaimed:

> There are the laws of sedition and the others. Let us take the law of sedition. *Now, I cannot conceive that that is going to function or will be allowed to function or can function in future, unless* it comes under the other clauses of *endangering the security of the state* etc. etc.[64]

This clearly points to the fact that the only version of sedition which Article 19 would tolerate, even after the First Amendment, was in respect of those activities which led to the destabilization of the State. This point emphasized by Nehru was consistent with the Constituent Assembly's vision that the Constitution could only treat such actions as sedition which led to acts which endangered State security and stability. Importantly, this also shows that the addition of 'public order' in Article 19(2) was not supposed to make any difference to the future of Section 124A.

Nehru was right. Both the Supreme Court (in the *Romesh Thappar* case) and the Punjab High Court (in the *Tara Singh* case) had clearly declared that Section 124A had absolutely nothing to do with the security of the State and had no connection with preserving it, for it only punished the excitement of disaffection against the government. It was a law which, by imprisoning freethinking Indians, applied a balm to the 'wounded vanity' of governments.

If this categorical statement of Nehru's was not enough, on 29 May 1951, when Parliament was discussing the Select Committee's report, just before the clock struck eleven, Nehru made his thoughts on Section 124A and sedition clarion clear:

> Take again section 124A of the Indian Penal Code. Now so far as I am concerned that particular section is *highly objectionable and obnoxious* and it *should have no place both for practical and historical reasons*, if you like, in any body of laws that we might pass. *The sooner we get rid of it the better.* We might deal with that matter in other ways, in more limited ways, as every other country does but that particular thing as it is *should have no place, because all of us have had enough experience of it in a variety of ways and apart from the logic of the situation, our urges are against it.*[65]

Nehru then added:

> *I do not think myself that these changes that we bring about validate the thing to any large extent.* I do not think so, because the whole thing has to be interpreted by a court of law in the full context, not only of this thing but other things as well. Suppose you pass an amendment of the constitution to a particular article. *Surely that particular article does not put an end to the rest of the Constitution, the spirit, the language, the objective and the rest?* It only clarifies an issue in regard to that particular article.[66]

In 1958, in the *Ram Nandan* case,[67] a Full Bench of the Allahabad High Court comprising Justices M.C. Desai, R.N. Gurtu and N.U. Beg struck down Section 124A as not being saved by the new Article 19(2). This decision was overturned by the Supreme Court in the *Kedar Nath Singh* case. But in *Ram Nandan*, the Full Bench relied on this portion of Nehru's speech in Parliament to declare that 'sedition' was always treated as a ground which was outside of 'public order.' Thus, despite the First Amendment to the Constitution, the fact that 'sedition' was not added to Article 19(2) clearly demonstrated that the law was not revived, even though 'public order' was a part of Article 19(2).[68]

The restructuring of Article 19(2), which included the addition of 'public order,' was not supposed to make much of a difference to Section 124A or, as Nehru pejoratively called it, 'the thing' (perhaps so revolted by the provision that he preferred not to mention it in formal terms).

During the debates in Parliament, there had been some doubts over the precise list of laws which were sought to be saved by the amendment of Article 19(2). To these demands, Nehru had remarked that it was impossible to exhaustively catalogue every single law which would be saved by the changes made to the free speech right by the First Amendment.[69] Yet, it was evident that sedition was not part of the catalogue of laws saved by Article 19(2).

It is surprising that in *Kedar Nath Singh*, the Supreme Court did not delve into the debates which occurred when the First Amendment Bill was debated in Parliament. The debates illuminated an important aspect of the amendment process—the addition of new restrictions in Article 19(2) were not related to sedition at all. Nehru's interventions in the deliberations also demonstrated that the understanding of the Constituent Assembly—that for something to be treated as sedition it must affect State security—would remain unaltered even after the First Amendment.

7
The Decisive Distinction

Sedition, State Security and Public Order

IT IS IMPORTANT TO EXPLORE WHY, UNDER THE CONSTITUTION, 'SEDITION' (as defined in Section 124A) is unrelated to 'public order' when it comes to the enumerated grounds in Article 19(2). For this, we must turn to history to understand the decisive distinction which the Constitution drew between sedition and public order.

As we saw, the earliest occasion on which the Constituent Assembly dealt with sedition was when the Advisory Committee prepared its Interim Report on Fundamental Rights in April 1947. In the charter of 'Justiciable Fundamental Rights' which accompanied the Interim Report, the Advisory Committee had stipulated that the freedom of speech, could be curbed on the broad grounds of public order, morality, and a declared emergency.

For the freedom of speech, the Advisory Committee also prepared an additional list of specific restrictions, including 'sedition'.[1] But on 30 April 1947, when the recommended clause on free speech was taken up by the Assembly, Patel announced that he was not going to move the specific list of restrictions that had been recommended.[2]

That is how sedition (as contained in Section 124A) was abandoned on the floor of the Assembly by Patel. What was approved by the Assembly on that day was a provision for curbing of free speech on three grounds only, including public order.[3]

This early vote on free speech made a clear distinction between sedition and public order, in that they operated in entirely different spheres. 'Public order' dealt with matters of public safety and local interests. 'Sedition' dealt only with Section 124A. Had public order covered sedition too, there would have been no need to separately mention 'sedition' in the list of restrictions on the freedom of speech, as had been proposed by the Advisory Committee in its Interim Report.

This distinction, between sedition and public order, was observed by B.N. Rau too. The freedom of speech and expression in Clause 15(1) of Rau's Draft Constitution of October 1947, was subject only to public order and morality. Next to the free speech clause, Rau had made a marginal noting that the source of inspiration for his free speech clause (as well as the other civil rights in Clause 15) was Article 40(6) of the Irish Constitution.[4]

Important to note is that in the Irish Constitution, the freedom of speech was subject to public order as well as sedition.[5] When Rau looked at the Irish Constitution, he only borrowed the ground of 'public order' and not the ground of sedition. Thus, in Rau's Draft Constitution too, the absence of 'sedition' clearly indicated that Section 124A was not to be a fetter on free speech.

In the Draft Constitution prepared by the Drafting Committee in 1948, a reversal occurred. Draft Article 13 contained specific civil rights, like the right to move freely across India and the right to practise one's choice of profession. Draft Article 13(1)(a) guaranteed the freedom of speech and expression, and draft Article 13(2) contained the grounds on which free speech could be restricted, in which 'sedition' was specifically enumerated as a curb on free speech. However, 'public order' as an enumerated ground in draft Article 13(2) was conspicuous by its absence.[6]

Public order was not to be a ground on which free speech could be curbed. In effect, even the Drafting Committee confirmed the thesis that 'sedition' and 'public order' were unrelated. More importantly, 'public order' was not the ground on which Section 124A was to be sustained. Due to this understanding, a separate ground of 'sedition' had to be enumerated as a restriction on the freedom of speech for Section 124A to remain valid. Sedition had nothing to with the preservation of public order and vice versa.

As we saw, when the Constituent Assembly took up the freedom of speech for discussion on 1 December 1948, K.M. Munshi spearheaded the effort to have sedition deleted. He succeeded because the next day Dr Ambedkar agreed with Munshi and decided to drop sedition as a curb on free speech. But Munshi did tell the Assembly that only a law which treated positive acts aimed at undermining State security or seeking to overthrow the State as sedition would be authorized by the Constitution as a curb on free speech.[7]

What Munshi achieved was to establish as a constitutional canon that speaking about the government in less than favourable terms had nothing to do with sedition, much less with public order. Simply exciting disaffection did not even remotely harm State security interests, let alone pose a threat to public order. As Munshi saw it, government regulation could apply only to such speech and expression which truly threatened the foundation of the State.[8]

Nonetheless, when the freedom of speech was under discussion, the Constituent Assembly wrestled with the idea of enumerating 'public order' as a ground to curb free speech. Just as the debates began on 1 December 1948, Damodar Swarup Seth, who represented the United Provinces, immediately moved Amendment No. 412, by which all the civil rights enumerated in draft Article 13, including the freedom of speech, were to be made subject only to public order or morality.[9]

As the debates progressed, the Assembly seemed to be making a move towards enumerating 'public order' as a curb for the other rights enumerated in draft Article 13, but not for free speech. For instance, Dr Ambedkar moved an amendment motion to make public order a ground for restricting the freedom of association,[10] which the Assembly approved.[11]

Seth's efforts proved unsuccessful, for on 2 December 1948 the Assembly rejected his amendment motion, which meant that the Assembly rejected the proposal of curbing of free speech on the ground of public order.[12]

This historical excursus is revealing. It shows that when 'sedition' was dropped from the list of restrictions on free speech by the Assembly on 30 April 1947, in effect Section 124A was dropped, even though the ground of 'public order' was retained. The fact that at one moment in time 'public order' as well as 'sedition' appeared as distinct grounds to restrict free speech lends credence to the idea that sedition and public order were unrelated and occupied different fields entirely.[13]

This is confirmed by the fact that in the Drafting Committee's Draft Constitution, 'sedition' was specifically enumerated as a curb on free speech, and 'public order' was not made a ground.

Ultimately, 'sedition' itself was removed by the Constituent Assembly—which is why under the Constitution sedition could only be a crime when it affected the very foundations of the State.

It is this which led the courts to declare Section 124A unconstitutional in 1950, because from its plain words it had no connection with State security or with preservation of the foundations of the Indian State. This was Munshi's vision for the freedom of speech, which received near- unanimous support in the Constituent Assembly.

Furthermore, even the Drafting Committee, as well as the Constituent Assembly, would have been mindful of the fact that sedition as defined in Section 124A had nothing to do with the preservation of public order. That was the reason why 'sedition' had to be enumerated as a specific head for restricting free speech. Otherwise, there was no question of Section 124A operating as a fetter on the freedom of speech and expression.

In the Drafting Committee's Draft Constitution which was presented to the Assembly in November 1948, the ground of 'public order' for curbing the freedom of speech was deleted, but 'sedition' was retained, with Section 124A in mind.[14] If sedition was subsumed under public order, then there would never have been the need for the Draft Constitution to spell out 'sedition' as a specific ground for curbing the freedom of speech and expression.

Importantly, the First Amendment to the Indian Constitution in 1951 did not delete 'security of the State' as an enumerated restriction in Article 19(2). After the First Amendment, both 'security of the State' and 'public order' were enumerated as distinct grounds for curbing free speech. That these two grounds coexisted next to each other in the new Article 19(2) only shows that public order meant something other than security of the State.

Concentric Circles

Indeed, for the purposes of Article 19(2), State security, public order, and law and order operate at entirely different levels and are not interrelated concepts. Security of the State may sometimes involve a public order dimension, but the converse is not always true. To explore the depth of this thesis, we must draw on the sagacious wisdom of one of India's greatest Supreme Court judges, Justice K. Subba Rao.

In 1960, a Constitution Bench of five justices in the *Ram Manohar Lohia* case resolved an important constitutional question: What impact did the addition of 'public order' in Article 19(2) have on the freedom of speech?[15] Justice Subba Rao (later, he served as Chief Justice of India from 30 June 1966 till 11 April 1967) authored the judgment, and in it he presented a sedulous answer to this important question.

Public order was an enormously capacious term and could take within its scope almost everything, ranging from a petty dispute to matters affecting State security. But when it came to free speech and the Constitution, this broad concept of public order was rejected.

Justice Subba Rao began with an assessment of the decision in the *Romesh Thappar* case, which held that in the initial iteration of Article 19(1)(a) and Article 19(2) in 1950, the Constituent Assembly chose matters affecting State security as the only concept from the broad framework of public order, as a ground to curb free speech. In other words, only an aggravated form of public disorder was accepted as a ground for restricting free speech.

This, however, created a constitutional vacuum, since acts of lesser significance which affected public order were outside the scope of Article 19(2). As we saw, in his dissent in the *Thappar-*

Bhushan cases, this had been Justice Fazl Ali's principal critique of Article 19(2). In view of this, according to Justice Subba Rao, what the First Amendment did was 'bring in offences involving breach of purely local significance within the scope of permissible restrictions'[16] enumerated in Article 19(2).

This distinction is important. The introduction of 'public order' was intended to apply to those situations in which the general safety and orderly life of the public was involved. It was not meant to subsume every sort of public order interest within it. To draw a contrast, Justice Subba Rao examined international practices. He observed that in the US, when it came to curbing free speech, a 'loud and raucous noise,' as well as 'utterances tending to incite an immediate breach of the peace or riot' were treated under the broad scope of public order.[17] And this was also the case in England.[18]

In stark contrast, all the restrictions which were enumerated in Article 19(2), ranging from defamation to State security, technically fell under the rubric of public order. However, since separate and distinct grounds to curb free speech were enumerated, it showed that public order was 'split up under different heads.'[19] The fact that 'public order' was enumerated alongside 'security of the State' could, according to Justice Subba Rao, mean only one thing:

> But the juxtaposition of the different grounds indicates that, though sometimes they tend to overlap, they must be ordinarily intended to exclude each other. *'Public Order' is therefore something which is demarcated from the others. In that limited sense, particularly in view of the history of the amendment,* it can be postulated that *'public order' is synonymous with public peace, safety and tranquillity.*[20]

Justice Subba Rao had thus given proper shape to the specific meaning that ought to be attributed to 'public order' in Article 19(2). The guiding principle, according to Justice Subba Rao, was that 'public order' was 'synonymous with public safety and public tranquillity: it is the absence of disorder involving breaches of local significance.' It did not deal with those matters involving 'national upheavals such as revolution, civil strife, war, affecting the security of the state.'[21]

In 1966, Justice Hidayatullah, as part of a Constitution Bench of five justices, drew on the body of jurisprudence on free speech and public order to create a picturesque illustration for understanding the different levels at which the concepts of State security, public order, as well as law and order operate:

> It will thus appear that just as 'public order' ... was said to comprehend disorders of *less gravity than those affecting 'security of state,'* 'law and order' also comprehends disorders of less gravity than those affecting public order. *One has to imagine three concentric circles. Law and order represents the largest circle within which is the next circle representing public order and the smallest circle represents security of State. It is then easy to see that an act may affect law and order but not public order just as an act may affect public order but not security of the State.*[22]

When it comes to public order, it may be tempting to think that matters affecting State security implicate public order, and thus by corollary sedition is a valid restriction on free speech within the scheme of public order. In his dissent in the *Thappar–Bhushan* cases, Justice Fazl Ali gave in to this temptation.

However, the design of Article 19(2), particularly after the First Amendment, very clearly indicates that the ground of 'public order' refers only to those matters where public safety and the orderly life of the public are involved. It does not relate to those aspects affecting broader matters of security of the State. That interest is dealt with under a specific and different head in Article 19(2) itself.

Seen in this light, it is clear that the Supreme Court in *Kedar Nath Singh* misunderstood the purport of the First Amendment introducing 'public order' in Article 19(2). One of the reasons for introducing public order as a restriction on the freedom of speech was to ensure that local laws on public order, public safety and public tranquillity, which had not yet been invalidated, would be saved, since these laws could now trace their roots to an enumerated restriction in Article 19(2). But in *Kedar Nath Singh*, this misunderstanding led to the mistaken conclusion that public order saved Section 124A.[23] Nothing could be further from that.[24]

Added to this is the fact that the emphatic declaration in 1960 by a Constitution Bench, speaking through Justice Subba Rao, that public order and matters of State security operate on different planes altogether and are unconnected for the purpose of Article 19(2) was simply not taken note of in the *Kedar Nath Singh* case.

It is a matter of deep dismay that in *Kedar Nath Singh*, the Supreme Court did not fully explore the history and purpose of the First Amendment and the freedom of speech and expression. Had it done that it would have been clear that public order was neither meant to, nor could have, breathed any life into Section 124A.

Section 124A remained unconstitutional even after the First Amendment. 'Public order' has nothing to with 'sedition' because public order cannot deal with matters affecting State security interest; for the purposes of the Constitution, they are dissociated and unconnected. Moreover, Section 124A has nothing to with State security.

Sedition has no link whatsoever with 'public order,' because that was never the ground on which Section 124A was sought to be sustained. Importantly, all this must be considered in the background of Dr Ambedkar's categorical statements during the debates on the First Amendment in Parliament, that the revival of laws which had been invalidated for violating the freedom of speech prior to the First Amendment, would only happen if the law could still find a home in the new Article 19(2).

Section 124A has no roots in Article 19(2), even after the First Amendment adding 'public order' to it. The only conclusion that can be drawn is that the enactment of the First Amendment to the Constitution made no difference to the fate of Section 124A. It was, and ought to have remained, as Nehru had repeatedly reminded Parliament, unconstitutional.

8

Reinvention

Importing Public Order into Sedition

DID THE CORE OF THE JUDGMENT IN *KEDAR NATH SINGH* REACH A constitutionally sustainable conclusion? It is critical to assess whether, in this framework, the Supreme Court's decision that Section 124A was triggered when the speech in question caused a public order disturbance was constitutionally sound. Here is what the Supreme Court did to save Section 124A.

The first point that the Court resolved was how it ought to read the two conflicting decisions—one of the Federal Court and the other of the Privy Council—on the meaning of Section 124A.[1] Lamentably, the Supreme Court resolved this point in an incomplete fashion. As we saw in the *Majumdar* case, the Federal Court took the position that Section 124A cannot be applied against speech which is purely critical of the government.

There had to be some indication that public order stood threatened before Section 124A was invoked. But the *Majumdar* case was overruled by the Privy Council in the *Bhalerao* case, where the Privy Council held that taking its plain meaning, Section 124A required no evidence of any consequence ensuing as a result of the seditious speech.

In *Kedar Nath Singh*, the Supreme Court observed that in view of a 'direct conflict' between these two decisions, 'either view can be taken' when it came to defining the meaning of Section 124A.[2] Now that both these options were on the table, the Supreme Court had to make a choice. Here the Court made its second move. It realized that Section 124A had been struck down in 1950 because it did not comply with Article 19(2). But with the First Amendment adding 'public order' to Article 19(2), there was now some hope.

The way out was that the Court declared Section 124A to be in the interest of public order. But did Section 124A have anything to do with public order? The Court thought so. It ruled that when Section 124A is examined in its entirety, it appeared that what it aimed to prevent was the outbreak of public disorder ensuing as a result of seditious speech and expression:

> The provisions of the sections read as a whole, along with the explanations, make it reasonably clear that the sections aim at rendering penal only such activities as would be intended, or have a tendency, to create disorder or disturbance of public peace by resort to violence. . . . It is only when the words, written or spoken, etc. which have the pernicious tendency or intention of creating public disorder or disturbance of law and order that the law steps in to prevent such activities in the interest of public order.[3]

The Court then added:

> So *construed*, the section, in our opinion, strikes the correct balance between individual fundamental rights and the interest of public order.[4]

The Court perhaps realized that it was taking a leap of faith in protecting Section 124A in that it was reading it down and reinterpreting it to apply to a specific set of circumstances which alone could trigger the law on sedition. That is why these observations were clothed in invocations of the need for judicial rectitude:

It is well settled that if certain provisions of law construed in one way would make them consistent with the Constitution, and another interpretation would render them unconstitutional, the Court would lean in favour of the former construction.[5]

Good faith aside, the Court's leap of faith in protecting Section 124A was wrong on principle and on precedent. On principle, it was wrong because the Court was fully aware that nothing in Section 124A—not a word—even remotely indicated that the crime of sedition was committed when the speech in question consequently led to public disorder.

If there was something to that effect in Section 124A, then that would have been a different matter, but there was not. In plain words, whether something happened as a result of a seditious speech was inconsequential for the purposes of Section 124A. To therefore uphold a law which was clearly inconsistent with Article 19(2) was wrong.

On precedent too it was wrong, because the judicial branch is prohibited from engaging in legislative action and in reworking legislations only to render them constitutional. If a law violates the Constitution, the courts ought to declare it unconstitutional.

Once it was clear that Section 124A only punished speech and expression which were critical of the government, regardless of every other consideration, then Section 124A could not possibly be in the interest of public order. As we have seen, simply saying something critical about the government or even the State and exciting disaffection has no bearing on public order.

With the singular motive of saving Section 124A from invalidation, the Court imported into Section 124A the requirement that public order must be threatened before Section 124A was triggered and a prosecution launched for sedition. This is how the Court drew the improbable connect between Section 124A, Article 19(2) and public order. But in doing so, the Court committed something that was categorically verboten: it donned the hat of the legislator and rewrote Section 124A to make it consistent with Article 19(2). Necessity truly became the mother of invention, or rather reinvention. And a law was made to somehow, and against all odds, prevail over a fundamental right.

Constitutional Power

The Indian Constitution divides power in a neat fashion. Under the scheme of separation of powers, it lies within the province of the legislature to make laws,[6] and it lies within the remit of the Supreme Court to declare the meaning of laws, and indeed of the Constitution.[7] These two functions are not interchangeable—which is why the Supreme Court views any move by the legislature to declare and define what the law of the land should be with extreme suspicion. The legislature has no power to enact legislations to directly nullify court decisions and upset the meaning of well-settled legal principles.[8]

Likewise, the Supreme Court has no power to rewrite laws and introduce words and phrases in them which it thinks they ought to contain. That is a purely legislative function. As the Supreme Court put it memorably in a 1955 decision, 'Our Constitution *does not contemplate assumption* by one organ or part of the State, *of functions that essentially belong to another*.'[9] These principles which nurture the separation of powers in the Indian Constitution are now so well recognized and deeply ingrained in Indian juristic thought that they are beyond dispute.[10]

Crucial to note is also another principle of constitutional jurisprudence. When a law in question does not deal with a particular aspect and makes no mention of it, it is impermissible for courts to expand the reach of the law, fill in these gaps and introduce requirements which are not present in the text of the law. Doubtless there will always be marginal situations where there is some ambiguity in the law or obvious errors in legislative drafting which can be corrected by courts to ensure that the legislation is rendered workable.[11]

Yet again, there will be situations in which courts can plausibly take the view that the law as it stands is constitutional, even though persuasive arguments are made that it is not. But under no circumstances may a court embark on a legislative enterprise to redefine a law to the extent that it bears little resemblance to what is actually contained in the text of the law.[12] And this principle must be followed even more strictly in the case of criminal laws which impose punishments.[13] Indeed, the Indian Constitution demands that if it is unconstitutional, the law in question must go.[14]

More importantly, to modify a plainly unconstitutional statute and to redefine it only for the purposes of rendering it constitutional is to cross the bounds of constitutional reason.

Consider the 1950 decision of the Supreme Court in the *Romesh Thappar* case by a Constitution Bench of six justices.

In that case, Section 9(1-A) of the Madras Maintenance of Public Order Act, 1949, a law which empowered the government to interfere with publications to protect public order, was struck down for violating the freedom of speech. To prevent the invalidation of this particular law, the government had implored the Court that the law must somehow be interpreted as being protected by Article 19(2), even though 'public order' was not a ground on which curbs could be imposed on the freedom of speech and expression.

The Supreme Court rejected this request for two important reasons. Once it was found that a law in question has no connection with Article 19(2), in that none of the enumerated restrictions covered it, then the law had to be declared unconstitutional. Moreover, and this is crucially important, even if part of a law can be saved by Article 19(2) but the remainder of it cannot, then in such a case the entire law has to be struck down.[15] The Constitution does not permit courts to disfigure a law only in the hope of saving it from invalidation. As the Supreme Court, speaking through Justice Patanjali Sastri clearly declared:

> Where a law purports to authorise the imposition of restrictions on a fundamental right in language wide enough to cover restrictions both within and without the limits of constitutionally permissible legislative action affecting such right, it is not possible to uphold it even so far as it may be applied within the constitutional limits, as it is not severable. So long as the possibility of its being applied for purposes not sanctioned by the Constitution cannot

be ruled out, it must be held to be wholly unconstitutional and void.[16]

To clarify this point, Justice Sastri also observed:

> In other words, clause (2) of Article 19 having allowed the imposition of restrictions on the freedom of speech and expression only in cases where danger to the State is involved, an enactment, which is capable of being applied to cases where no such danger could arise, cannot be held to be constitutional and valid to any extent.[17]

This early signal by the Supreme Court was followed in the later years. In 1955, the Supreme Court was called upon to consider the question of whether an exception can be invented for a law. A Constitution Bench of five justices of the Supreme Court, speaking through Chief Justice M.C. Mahajan, warned against such a method from being employed:

> [T]he Court has *no power to re-write the section. It has to be kept intact* . . . An exception or proviso can only be engrafted for the purpose of excluding from the substantive part of the section certain matters which but for the proviso would be within it. *But when there is no power to enact at all what is proposed to be embodied in the exception, there is no power to enact an exception by enacting a law which the Legislature is not competent to make.* The State has no power to make a law abridging fundamental rights and therefore *there is no power to engraft an exception by taking something out of a law which cannot be enacted.*[18]

Apart from this, the justices in *Kedar Nath Singh* had before them an immediate decision of the Supreme Court, where a law enacted after the First Amendment to the Indian Constitution was struck down for violating the freedom of speech.

On 25 September 1961, four months before the decision in the *Kedar Nath Singh* case, a Constitution Bench of five justices headed by Chief Justice B.P. Sinha announced its decision in *Sakal Papers v. Union of India*.[19] Four of the five justices in *Kedar Nath Singh*—Chief Justice Sinha, Justices A.K. Sarkar, N. Rajagopala Ayyangar and J.R. Mudholkar—were part of the Constitution Bench in *Sakal Papers*. It was Justice Mudholkar who authored the decision for a unanimous Constitution Bench.

At issue in *Sakal Papers* was the Newspaper (Price and Page) Act, 1956. The core provision under challenge, Section 3 of the Act, authorized the government to combat 'unfair competition among newspapers' by fixing the price of newspapers after taking into account the page length and laying down the quantum and extent to which advertisements could be carried in a newspaper.[20] Through this law, it was the government which had total commercial control over the newspaper's fiscal decisions.[21]

The Supreme Court made ringing declarations about the importance of a free press and how regulations such as these directly harmed the ability of newspapers to be in circulation, since the quantity that could be printed was stipulated by the government.[22]

In defending this law, the government came up with an innovative argument. It tried to convince the Court that the general interest of the public demanded that such a law be upheld since the upsurge of monopolies in the press would be controlled by this law. The government also suggested that in any case, regulations affecting the commercial side of a business cannot be questioned for violating the freedom of speech.

Article 19(1)(g) guarantees the right to conduct one's 'profession … occupation, trade or business.' Under Article 19(6), this right could be curbed 'in the interests of the general public.' In view of this, the government tried to convince the Supreme Court that if the regulation in question could be treated as a valid restriction on the freedom to conduct one's business activities, then the fact that the freedom of speech was affected was inconsequential.[23] This argument was nothing but an invitation to the Supreme Court to convert a law which was unconstitutional into a constitutionally valid law. The Supreme Court rejected this argument.

The Court reasoned that a law empowering the government to determine the number of pages a newspaper could have or to dictate that a newspaper must increase its price if it wanted to print more pages, was an insidious restriction on the freedom of speech. Conferring such powers on the government, in the Court's view, directly affected the circulation of newspapers.

In the *Romesh Thappar* case, the Supreme Court had cemented the position that the freedom to circulate a newspaper or journal was a core free speech right. A law harming this freedom ought to be struck down for violating the freedom of the press. Which is why in *Sakal Papers*, the Supreme Court was convinced that under no circumstances must such a law affecting free speech be declared constitutional, by viewing it purely as a regulation concerning a newspaper's commercial affairs. Under the garb of regulating business activities, a law could not erode the cherished fundamental right of the freedom of speech and expression.[24]

To caution future generations that the civil rights enumerated in Article 19 had to be guarded in the most zealous manner, the Supreme Court declared that a law which harms the freedom of speech should not be given a different spin or a different interpretation with the sole aim of saving it from unconstitutionality. As the Court declared:

> The impugned law far from being one, which merely interferes with the right of freedom of speech incidentally, does so directly though it seeks to achieve the end by purporting to regulate the business aspect of a newspaper. *Such a course is not permissible and the courts must be ever vigilant in guarding perhaps the most precious of all the freedoms guaranteed by our Constitution.*[25]

The Court added:

> The reason for this is obvious. *The freedom of speech and expression of opinion is of paramount importance under a democratic Constitution which envisages changes in the composition of legislatures and governments and must be preserved.* . . . but since its object is to affect directly the right of circulation of newspapers which would necessarily undermine their power to influence public opinion *it cannot but be regarded as a dangerous weapon which is capable of being used against democracy itself.*[26]

However, the Supreme Court was not done yet. As a parting statement, Justice Mudholkar once again declared that the Constitution demands that if a restriction is imposed on fundamental rights, the restriction itself must be sanctioned by the Constitution. A law can never be a rightful curb if it is constitutionally unauthorized, regardless of the interest it seeks to attain. The freedom of speech is not subservient to a generally proclaimed public interest:

> The legitimacy of the result intended to be achieved does not necessarily imply that every means to achieve it is permissible; for even if the end is desirable and permissible, *the means employed must not transgress the limits laid down by the Constitution*, if they directly impinge on any of the fundamental rights guaranteed by the Constitution *it is no answer* when the constitutionality of the measure is challenged that apart from the fundamental right infringed the provision is otherwise legal.[27]

In September 1961, Justice Mudholkar writing for a unanimous Constitution Bench—in prose which deserves to belong in the pantheon of decisions which are treated as 'law as literature'—had clearly warned that when it came to the freedom of speech and expression, no court must ever go down the path of manipulating a law to render it constitutional. So much so, even if a law plainly appears to deal with an entirely different subject matter but in actuality harms free speech rights, then the law must be declared invalid for violating the freedom of speech.

That a law may otherwise be sustained is no answer to the argument that the law is unconstitutional. But the lesson of September 1961 was not even alluded to by the Supreme Court in *Kedar Nath Singh*. The justices who decided *Sakal Papers* glossed over their own prescient warnings of being protective of free speech and embarked on a creative exercise to somehow render the law on sedition consistent with the Constitution.

Yet, the *Sakal Papers* case is not an isolated example. In January 1960, a Constitution Bench of five justices headed by Chief Justice

B.P. Sinha struck down a provision of a 1932 Act which punished anyone who encouraged another not to pay a liability.

Ram Manohar Lohia was a leading figure in the Indian socialist movement, and sometime in the 1950s he began to organize the masses in the state of Uttar Pradesh to not pay an increased levy imposed on irrigation rates. For this, he was prosecuted under the UP Special Powers Act of 1932, which in Section 3 made it an offence for anyone to encourage in any way another not to pay any liability.[28]

Speaking for the Court, Justice Subba Rao reasoned that this colonial law found no hope in Article 19(2) because it was patently overbroad. Justice Subba Rao observed that this was a law which 'takes in the innocent and the guilty persons, *bona fide* and *mala fide* advice.... In short, no person, whether legal adviser or a friend or a well-wisher of a person instigated, can escape the tentacles of this section.'[29]

From here, Justice Subba Rao found it relatively uncomplicated to hold that such overbreadth targets even 'innocuous speech.'[30] Such a provision of law can never be in service of preserving public order, for the simple reason that encouraging another to not discharge a liability has no impact on the state of public tranquillity.[31] The Court went on to declare the law unconstitutional for violating the freedom of speech and expression.[32]

Faced with this inevitability, the government asked the Supreme Court to interpret this law as being consistent with Article 19(2). As Justice Subba Rao noted, the purpose of this request was to somehow save the law from the 'vice of unconstitutionality.'[33] Justice Subba Rao rejected this request.

He declared that jurisprudential tradition condemned the manipulation of a law which was unconstitutional, only in the hope of ensuring that it was somehow 'salvaged.'[34] Here was a law which was bewilderingly overbroad; it had no connection with protecting any public order interest;[35] and, the judicial redrafting of a law only to render it constitutional was to ask for the impossible.[36]

The government was not done yet. It redoubled its efforts and made an 'impassioned appeal' to the Court that it would ensure that the law would be 're-drafted' to ensure that it conformed with Article 19(2).[37] Justice Subba Rao yet again rejected this request. 'It is not within the Court's province,' Justice Subba Rao declared, 'to express or give advice or make general observations on situations that are not presented to it in a particular case.'[38]

It lies within the province of the legislature to make laws which comply with the Constitution, and it is the task of the judiciary to decide whether the law is constitutional. Justice Subba Rao established a carefully calibrated principle—that there is no question of a partnership being forged where the highest court of the land will give the State a second chance to correct laws which the Court finds patently unconstitutional, much less give the State 'advice.'[39]

Then there are recent examples too, where the Supreme Court decided not to judicially legislate when the freedom of speech was involved. In *Shreya Singhal v. Union of India*,[40] the Supreme Court reviewed the constitutionality of Section 66A of the Information Technology Act and ultimately declared it unconstitutional for violating the freedom of speech. But at one point, and just like in the cases of *Romesh Thappar* and *Ram Manohar Lohia*, the government implored the Supreme Court to save the law by 'read[ing] into Section 66A each of the subject matters contained in Article 19(2).'[41]

What this asked the Supreme Court to do was to redefine a plainly unconstitutional law only to make it constitutional. This request was rejected by the Supreme Court. As Justice Nariman held, the only way Section 66A could be interpreted as including aspects or applying to matters which obviously were not part of it, only in the hope of saving it from invalidation, was by doing 'complete violence' to this provision of law.[42]

As the Supreme Court saw it, reinterpretation of the law in a bid to render it constitutional was tantamount to 'a wholesale substitution of the provision.'[43] When it came to Section 66A, the Supreme Court rejected any invitation to give a new and constitutionally sustainable meaning to the law by importing a variety of requirements into it. It chose rather to declare it unconstitutional upon finding that Section 66A was grossly incompliant with Article 19(2).

One of the most intriguing aspects of the decision in *Kedar Nath Singh* is that the Supreme Court was more than aware that if Section 124A was taken at its face value, it was clearly unconstitutional and beyond the purview of Article 19(2). Chief Justice Sinha was conscious of this and held that if Section 124A was given its 'literal meaning' then it was evident that the law was not in service on any of the enumerated grounds in Article 19(2):

> [I]f on the other hand we give *a literal meaning to the words of the section*, divorced from all the antecedent background in which the law of sedition has grown . . . *it will be true to say that the section is not only within but also very much beyond the limits laid down in cl. (2) aforesaid*.[44]

Here we have the most honest admission from the Court itself that, plainly speaking, nothing in Section 124A related to either preserving State security interests or even public order interests. In other words, nothing in Article 19(2) saved Section 124A, even after the First Amendment to the Indian Constitution.

Moreover, by saying that Section 124A was 'much beyond the limits' of Article 19(2), what Chief Justice Sinha possibly alluded to was the fact that Section 124A would not be a reasonable restriction on the freedom of speech if it was given its 'literal meaning.' What we then have is the Supreme Court admitting that Section 124A is not at all saved by Article 19(2)

However, once the Court arrived at this conclusion, the next logical step would have been to declare Section 124A unconstitutional. That would have been in accord with the fine tradition of the Supreme Court strongly siding with the citizens in their endeavour to speak, write and express themselves more freely. But the opposite happened.

Chief Justice Sinha decided that something must be done to somehow render Section 124A constitutional, knowing fully well that it was unconstitutional on its face. That was done by the Court announcing that Section 124A could only be triggered when the speech and expression had the tendency of harming public order. The Court grafted this requirement onto Section 124A. After that, the Court read this into Article 19(2) to declare that, with this particular requirement, Section 124A was fully compatible with 'public order' in Article 19(2).[45]

To be sure, the Court in *Kedar Nath Singh* had before it a note of caution about the perils of redefining Section 124A only to render it constitutional. In *Ram Nandan*, the Full Bench of the Allahabad High Court had held that Section 124A was unconstitutional because it did not concern itself with preventing harm to public order as a result of the speech and expression which excited disaffection.

The First Union Cabinet of Independent India.

Joachim and Violet Alva with Jawaharlal Nehru.

Violet Alva with John F. Kennedy at the White House (1963).

Opening of the Joint Houses of Parliament (1969).

REGISTERED No. EP-503

The Gazette  of India

EXTRAORDINARY
PART II—Section 1
PUBLISHED BY AUTHORITY

NEW DELHI, MONDAY, JUNE 18, 1951

MINISTRY OF LAW

New Delhi, the 18th June, 1951

The following Act of Parliament received the assent of the President on the 18th June, 1951 and is hereby published for general information:—

THE CONSTITUTION (FIRST AMENDMENT) ACT, 1951

An Act to amend the Constitution of India.

[18th June, 1951]

BE it enacted by Parliament as follows:—

1. **Short title.**—This Act may be called the Constitution (First Amendment) Act, 1951.

2. **Amendment of article 15.**—To article 15 of the Constitution, the following clause shall be added:—

"(4) Nothing in this article or in clause (2) of article 29 shall prevent the State from making any special provision for the advancement of any socially and educationally backward classes of citizens or for the Scheduled Castes and the Scheduled Tribes."

3. **Amendment of article 19 and validation of certain laws.**—(1) In article 19 of the Constitution,—

(a) for clause (2), the following clause shall be substituted, and the said clause shall be deemed always to have been enacted in the following form, namely:—

"(2) Nothing in sub-clause (a) of clause (1) shall affect the operation of any existing law, or prevent the State from making any law, in so far as such law imposes reasonable restrictions on the exercise of the right conferred by the said sub-clause in the interests of the security of the State, friendly relations with foreign States, public order, decency or morality, or in relation to contempt of court, defamation or incitement to an offence.";

(203)

The Full Bench noted that it would be easy to render Section 124A constitutional by reading into it the requirement that sedition would only be punishable when public order was deleteriously affected. But the Full Bench warned that this result could only be achieved by courts crossing all limits of judicial review, and judicially amending a statute only to make it constitutional:

> What has made the present section vulnerable is the fact that it makes a mere creation of bad feelings towards the government an offence. It is quite easy to bring this section into line with the requirements of the Constitution. It could be done by adding a qualification to the effect that the acts prescribed in section 124-A, I.P.C. would be punishable only when they excite public disorder or create a reasonable anticipation or likelihood of exciting such disorder, or have a tendency in that direction. The addition of some such words would easily cure the defect.[46]

The Full Bench added:

> The section itself, however, does not contain any such qualification or words. It is not possible for the Court to add the words containing that qualification into this section for the purpose of validating this section. . . . It is not the function of the Court to add words and remodel law, if the law itself lacks words which might go to validate it. Nor is it possible for the Court to construe law in a manner not warranted by the clear terms of the section.[47]

At once we can see the error in which the Court in *Kedar Nath Singh* fell. Section 124A had nothing to do with public order, and thus the law was unrelated to Article 19(2). That should have been the end of the matter as far as any doubts about its constitutionality were concerned. For this proposition, the decisions of the Supreme Court that should have been treated as a guiding light were *Romesh Thappar*, *Ram Manohar Lohia*, and *Sakal Papers*. That was not done.

Rather, the Court reinvented Section 124A: it held that Section 124A was in pursuance of promoting public order, and hence only such speech which disturbed public order would fall within the four corners of this law. As we have seen so far, Section 124A had absolutely nothing in it—not a single letter, let alone a word—which suggested that it was aimed at maintaining public order.

Yet it was the absence of this particular requirement that impelled the Court in *Kedar Nath Singh* to reinvent Section 124A to confer constitutional viability on it.

A Promise to Uphold Rights

Crucially, the *Kedar Nath Singh* case was decided by a bench of five justices. It was numerically smaller than the bench in the *Romesh Thappar* case, which comprised six justices, and judicial discipline demanded that the holding in *Romesh Thappar*—that a law cannot be disfigured beyond recognition only to save it from unconstitutionality—controlled the Supreme Court in *Kedar Nath Singh*.

It is a well-established canon of constitutional law that the decision of a larger bench must always be followed by a smaller bench, unless the numerically smaller bench identifies serious drawbacks in the judicial precedent in question or has some reason to believe that there are distinguishing factors which advise against mechanically applying the precedent in question. It is unthinkable to have a legal system where decisions of the Supreme Court have no precedential value.

At the level of the Supreme Court too, smaller benches are duty-bound to follow the decisions of a larger bench. If any errors are identified in a decision, then the proper course is to make a reference asking for a numerically larger bench to settle the question of law once and for all. If this practice is not followed, there will be chaos because the legal system will be beset with a long line of decisions which do not settle the law but speak at cross purposes and entirely unsettle the system.[48]

The justices in *Kedar Nath Singh* were duty-bound and constitutionally obligated to follow the decision in the *Romesh Thappar* case and could not simply ignore the important points of constitutional law that had been laid down. But that did not happen. On the other hand, in outright disregard of the cautionary principle enunciated by the Supreme Court in *Romesh Thappar*—that courts must desist from playing around with the meaning of laws—the bench in *Kedar Nath Singh* launched into a legislative enterprise to somehow save the law on sedition.

In *Kedar Nath Singh*, the Supreme Court, to save sedition, chose to adopt the Federal Court's line of reasoning on the meaning of Section 124A and read in the requirement that some form of public disorder must ensue before Section 124A was triggered. This was used by the Supreme Court to hold that by stipulating this threshold requirement, Section 124A became relatable to the ground of 'public order' in Article 19(2). But the Federal Court had decided its case in an era when India did not have a written constitution.

Under the Government of India Act of 1935, the Federal Court had no power to declare legislation unconstitutional; it had only the power to interpret the meaning of laws. Consistent with that function, Chief Justice Gwyer of the Federal Court attempted to narrow the meaning of Section 124A and reduce the law's impact by reading into it the requirement that there had to be a showing of public order being threatened before Section 124A was applied.

The Supreme Court has the power to strike down laws if they contravene the Constitution. After all, the duty of the Supreme Court is not to uphold laws but to *uphold and protect fundamental rights*.[49] The creation of a Supreme Court which would have the pre-eminent power to invalidate laws and tell Parliament that it had made an error in lawmaking was an enormous achievement. In the Constituent Assembly, Sardar Patel had extolled the virtue of this progressive stride by proclaiming, 'If we provide for fundamental rights, *it is necessary we must provide also for a remedy*.'[50]

In 1952, a Constitution Bench of five justices declared that with the Constitution guaranteeing fundamental rights to the people of India, the structure of the Constitution ordained that the courts were the ultimate arbiters of whether a law was constitutional. This was a radical vision which was sanctified in the Constitution:

> If, then, the courts in the country face up to such important and none too easy task, it is not out of any desire to tilt at legislative authority in a crusader's spirit, but in discharge of a duty plainly laid upon them by the Constitution. This is especially true as regards the 'fundamental rights,' as to which this Court has been assigned the role of a sentinel on the qui vive. While the Court naturally attaches great weight to the legislative judgment, it cannot desert its

own duty to determine finally the constitutionality of an impugned statute.[51]

Nonetheless, the Supreme Court chose not to do that. It chose not to uphold fundamental rights. It chose not to remedy their violations. Rather, it chose to somehow save Section 124A by redefining it altogether.

To be sure—and this point bears re-emphasis—Section 124A did not contain a single word which indicated that the offence of sedition was committed when seditious speech resulted in public disorder. None other than the Supreme Court in *Kedar Nath Singh* recognized this.

From a constitutional perspective, this omission was enough to declare Section 124A unconstitutional. But, counter-intuitively, it somehow became the dubious basis for breathing life into Section 124A.

A Modern Parallel

When Section 124A is reviewed, any complaint that it is unconstitutional may face a legitimate objection: that the general interest of preserving 'public order' requires such a law, or that the interests of preserving the 'sovereignty and integrity of India'; 'security of the State'; and the need for preventing the 'incitement of an offence' justify Section 124A. A modern parallel can help in overcoming this objection. It is the decision of the Supreme Court in *Shreya Singhal*.

In 2009, Parliament amended the Information Technology Act of 2000. This legislative amendment introduced a new provision—Section 66A. It quickly acquired public notoriety, for it punished any person who used the means of electronic communication to send a message to anyone which was 'grossly offensive' or had a 'menacing character' or was knowingly 'false', which led to 'annoyance, inconvenience, danger, obstruction, insult, injury, criminal intimidation, *enmity, hatred, or ill-will*.'[51] This crime was punishable with a three-year jail term. Justice R.F. Nariman who authored the judgment, struck down Section 66A for violating the freedom of speech.

The reason why Section 66A of the IT Act is a parallel with Section 124A is because the former provision of law punished speech and writings which stoked 'enmity,' 'hatred' and 'ill-will,' which are the same words and phrases contained in the law on sedition. The constitutional principles which became the basis for the judgment in the *Shreya Singhal* case apply equally to Section 124A given the common features between the two provisions.

Justice Nariman emphasized that as a general constitutional principle, the regulation in question must have some rational connection with achieving the interests enumerated in Article 19(2) to be valid. A regulation cannot simply recite that it is in the interest of public order but in reality have nothing to with the preservation of public order and tranquillity.[53]

When judged by this standard, it was evident to the Supreme Court that Section 66A did not consider whether public order would be harmed as a result of the electronic communication. Nothing in the law stipulated that punishment would follow only if public order was affected as a result of the messages being sent. Seen in this light, Section 66A simply punished the communication of messages. For Justice Nariman, this was sufficient to hold that Section 66A could not possibly take cover under the head of 'public order' in Article 19(2):

The section makes no distinction between mass dissemination and dissemination to one person. Further, *the section does not require that such message should have a clear tendency to disrupt public order*. Such message *need not have any potential* which could disturb the community at large.[54]

Justice Nariman added:

The nexus between the message and action that may be taken based on the message is conspicuously absent—there is no ingredient in this offence of inciting anybody to do anything which a reasonable man would then say would have the tendency of being an immediate threat to public safety or tranquillity. *On all these counts, it is clear that the section has no proximate relationship to public order whatsoever.*[55]

In the context of the ground of 'incitement to an offence' in Article 19(2), Justice Nariman reasoned that Section 66A was not saved by it either, for the simple reason that nothing in Section 66A incited anybody to commit an offence.[56] Everything said about Section 66A being inconsistent with the grounds of 'public order' as well as 'incitement to an offence' in Article 19(2) applied equally to Section 124A.

We have seen so far that by its bare words the law on sedition has nothing to with public order being harmed. That public order is disturbed as a result of the seditious speech is not even an ingredient in the offence of sedition. A conviction for sedition is to be granted looking solely at what was expressed, and not at what happens thereafter.

Indeed, in 1958, a Full Bench of the Allahabad High Court in the *Ram Nandan* case presented a sophisticated analysis of how sedition was incompatible with Article 19 of the Constitution.[57] All three justices comprising the Full Bench, who wrote separate judgments, concluded that for Section 124A it was immaterial if public disorder occurred as a result of the excitement of disaffection.

The aim of sedition was to suppress the legitimate excitement of disaffection against governments, which, under the Constitution, can never be suppressed. As the Full Bench saw it, preserving public order interests was not the goal of Section 124A and thus it was a provision of law which was not in service of the enumerated grounds in Article 19(2).[58]

The Full Bench also warned that simply because the First Amendment had changed Article 19(2), it did not mean that the freedom of speech and expression itself was relegated to a secondary position and that laws of all kinds would pass muster under the new Article 19(2). To think otherwise, the Full Bench observed, 'would be against the spirit of the Constitution, that the amendment effected endowed the Legislature with such ample powers that the very fundamental right guaranteed could be completely nullified.'[59] Unfortunately, the Supreme Court overruled this judgment in the *Kedar Nath Singh* case without engaging with it.

It is clear that Section 124A does not deal with consequences. It is unconcerned with them. It purely and solely punishes speech and expression which excite disaffection, enmity and ill-will against the government. According to the *Shreya Singhal* standard, a law such as this has no connection whatsoever with the preservation of public order or, for that matter, with any other ground in Article 19(2). Seen in this light, the law on sedition as contained in Section 124A is unconstitutional, because it is not in service of any public order interest.

So far as the ground of 'incitement to an offence' in Article 19(2) is concerned, nothing in Section 124A can be understood as dealing with a class of speech which incites others to commit a crime. Here too, a conviction for sedition is not contingent on whether any person has been incited to do anything violent. This goes to show that the 'incitement to an offence' ground in Article 19(2) cannot save Section 124A.

9
Triumph of Democracy

THIS CHAPTER PROPOSES THAT WITHIN THE SCHEME OF THE INDIAN Constitution, the law on sedition is an anomaly because it severely constricts the ability of the people to engage in political speech. The single-most important factor that is needed to ensure the survival of Indian democracy is a people who engage in political speech and use the power of their thoughts to keep a continued check on those who have been elected to public office and charged with the supreme responsibility of governing the nation.

At its core, the fundamental right to freedom of speech and expression ought to guarantee an especial level of protection to political speech. By its bare text, Section 124A is specifically targeted against such political speech, and its historical journey provides the clearest evidence for it. The law on sedition constricts free political speech in an insidious manner, which is constitutionally intolerable.[1]

It is essential that the freedom of speech and expression in the Constitution is understood and interpreted as placing a very high premium on the abiding importance of political speech and its salient role in ensuring that the people of India can become equal partners in the process of democratic discussion and change.

The distinctive value of political speech lies in its role in preserving the institution of democracy, in holding those in power accountable long after the people have cast their votes at the ballot box, and in seeking the reordering of public institutions and public office. Its importance also lies in bringing about the transformation of orthodox views and in advocating for the realization of the liberal vision of the Constitution.

This is to ensure that those in government and indeed in a position of power are bound to obey the terms of the Constitution and implement it with some care to achieve particular progressive ends. After all, the Constitution cannot be rendered moribund. It is a foundational document to be used by the people to keep a check on events and on the people impacting their lives in the most fundamental and pervasive manner.

To be sure, Indian courts have often emphasized the importance of political speech and its role in strengthening democracy. Yet that recognition has not yet yielded a surer foundation for elevating political speech to a level where we understand political speech on its own terms rather than as a mere illustration or an instantiation of what free speech involves.

Drawing on global political theory, the history of the free speech right as well as its jurisprudence in India, this chapter proposes the idea that political speech is a core free speech right. The proposals made here are purely in the context of political speech directed against the government.

This chapter presents a road map to understand why sedition in the form of Section 124A is fundamentally incompatible with the freedom of speech precisely because it is too heavy a fetter on political speech. Only when political speech is elevated above matters of ordinary regulation can the people experience the true freedom of voicing their opinion against the powers that be.

The framework set out here is in respect of political speech alone. It is not a general defence of granting near-absolute protection to dangerous forms of speech, such as hate speech, and speech and expressions which by their content speak against groups and communities in a divisive manner with the aim of seeking their social isolation. As we shall see, it is possible to think of a framework in which political speech that affects democratic well-being is granted a much higher level of protection than other types of speech.

James Fitzjames Stephen's Democratic Objection to Sedition

The enactment of Section 124A in 1870 and its subsequent restructuring in 1898 were tied in with the idea that India was a country whose people must obey the British Crown and the British government in India. Indians were subjects and had no right to criticize their rulers—so much so that when Tilak criticized the Epidemic Diseases Act, which the British government had enacted to battle the plague ravaging India at that time, he was hauled up for sedition in 1897 and promptly sent to jail. No one could dare question the motives of the colonial government. But when India gave itself its Constitution in 1950, there was a radical reordering of institutions.

It was the people who would cast their votes and elect their political representatives. There was no longer any concept of a ruler and subjects being part of the Constitution. A new vocabulary of government and governance was introduced by the Constitution, whose central tenet was that the voice of the people would be controlling in matters of democracy. As Granville Austin observes:

> Adult suffrage gave a voice, indeed power, to millions who had previously to depend on the whim of others for even a vague representation of their interests. Direct elections brought—or could bring—national life and consciousness to individuals in the village.[2]

However, long before India embarked on the path of becoming a democratic republic, the father of sedition in India, James Fitzjames Stephen had written extensively on how a law on sedition is a complete aberration in democracies.

Stephen had brought Section 124A into the fold of the IPC in 1870. Some years after that, Stephen authored his magnum opus, *A History of the Criminal Law in England*. Writing in 1883, Stephen made many interesting observations about sedition and the relationship of the crime with the political system in place.

According to Stephen, when the social system conceives of a ruler (and here he was speaking of England and the monarchy) who by their high standing is considered 'wise and good,' it is 'wrong to censure him openly.'[3] The crime of sedition was justified by Stephen because in such a system the benevolent ruler must always remain in the highest esteem of the subjects and which demands nothing but unquestioned deference. As Stephen observed:

> If the ruler is regarded as the superior of the subject, as being by the nature of his position presumably wise and

good, the rightful ruler and guide of the whole population, it must necessarily follow that it is wrong to censure him openly, that even if he is mistaken his mistakes should be pointed out with utmost respect, and that whether mistaken or not no censure should be cast upon him likely or designed to diminish his authority.[4]

As we saw, Stephen was doubtless an ardent monarchist and his views on preserving the British government in India, which was ruling directly under the paramountcy of the British Crown, shone through when he spearheaded the effort to make sedition a crime in 1870.

Nevertheless, Stephen himself seemed to believe that sedition could not be a crime in a society based on pure democracy. In such a system, the ruler is not a benevolent and superior authority but a representative of the people. Therefore, rightly speaking, the people cannot be prosecuted and punished for the unpleasant comments directed against their representatives. Democracy, Stephen argued, entirely upended the very justification for sedition:

> If on the other hand the ruler is regarded as the agent and servant, and the subject as the wise and good master who is obliged to delegate his power to the so-called ruler because being a multitude he cannot use it himself, *it is obvious that this sentiment must be reversed.*[5]

Stephen went on to say that when the people elect their government, it lies within the province of public opinion to be openly critical of elected representatives, since they are being critical of those who are to serve the people. In a democracy, there is no question of punishing the people who air their grievances against the government:

> *Every member of the public who censures the ruler* for the time being exercises in his own person *the right which belongs to the whole of which he forms a part. He is finding fault with his servant.* If others think differently they can take the other side of the dispute, and the utmost that can happen is that the *servant will be dismissed and another put in his place, or perhaps that the arrangements of the household will be modified. To those who hold this view fully and carry it out to all its consequences there can be no such offence of sedition.*[6]

Stephen was not done yet. He was candid enough to note that if one speaks of a political system in which there are elected representatives, then to say that sedition can be a crime in a democracy would be to speak at cross purposes. As Stephen saw it, short of stoking immediate violence, speech of whatever kind against an elected government could not possibly be made a crime:

> There may indeed be breaches of the peace which may destroy or endanger life, limb, or property, and there may be incitements to such offences, but *no imaginable censure of the government, short of a censure which has the immediate tendency to produce a breach of the peace, ought to be regarded as criminal.*[7]

Here, we literally have it from the horse's mouth. The person who championed sedition in 1870 and wanted unquestioned obedience from the Indian people to the British government in India himself acknowledged that in a democratic system, where there is no rightful monarch but a body of elected representatives, the existence of sedition was an aberration. But above all, Stephen was firm in his belief that in a democracy, political speech could not be muzzled under the ruse of preventing sedition.

It is indeed a matter of grim irony that Stephen, the father of sedition in India, should provide such a wide-ranging exposition on sedition being a misfit in democracies, when Chief Justice B.P. Sinha, speaking for the Supreme Court in *Kedar Nath Singh*, was moved to uphold the constitutional validity of sedition in a sovereign and democratic India.

The Constituent Assembly and the Democratic Objection to Sedition

Turning to the deliberations in the Constituent Assembly, it is striking to note the sheer urgency which informed the debates on the question of political speech and sedition. When K.M. Munshi addressed the Assembly on 1 December 1948 to make his arguments as to why sedition must be abandoned, he placed great emphasis on the ability of the citizens to engage in free and frank political speech. In a forthright manner, Munshi told the Assembly:

> But the public opinion has changed considerably since and now that we have a democratic Government a *line must be drawn between criticism of the Government which should be welcome* and incitement which would undermine the security or order on which civilized life is based, or which is calculated to overthrow the State.[8]

Munshi was certain that so long as sedition remained a crime, freedom in the sphere of political speech would be a chimera. He was clear that the new republic which the Constitution would inaugurate was founded on the idea of a republican form of government and that it is in the nature of democracy for governments to change.

Munshi's greatest contribution came in establishing as a constitutional truth that democracy demands the free flow of political speech. Indian democracy could not do without free political speech. Which is why political speech must be carefully nurtured by the Constitution to ensure that Indian democracy itself stays alive:

> As a matter of fact *the essence of democracy is Criticism of Government*. The party system which *necessarily involves an advocacy of the replacement of one Government by another is its only bulwark; the advocacy of a different system of Government should be welcome because that gives vitality to a democracy.*[9]

M. Ananthasayanam Ayyangar, a member from Madras, too believed that, given its history, sedition had rightly acquired an infamous reputation and in free India, the law on sedition needed to be reworked. Like Munshi, Ayyangar too believed that the law ought to only curb such speech and expression by which 'the entire state is sought to be overthrown or undermined by force or otherwise, leading to public disorder.'[10]

He believed that free discussion of political affairs must not to be muzzled by the Constitution. '[A]ny *attack on the government itself,*' said Ayyangar, '*ought not to be made* an offence under the law.'[11] Ayyangar had a unique formulation of what 'overthrow' of the government meant. As he told the Assembly:

> If we find that the government for the time being has a knack of entrenching itself, however hard its administration might be *it must be the fundamental right of every citizen in the country to overthrow that government without violence, by persuading the people, by exposing its faults in the administration, its method of working and so on.*[12]

Thus, according to Ayyangar, the people of India had to have the freedom to say whatever they wanted against the government, in whatever form and in whatever measure, so long as the end which was to be achieved was a change in the government or in the method of governance.

In the Assembly, Munshi and Ayyangar had laid the groundwork for recognizing the constitutional principle that the freedom of speech ought to be a right which creates the maximum space for the free flow of political speech with the least restrictive form of hindrances.

This is the foundational conception for free political speech being integral to democracy and for good governance being demanded by the people. Treating sedition as an obstacle in the path of political development displays an extraordinarily high level of constitutional reason for robust protection being granted to political speech.

This vision, of the transformed and fundamentally reordered political landscape of India where the government is the agent of the electorate, who have installed them in office, firmly secured the profound principle that making sedition a crime in free India was unthinkable. It would stultify and paralyse political speech.

No constitution can tolerate a system where the people are treated as criminals only because they choose to exercise their freedom of speech and expression to direct their criticism, and indeed their angst and ire, against the government.

Sedition and Democracy: The International Perspective

From an international perspective, nations which encountered sedition did away with it to ensure that political speech remained unhindered. Take the United States of America first. The US and India are historical siblings in more than one sense. Both nations were in the vice-like grip of the same colonial power, and both nations, after attaining freedom, embarked on a path to draft a constitution which had at its heart a democratically elected, republican form of government.

When it came to the Indian Constitution, the framers were clear that the US Constitution would be treated as a guiding light. Indeed, when Dr Sachchidananda Sinha delivered his inaugural address as the Constituent Assembly's temporary chairman on 9 December 1946, he specifically took the example of the US Constitution as a document which had been recognized globally 'as a model for framing independent federal constitutions,' and for which reason it must be 'carefully studied' by the Assembly.[13]

Nowhere was this truer than in the realm of crafting the right to free speech.[14] In fact, the Indian Supreme Court has categorically acknowledged that much of American jurisprudence on free speech holds enormous persuasive value for India.[15] Although historical siblings, when it came to sedition the US went along a different trajectory altogether.

In 1798, the US Congress enacted the Sedition Act.[16] Within a few months, the state of Virginia hit back with a resolution, the authorship of which is attributed to James Madison,[17] condemning the enactment of the Sedition Act. Propounding that a law on sedition was expressly barred by the 1st Amendment to the US Constitution, which declares that the US Congress cannot make a law abridging the freedom of speech, the resolution proclaimed that the Sedition Act 'ought to produce universal alarm, because it is levelled against that *right of freely examining public characters and measures, and of free communication among the people* thereon, which has ever been justly deemed, the only effectual guardian of every other right.'[18]

The denunciation of the Sedition Act was founded on the idea that the 1st Amendment placed a very high premium on political speech, deeming it integral to the preservation of democracy.

In 1964, the US Supreme Court announced its decision in the famous case of *New York Times v. Sullivan*.[19] That was a decision which declared that public officials could not institute defamation proceedings against those who examine the conduct of public officials. Justice Brennan authored the decision for a unanimous Court, and a large portion of the decision was devoted to examining why a crime such as sedition is fundamentally incompatible with a democracy which guarantees the freedom of speech.

Justice Brennan began his assessment by declaring that the form taken by speech involving discussion of issues of public importance cannot be the baseline by which the state determines whether the speech is to be proscribed. In other words, it was not for the state to decide the language of choice of the citizens who expressed their opinions. As Justice Brennan saw it, the fundamental principle secured by the free speech guarantee was 'the principle that *debate on public issues* should be *uninhibited, robust*, wide-open, and that it may *well include vehement, caustic and sometimes unpleasantly sharp attacks* on government and public officials.'[20]

Drawing on the words of James Madison, Justice Brennan declared that the discussion of matters touching on public importance will inevitably be in highly intense terms. As Justice Brennan noted, Madison had said, 'some degree of abuse is inseparable from the proper use of everything; and in no instance is this more true than in that of the press.'[21]

When it came to the Sedition Act of 1798, Justice Brennan declared that it was a law which 'first crystallized a national awareness of the central meaning of the First Amendment.'[22] Madison's report in response to the Sedition Act urged that it was unconstitutional for the government to make a law which regulated how the people were to voice their opinions against the State.

The very concept of a democratic and republican form of government negated the idea that the government is superior to the people, and that, in turn, negated any concept of using sedition to silence the voice of the people. As Justice Brennan declared:

> Madison prepared the Report in support of the protest. His premise was that the Constitution created a form of government under which 'The people, not the government, possess the absolute sovereignty.' The structure of the government dispersed power in reflection of the people's distrust of concentrated power, and of power itself at all levels. *This form of government was 'altogether different' from the British form, under which the Crown was sovereign and the people were subjects.* 'Is it not natural and necessary, under such different circumstances,' he asked, 'that a different degree of freedom in the use of the press should be contemplated?'[23]

Justice Brennan observed that although by its own terms the Sedition Act came to an end in 1801, there had been deep resentment against this law.[24] When Thomas Jefferson became President in 1800, he granted executive clemency to all those who had been swept away by the tide of the Sedition Act.[25] In 1840, the penalties which were collected under the 1798 Sedition Act were 'repaid by Act of Congress on the ground that it was unconstitutional'.[26]

This led Justice Brennan to observe that even the greatest justices of the US Supreme Court, such as Justices Holmes, Brandeis, and Jackson, had always believed that the Sedition Act was contrary to the 1st Amendment to the US Constitution.[27] As Justice Brennan held, the reason why there was near unanimity in the belief that the Sedition Act violated the freedom of speech was due to a 'broad consensus that the Act, *because of the restraint it imposed upon criticism of government and public officials*, was inconsistent with the First Amendment'.[28] Incidentally, during World War I, the US Congress enacted the Sedition Act in 1918, but it was treated as a war-time measure and repealed within two years.[29]

The enduring teachings from Justice Brennan's masterful decision in *The New York Times* is that the First Amendment to the US Constitution at its core granted a special level of protection to the discussion of public affairs and a law on sedition injuriously affected the free discussion of matters affecting governance and democracy. Democracy, the very system by which a government is elected by the people, is a system which expressly bars a law on sedition.

In England, too, the crimes of sedition and seditious libel were done away with in 2009, by Section 73 of the Coroners and Justice Act.[30] This provision of law pithily declared that the 'offences of sedition and seditious libel' were 'abolished' from the 'common law of England and Wales and the common law of Northern Ireland'.[31] Two important factors motivated the repeal of sedition.

It was realized that sedition was much too heavy a burden on the freedom of speech and would be inconsistent with the Human Rights Act of 1998. More importantly, the move of doing away with sedition was intended to inspire other countries, which are part of the common law tradition, to themselves take steps to get rid of sedition and truly unshackle free speech.[32] It was supposed to be a persuasive nudge to other nations, which would include India, to follow suit and to also do away with the crime of sedition. As Claire Ward, the Parliamentary Under Secretary for the Ministry of Justice, put it:

> Sedition and seditious and defamatory libel are arcane offences—from a bygone era when freedom of expression wasn't seen as the right it is today ... The existence of these obsolete offences in this country had been used by other countries as justification for the retention of similar laws which have been actively used to suppress political dissent and restrict press freedom ... Abolishing these offences will allow the UK to take a lead in challenging similar laws in other countries, where they are used to suppress free speech.[33]

Turning to global political theory, a strong case can be made for the broad guarantee of free speech creating a special zone of protection for political speech, where the expression of views is meant to bring about transformation of the status quo. Hannah Arendt postulated that the value of speech lies in reminding others about the true state of the world, because what one experiences is almost always from one's own perspective. To use the power of speech to alter the world view of people and show them that the world may not be what one considers it to be is an important purpose that free speech serves.[34] 'Only in the freedom of our speaking,' wrote Arendt, 'does the world ... emerge in its objectivity and visibility.'[35]

In the context of seditious speech and the US Constitution, Ernst Freund[36] propounded the idea that tempering free speech with ordinary criminal law principles was an idea filled with tension, for it struck at the ability of the people to engage in political matters. 'So long as we apply the notoriously loose common law doctrines of conspiracy and incitement to offense of a political character,' Freund wrote, 'we are *adrift on a sea of doubt and conjecture*.'[37] Freund placed enormous faith in the idea that the free flow of discussion on matters affecting the nation ought to be unhindered. Freund believed that speech on political matters will undoubtedly involve contrary and opposing viewpoints, and to impose uniformity in what could be said against the state strikes at the very heart of free speech:

> The peril resulting to the national cause from toleration of adverse opinion is largely imaginary; in any event it is slight as compared with the permanent danger of intolerance to free institutions. . . . *Toleration of adverse opinion is not a matter of generosity, but of political prudence.*[38]

Alexander Bickel, one of the most influential scholars in the field of constitutional studies, propounded the principle that the development of free speech, particularly in the era after World War II, asserted the idea that political speech was central to any meaningful understanding of the freedom of speech.[39]

Writing in the context of the 1st Amendment to the US Constitution, Bickel presciently observed that the Constitution must 'protect and indeed encourage speech so long as it serves to make the political process work, seeking to achieve objectives through the political process by persuading a majority of voters.'[40] Political speech is crucially important, for it created a platform by which the people can engage in the 'exchange of views, the ventilation of desires and demands.'[41]

Yet Bickel was careful to note that although political speech ought to be guarded closely, what can be regulated is the type of speech and expression which intends to 'supplant, disrupt, or coerce the process, as by overthrowing the government, by rioting or by other forms of violence.'[42] Bickel also entered a second caveat: political speech becomes subject to regulation when it aims to break laws, for that is a 'violation of majority decisions embodied in law.'[43]

To be sure, Bickel's second caveat is inconsistent with much of the jurisprudence on free speech, particularly because, and as we shall see, the espousal of political claims through political speech invariably involves a clash with a law that regulates it. And if the position is that violation of law is a ground for curbing all political speech, then that answers the question rather than asking it. For the question of singular importance is: What are the necessary conditions for free speech to thrive? However, Bickel's second caveat will ensure the certain death of all political speech.

The most sophisticated argument in favour of granting an absolute level of protection to speech which concerns politics and democracy was put forth by Alexander Meiklejohn in 1961.[44] Speaking in the context of the 1st Amendment to the US Constitution, Meiklejohn proposed that the people who elect a government to power are in truth 'the governors,' because it is they who have installed people in public office.[45] And if sovereignty resides only in the people, then all 'those activities of thought and communication by which we "govern"' are immune from State regulation.[46] They cannot be touched by the lawmaking powers of the government.[47]

The relevance of political speech assumes importance, as per Meiklejohn, if the conception of democracy is grounded in the idea of 'self-government.'[48] Political speech helps the people to 'understand the issues' which the country needs to resolve. Political speech is that valuable tool by which the people 'pass judgment upon the decisions' which have been taken by those whom the people have elected to public office.[49] Finally, political speech allows people to marshal their thoughts and opinions to discuss and even impugn governmental decisions, with the ultimate purpose of ensuring 'greater wisdom and effectiveness' in them.[50]

The idea of democratic and political progress rejects governmental overreach in matters concerning political speech. As Meiklejohn saw it:

> What I have said is that the First Amendment, as seen in its constitutional setting, forbids Congress to abridge the freedom of a citizen's speech, press, peaceable assembly, or petition, whenever those activities are utilized for the governing of the nation.[51]

Cass Sunstein proposes that to give effect to the freedom of speech, it is important to consider the free speech guarantee as granting core constitutional protection to political speech. This right can only be abridged on a showing of extraordinary and compelling reasons. Speaking in the context of the 1st Amendment to the

US Constitution, Sunstein suggests that it is political speech which must receive an especially higher level of protection.[52] In his work, Sunstein singled out the Sedition Act enacted during World War I as doing the greatest harm to the freedom of speech guaranteed by the 1st Amendment to the US Constitution and to democracy itself. A law on sedition inflicted incalculable harm on democracy:

> The Sedition Act operated as a formidable barrier to public criticism of government, including dissenting opinions published in popular newspapers. In contemporary textbooks, as well as in modern Supreme Court opinions, the Sedition Act is commonly described as an act of evil and unquestionably unconstitutional censorship.[53]

Political Speech and Indian Jurisprudence

The idea that political speech requires a special degree of protection is firmly rooted in Indian jurisprudence. When the Constitution came to life in 1950, it fell on the shoulders of the Supreme Court to interpret its meaning, and in those early years it came out strongly in favour of granting a high level of protection to political speech.

In the *Romesh Thappar* case in 1950, which was the very first decision on the meaning of the freedom of speech, the Supreme Court emphatically declared that the Constitution decidedly imposed 'narrow and stringent limits'[54] on how the State could regulate free speech. This was because the Constituent Assembly had acknowledged that for the people of India to be a responsive people, it was the duty of the press to engage in political speech. '[W]ithout free political discussion,' the Supreme Court declared, '*no public education*, so *essential* for the *proper functioning* of the *processes of popular government* is possible.'⁵⁵

In 1958, a Full Bench of the Allahabad High Court invalidated Section 124A—a decision which was overturned by the Supreme Court in *Kedar Nath Singh*. In dealing with Section 124A, the Full Bench placed great emphasis on the fact that democracy and a system of elected government negate any law which punishes citizens from exciting disaffection against their elected representatives. The powers which governments enjoy are only possible because the people decide to elect their representatives.

As the Full Bench saw it, the Indian Constitution radically altered the relationship between the government and the people in that democracy connotes the triumph of the power of the people. In such a system, the people cannot be held down by a law which punishes their ability to question those who hold public office.⁵⁶

Twelve years later, in its decision in the case of *Ram Manohar Lohia*, a Constitution Bench of the Supreme Court, speaking through Justice Subba Rao, sanctified the constitutional principle that the freedom of speech and expression guarantees the freedom to dissent, the freedom to agitate, and even the freedom to engage in civil disobedience. For the Supreme Court, it was the goal of preserving democracy itself which required the promotion of political speech:

> It is said that in a democratic set-up there is no scope for agitational approach and that if a law is bad the only course is to get it modified by democratic process and that any instigation to break the law is in itself a disturbance of public order. If this argument without obvious limitation is accepted, it would *destroy the right to freedom of speech which is the very foundation of democratic life*.⁵⁷

Two years later, in 1962, the Supreme Court in the *Sakal Papers* case came out strongly in favour of political speech. The Supreme Court held that the State cannot exercise its lawmaking powers to control the press. It reasoned that the democratic process, and indeed the process of the people changing the composition of the government, required a very high level of protection to be granted to the free speech right; a right which the Court termed 'the most precious of all the freedoms guaranteed by the Constitution.'[58] 'The freedom of speech and expression of opinion is of paramount importance under a democratic Constitution,' the Supreme Court declared, 'which *envisages changes* in the composition of legislatures and governments *and must be preserved*.'[59]

This is a ringing declaration by the Supreme Court that free speech is a right which improves the state of Indian democracy and politics, and that for democracy to survive it was essential that free speech be provided adequate breathing space lest democracy should itself be paralyzed. In the case before it, the Court viewed the Newspaper (Price and Page) Act of 1956, which gave the government broad powers to control just how much a newspaper could publish and how it was to be circulated, as harming political discussion and, in turn, democracy:

> No doubt, the law in question was made upon the recommendation of the Press Commission but since *its object is to affect directly the right of circulation of newspapers which would necessarily undermine their power to influence public opinion it cannot but be regarded as a dangerous weapon which is capable of being used against democracy itself.*[60]

In 2021, the Supreme Court yet again made a ringing declaration on the value of free speech, political speech, and their role in enhancing democracy. In *Amish Devgan v. Union of India*,[61] the Supreme Court, speaking through Justice Sanjiv Khanna, declared that the core right guaranteed by Article 19(1)(a) is political speech. The democratic process is only strengthened when the people have the freedom to engage in the most critical assessment of the government without fear of any reprisal against them by the State. This conception led the Supreme Court to announce that all forms of political speech, whether sober or rough or even patently incorrect, deserve constitutional protection.

Moreover, the Supreme Court recognized that when people engage in political speech, they may say things which may not be entirely true. Nonetheless, since the freedom of speech must empower people to give vent to their feelings against the government, the fact that what has been said may not be entirely correct can never furnish an adequate justification for hounding people through the mechanism of criminal law. As the Supreme Court declared:

> Freedom to express and speak is the most important condition for political democracy. *Law and policies are not democratic unless they have been made and subjected to democratic process including questioning and criticism. Dissent and criticism of the elected Government's policy, when puissant, deceptive or even false would be ethically wrong, but would not invite penal action.* Elected representatives in power have the right to respond and dispel suspicion. The 'market place of ideas' and 'pursuit of truth' principle are fully applicable.[62]

This conception of free political speech being placed on the highest pedestal of constitutional protection was tied in with the idea that the State has no business regulating political speech at all. This is because the State suffers from default bias, in that it seeks to regulate speech which is critical of it.

Viewed from this perspective, the State will always be inclined to stifle political speech which is aimed against the government. Moreover, the free flow of political speech also demands that the State does not erect unnecessary barriers in the path of free speech in the name of imposing reasonable restrictions. Government regulation must be the least when political speech is involved, for any steps by the State to interfere with political speech are entirely unwelcome. As the Supreme Court declared:

> Government should be left out from adjudicating what is true or false, good or bad, valid or invalid as these aspects should be left for open discussion in the public domain. This justification is also premised on the conviction that freedom of speech serves an *indispensable function in democratic governance without which the citizens cannot successfully carry out the task to convey and receive ideas. Political speech relating to government policies requires greater protection for preservation and promotion of democracy.* Falsity of the accusation would not be sufficient to constitute criminal offence of 'hate speech.'[63]

The pre-eminent scholar of the Indian Constitution, H.M. Seervai, in his classic work *Constitutional Law of India*, drew a direct connection between the freedom of speech and expression, and the preservation of Indian democracy. As Seervai saw it, the bedrock of Indian democracy is that governmental affairs are to be discussed in the most open manner to ensure that the people are able to interrogate the method of governance itself. As Seervai put it:

> The freedom of thought and expression, and the freedom of the press, are not only valuable freedoms in themselves, but are basic to a democratic form of Govt. which proceeds on the theory that problems of Govt. can be solved by the free exchange of thought and by public discussion.[64]

Ultimately, it is the people who must have the final say on aspects concerning the political system, whose activities affect them in the most profound and fundamental way. To limit free discussion of political affairs is an anathema to the freedom of speech and expression. This is the vision of free speech that is recognized in Indian juristic thought.

The Value of Political Speech

In thinking of the heuristic tools and the normative justifications that are essential to recognize and elevate political speech to a high level of importance, it is useful to draw on the framework developed by Cass Sunstein in his book *Democracy and the Problem of Free Speech*.

Sunstein begins by suggesting that any objective assessment cannot deny the reality that a responsive democracy requires strong protection for free speech. 'The right to free speech,' Sunstein suggests, 'is hardly in tension with democracy; it is a precondition for it.'[65]

In Sunstein's conception, political speech denotes speech which '*is both intended and received as a contribution to public deliberation about some issue*.'[66] Importantly, the way in which free speech is conceived is directly tied to the nature of restrictions which we think can permissibly be imposed.

If we believe that all speech must be regulated only from the point of view of the harm or effect that it has, a large segment of political speech can stand excluded from the purview of constitutional protection. This is because governments can designate political speech as likely to inflict undue harm on the State apparatus and use this as a ruse to quell speech which is critical of governmental conduct and State action.[67]

Sunstein makes a preference for a value-based approach to political speech. There is an important value addition which political speech makes to 'deliberative democracy,' which deserves a level of constitutional protection in which the maximum space is created for political speech, coupled with the most minimal levels of State intrusion.

Sunstein's main thesis is that it is the 'Value' of political speech in furthering democratic ideals which must always be considered when thinking of the justification for why political speech ought to be protected, rather than focusing on the possible drawbacks which might be associated with political speech.

Applying this to the 1st Amendment to the US Constitution which guarantees the freedom of speech, Sunstein advances a framework in which he deems the 1st Amendment to be a 'two-tier' constitutional guarantee.

The first tier is occupied by political speech which is 'high value.' Since the value of political speech is the highest in terms of the furthering of democratic ideals, Sunstein proposes that 'political speech is firmly protected; it may be regulated only on the basis of the strongest showing of harm.'[68]

The second tier comprises 'low-value' speech, which includes commercial speech, obscenity and the like, in respect of which the nature of regulation requires a different legal approach.[69]

By separating political speech from all other forms of speech, Sunstein proposes that we can focus more clearly and more specifically on developing robust means of promoting political speech. More importantly, the purpose of introducing this tiered approach to free speech is to create a logical justification for establishing the guiding principle that in regulating political speech the State has to overcome an extraordinarily high burden before any curb can be imposed.

Ordinary justifications, such as there being a rational reason for curbing political speech or that State efforts at achieving particular ends will be harmed by free speech, are rendered untenable grounds for curbing political speech. There is, after all, a distinct advantage in political speech enjoying complete freedom if we think of it as possessing a high level of value which contributes to democracy.[70]

In advancing this framework, Sunstein enlists four justifications. To begin with, as a historical matter (from the perspective of both the framers of the US Constitution as well as the jurisprudence of the US Supreme Court), political speech was always treated as being the core form of speech which the US Constitution protects. Indeed, the 1st Amendment was framed with the specific aim of ensuring that the government is never authorized to outlaw 'political ideas of which it disapproved.'[71]

Moreover, even the US Supreme Court has made important declarations to further political speech and stop governmental action which directly harms the free flow of political speech. Looked at from a historical perspective, there is much support for the idea that political speech is deserving of a high level of protection.[72]

Related to this is the second justification. Since political speech is critical for the enhancement and betterment of the conditions of democracy, it is logical that political speech requires a special degree of heightened protection. It goes to reaffirm the basic principle 'that speech that bears on political life is entitled to the fullest protection of the free speech principle.'[73]

The third justification is that State regulation of political speech must always be viewed from a different perspective, and indeed with suspicion. Political speech is almost always directed against the government, and since the State is at the receiving end, any measure which seeks to control political speech 'raises the distinctive spectre of government censorship harmful to its own self-interest.'[74]

When contrasted with all other forms of speech, it is political speech which seeks to hold the government accountable. And particularly when political speech demands governmental accountability, we must approach any regulation seeking to curb the channel of free speech by which governmental action is held up to a standard of accountability tentatively:

> An insistence that government's burden is greatest for regulating political speech is based on a sensible view of government's incentive. It is in this setting that *government is most likely to be biased or to be acting on the basis of illegitimate, venal or partial considerations*. Government is *rightly distrusted* when it is regulating speech that might harm its own interests; and when the speech at issue is political, its own interests are almost always at stake. It follows that the *premise of distrust of government is strongest when politics is at issue*. And *when the premise of distrust is strongest, the burden of justification is highest*.[75]

Finally, a conception of political speech as being a core part of free speech helps in counteracting much regulation which effectively inflicts serious injury on the 'democratic process' itself. Political speech is not merely an expression of an opinion but also endeavours to generate change. And when political speech is capable of bringing about democratic change, any curb on political speech has the real effect of 'impairing the ordinary channels for political change.'[76]

Political speech is the 'democratic corrective' which is guaranteed by the US Constitution, and when regulation harms political speech, it creates a system where the 'process of political deliberation' and 'democratic debate' are almost always never fully realized.[77]

The elevation of core political speech to the top tier of the freedom of speech and expression is fully compatible with the scheme of the Indian Constitution; indeed, the Constitution demands so. The framers of the Constitution themselves had a distinct conception of political speech being crucial to the health and state of Indian democracy, and of not permitting a law such as Section 124A to be valid in the eyes of the Constitution.

As we saw, the speeches of K.M. Munshi, Ananthasayanam Ayyangar, Pandit Thakur Dass Bhargava and T.T. Krishnamachari in the debates on free speech in the Constituent Assembly asserted the central idea that it was political speech that was principally to be secured by the freedom of speech and expression.

For the citizens of India to be responsive and alert, they must have the full capability of using the power of their thoughts to bring about change in the nature of governance and in the government itself. Political change is central to the life of a democratic republic, and political speech is an important means of achieving that end.

Fortunately, the Indian Supreme Court itself has articulated and often re-emphasized, from 1950 itself, the constitutional credo that the guiding principle of the free speech right in the Constitution is to ensure that political speech is closely safeguarded.

In his judgment in *Shreya Singhal*, Justice Nariman drew on the rich body of Indian jurisprudence and the declarations on the importance of political speech to develop a framework in which free speech can truly flourish.

The freedom of speech and expression has three broad fundamental components: 'Discussion, Advocacy, and Incitement.'[78] 'Mere discussion or even advocacy of a particular cause no matter how unpopular,' Justice Nariman declared, 'is at the heart of Article 19(1)(a).'[79] As we have seen, Indian jurisprudence has also articulated the idea that governmental regulation of political speech must be analysed rigorously because of the inherent bias in the nature of such regulation, since it is the government which attempts to curb and prevent the airing of views which are critical of it. We thus have the makings of a jurisprudence which places political speech on a plane of high importance.

There is no room for equivocation. The Indian Constitution demands that political speech must receive the highest level of protection. It secures the libertarian idea that political speech is a means of ushering in political change. The Constitution cherishes the idea that state regulation is always suspect when it is directed against political speech. And, it cements as a constitutional canon that short of showing exceptional justification for regulation, political speech is above governmental regulation. The tradition of the free speech guarantee leans in favour of granting strong, if not near-absolute, protection to political speech.

10
Putting the Soul in a Lifeless Article

———•———

It is important to explore exactly how the phrase 'reasonable restrictions' entered Article 19(2) and the constitutional revolution it ushered. The conception of the freedom of speech guaranteeing absolute protection to political speech rests on the use of 'reasonable restrictions' as the fulcrum to place political speech on an elevated platform within the normative framework of Article 19(1)(a) and Article 19(2). The story of this phrase begins with the First Amendment to the Indian Constitution.

A Moment of Victory

When the First Amendment Bill was being discussed in the Provisional Parliament on 16 May 1951, Pandit Thakur Dass Bhargava had delivered a long speech. At one point, Bhargava made an important recommendation which would prove to be the saving grace for free speech in India.

He proposed that since Parliament was getting a second shot at changing the Constitution which the very same Parliament had passed in its capacity as the Constituent Assembly, it was worth ensuring that the phrase 'reasonable restrictions' was introduced in Article 19(2).[1] Incidentally, this was Bhargava's third attempt at including the principle of reasonableness in Article 19(2).

In the Constitution which came to life on 26 January 1950, seven civil rights were enumerated in Article 19, like the freedom of association. For each of these there was a corresponding clause by which the right could be curbed.

When the Constituent Assembly took up Article 19 (then draft Article 13) for debate on 1 December 1948, Bhargava had moved an amendment motion in which he proposed that in addition to enumerating the specific grounds on which each of the civil rights could be restricted, the Constitution must also specify that only 'reasonable restrictions' could be imposed on these rights.[2]

The importance of qualifying the ability of the State to impose limitations, particularly on the freedom of speech, with the word 'reasonable' was that the fundamental rights would have some constitutional force in them rather than being a mere collection of moral principles in the Constitution. There was a need for introducing some balance. Otherwise, there would be no outer limit in terms of the kind of restrictions the State could impose on civil liberties.

To invest in the judiciary the power to substantively review the restrictions in respect of the rights enumerated in Article 19, Bhargava proposed the introduction of the phrase 'reasonable restrictions' in all the clauses in Article 19 which contained the grounds on which the liberty rights could be curbed. Bhargava told the Assembly that this phrase would put the 'soul' into an otherwise 'lifeless' set of civil rights.[3] Passionately putting his case before the Constituent Assembly, Bhargava proclaimed:

> If you put the word 'reasonable' there, the court will have to see whether a particular Act is in the interests of the public and secondly whether the restrictions imposed by the legislatures are reasonable, proper and necessary in the circumstances of the case. The courts shall have to go into the question and it will not be the legislature and the executive who could play with the fundamental rights of the people. It is the courts which will have the final say.[4]

Thus, it was the word 'reasonable' which would empower the judiciary to inquire whether a law was proper, motivated by good reasons, just and fair, and whether the restrictions imposed on any of the rights in Article 19, including the freedom of speech, were proportionate and necessary.

Essentially, Bhargava's proposal sought to ensure that when it came to judicial review of the civil rights enumerated in Article 19, the standard of review would be akin to due process review, which is the most rigorous form of judicial review.[5] Putting the word 'reasonable' was, according to Bhargava, to confer on 'courts the final authority to say whether the restrictions put are reasonable or reasonably necessary or not.'[6]

The next day, on 2 December 1948, the Constituent Assembly voted on all the amendments that had been proposed to Article 19 (then draft Article 13). When it came to accepting Bhargava's amendments, the Assembly agreed to introduce the phrase 'reasonable restrictions' in respect of all the civil rights, except freedom of speech.[7]

For free speech, the Assembly did not stipulate that a law curbing it must be 'reasonable', even though the other civil rights, such as the freedom of association, the freedom to choose one's work, and the right to property, could only be subject to reasonable restrictions.[8]

However, Bhargava remained undaunted, and he redoubled his efforts to ensure that for the freedom of speech, Article 19(2) (then draft Article 13(2)) also spoke of reasonable restrictions. Almost a year after the Assembly had discussed the freedom of speech, on 17 October 1949, the Assembly once again took up the freedom of speech and expression right for debate. On that day, Bhargava again tried to introduce the word 'reasonable' in Article 19(2).

The absence of the 'reasonable restrictions' standard of review in respect of free speech alone, Bhargava told the Assembly, would have devastating consequences, because 'a legislature has been given full powers to place any kind of restriction, reasonable or unreasonable.'[9]

Bhargava believed that the Assembly perhaps had decided not to introduce the word 'reasonable' in Article 19(2) because 'sedition' had been deleted and, at any rate, the grounds for curbing free speech were mentioned in very specific terms. The manner in which Article 19(2) was structured was in contrast to the structuring of some of the other rights in Article 19, which used broadly defined phrases such as 'public interest' when dealing with the grounds on which curbs could be imposed.[10]

For Bhargava, specific definitions in Article 19(2) did not mean that the State should have a free pass to curb free speech in whatever manner it liked, without anyone asking any questions. The freedom of speech was an all-important right, and if the State was given the power to curb it, then it followed logically that the courts must have the corresponding power to review the nature of the restrictions that had been imposed.[11] As Bhargava told the Assembly:

> All these matters will be rationalized to a certain extent and instead of reducing the rights and privileges of citizens of the Republic it would be better if we enlarge their liberties, and I therefore suggest that instead of the words 'any law' the words 'any reasonable law' may be substituted.[12]

Bhargava was still unsuccessful. On this occasion too, he could not convince the Assembly, and his efforts proved unfruitful.[13] As a result of this, in 1950, in respect of the freedom of speech and expression, the Constitution allowed the State to impose whatever kind of restrictions it desired, so long as the subject matter of the restriction was traceable to an enumerated ground in Article 19(2). No questions could ever be asked as to whether the nature of the restriction itself was reasonable.

This was a major problem with the fundamental right to freedom of speech and expression which was approved by the Constituent Assembly, because nothing in the Constitution remotely suggested, 'how far a law will be permitted to go in restraining free speech.'[14] The absence of this limiting principle made an amendment to Article 19 and the introduction of the reasonableness standard of review inevitable.[15]

Now, in 1951, Bhargava launched his third and possibly final attempt at infusing in Article 19(2) a modicum of rationality, so that the State did not have an open-ended invitation to curb free speech to whatever extent it wished. 'I want that the liberties of the citizen of this country should be protected,' beseeched Bhargava, 'and unless and until the word "reasonable" is placed before the word "restrictions" it would not ensure that liberty.'[16]

The fundamental purpose of introducing the phrase 'reasonable restrictions' in Article 19(2) was to forevermore ensure that in curbing free speech, the State would never cross the 'limits prescribed for them by virtue of this Constitution.'[17] This was a demand which Bhargava would reiterate on most occasions when he addressed Parliament on the First Amendment.[18]

Bhargava's demand resonated with others. When Dr Ambedkar addressed Parliament on 18 May 1951, he straight away agreed that Bhargava's demand was fit to be considered by the Select Committee as well as by Parliament itself.[19]

Indeed, when the proposals for the First Amendment Bill were being vetted by the Cabinet in April 1951, Dr Ambedkar, as well as India's first Attorney General, M.C. Setalvad, had recommended that the phrase 'reasonable restrictions' be added to Article 19(2). Dr Ambedkar felt that this was necessary, or else 'the State would have the power altogether to deny freedom of speech and expression to the citizen.' At that time, this recommendation was not accepted.[20]

In Parliament, when the First Amendment Bill went to the Select Committee, the result of the deliberations revealed that the Select Committee decided to add the phrase 'reasonable restrictions' in Article 19(2).[21] Eventually, Parliament approved this, when it passed the First Amendment to the Constitution. In this third attempt, Bhargava proved victorious.

The true import of the constitutional revolution ushered in by the phrase 'reasonable restrictions' in Article 19, was recognized in an early decision of the Supreme Court in 1950. In the case of *Chintaman Rao*, the Supreme Court declared that when it came to examining whether a restriction was reasonable, the Court had to mandatorily undertake a most rigorous analysis of the measure in question:

> The phrase 'reasonable restriction' connotes that the limitation imposed on a person in enjoyment of the right should not be arbitrary or of an excessive nature, beyond what is required in the interests of the public. The word 'reasonable' *implies intelligent care and deliberation, that is, the choice of a course which reason dictates. Legislation which arbitrarily or excessively invades the right cannot be said to contain the quality of reasonableness* and unless it strikes a proper balance between the freedom guaranteed in Article 19(1)(g) and the social control permitted by clause (6) of Article 19, it must be held to be wanting in that quality.[22]

The use of 'reasonable restrictions' indicates that when a court reviews a curb on free speech, it must apply due process review, which is the most rigorous form of review available to a constitutional court. As Bhargava had pointed out in the Constituent Assembly on 17 October 1949, it was fully possible for laws to be passed in a state of 'ignorance, passion, panic and prejudice which look reasonable to some and unreasonable to others.'[23] The reasonable restrictions standard would help courts to see through such laws and judge them for what they were truly worth.[24]

In 1985, the wide powers conferred by the reasonable restrictions standard of review was used by the Supreme Court in the *Indian Express Newspapers* case, to question onerous regulations which were imposed on the freedom of the press. Drawing a direct connection between the freedom of speech and its role in enhancing democracy, the Court declared that it was 'reasonable restrictions' standard of review which would ensure the continued vitality of the freedom of speech:

> The Government should strike *a just and reasonable balance* between the need for ensuring the right of people to freedom of speech and expression on the one hand and the need to impose social control on the business of publication of a newspaper on the other. In other words, the Government must at all material times *be conscious of the fact* that it is dealing with an activity protected by Article 19(1)(a) of the Constitution *which is vital to our democratic existence.*[25]

The Court added:

> In deciding the reasonableness of restrictions imposed on any fundamental right the *Court should take into consideration the nature of the right alleged to have been infringed, the underlying purpose of the restrictions imposed, the disproportion of the imposition and the prevailing conditions at the relevant time including the social values whose needs are sought to be satisfied by means of the restrictions.*[26]

In Indian scholarship, many have taken the view that the phrase 'reasonable restrictions' in Article 19 really means due process review of the restrictions imposed. One of the leading commentators on the Indian Constitution, Charles Henry Alexandrowicz wrote as early as in 1957 that the word 'reasonable' implies that it is the constitutional courts which will decide whether a restriction is constitutionally proper. In taking that decision the Indian justices exercise expansive powers of review, on par with their counterparts in the US Supreme Court:

> ...[B]ut it is open to the judges to review the reasonableness of restrictions and constitutionality of the respective laws, which gives them *mutatis mutandis* the same power in relation to article 19 which American judges *enjoy generally under the due-process-of-law clause.*[27]

Another scholar of the Indian Constitution, P.K. Tripathi from the Faculty of Law at Delhi University, also made a strong case for the phrase 'reasonable restrictions' being synonymous with due process review:

> In fact, *no constitution which secures liberties by providing for judicial review* of executive and legislative action on the basis of judicially supervised standards of reasonableness *can simply succeed in avoiding the doctrines of 'due process'* and 'police powers.' Because, as Bhargava and other members of the Constituent Assembly *rightly understood, 'due process' is none other than the test of 'reasonableness'* applied by the judiciary in assessing the quality of the legislative measures affecting the liberty of the individual.[28]

Commenting on the selection of the word 'reasonable' for the civil rights contained in Article 19, Tripathi argued that many in the Assembly were well aware that the word 'reasonable' would bring with it the 'due process' standard of review. As Tripathi saw it:

They were also at least vaguely aware that in the United States the Constitution has carried out the experiment of authorizing the judges to apply the standards, and the results there obtained encourage emulation. And they all knew that the "due process" clause was the key to the enforcement of judicially supervised standards. Some among them, like Bhargava, were certainly more knowledgeable and were able to see that the same standards can be enforced by using either the expression 'due process' or the expression 'reasonable.' In either case, the standards are determined and the lines of demarcation between freedom and permissible restraint are drawn by the judges.[29]

Essentially, that one word—reasonable—ensured that in the scheme of the Indian Constitution civil rights would enjoy heightened due process protection.[30]

H.M. Seervai, however, had a different point of view. According to him, any inquiry into the measure restricting a right in Article 19 must not be akin to due process review as it is known under the US Constitution, because 'due process does not apply to our Constitution.'[31] Rather, the proper test to be applied is 'whether a reasonable man would necessarily consider them unreasonable.'[32]

Yet, in describing the method by which courts must review the restrictions imposed on civil liberties, Seervai ended up using the language of due process review. In saying that courts must scrutinize '[t]he reasonableness of both the substantive and the procedural provisions of the law,' and that it is crucial to see whether the 'law provides crucial safeguards,'[33] is to speak the language of due process review.

At any rate, for all purposes today, due process rights are very much recognized as being a part of Article 19, as well as of Article 21 of the Constitution, which guarantees the fundamental right to life and personal liberty.[34]

The presence of 'reasonable restrictions' in Article 19(2) shows that the State's proffered justification for a law such as sedition is not to be taken at face value. No one put this point better than Jawaharlal Nehru.

During the deliberations on the First Amendment, Nehru applauded the introduction of the 'reasonable restrictions' standard in Article 19(2) and recognized it as a moment of enormous constitutional importance. According to him, the presence of this phrase clearly conferred on the judicial branch '*direct authority*' to judge the constitutional validity of any regulation imposed on the freedom of speech.[35] The addition of that one word—'reasonable'—according to Nehru, transformed Article 19(2). It was a 'major change' which rendered State action affecting free speech 'patently justiciable.'[36]

Under the framework of the Constitution, the Supreme Court and the high courts are constitutionally bound to rigorously probe the rationale, justification, feasibility as well as the purported merits of a law. The State cannot get over this requirement by simply invoking the interest of State security.

In the name of imposing restrictions, the right cannot be gobbled up. As a result of reasonable restrictions becoming part of Article 19(2), power was divided. It fell within the remit of the State's powers to formulate the nature of restrictions, and it was left to the judicial branch to decide whether a restriction was constitutionally reasonable.

The full power of the phrase 'reasonable restrictions' was on display in the years which followed the passage of the First

Amendment. In 1958, the Supreme Court declared a State law which affected the liberty of the press as unconstitutional, for it was unreasonable.

In *Virendra v. State of Punjab*,[37] a Constitution Bench of five justices headed by Chief Justice S.R. Das had to decide whether a certain provision of the Punjab Special Powers (Press) Act of 1956 was consistent with Article 19(2). Section 3 of that Act empowered the state of Punjab to bar the publication and distribution of a newspaper in the state on the ground of public order, among several other grounds.[38] The Supreme Court, speaking through Chief Justice Das, declared this provision of law unconstitutional for violating the freedom of speech and expression.

Applying the rigorous principles contained in the powerful phrase 'reasonable restrictions,' the Court reasoned that the law was 'unreasonable' and utterly disproportionate. As the Court saw it, the law did not provide a 'time limit' for which a newspaper could be banned, and thus any order barring the circulation of newspapers in the state could potentially be permanent. Further, the law did not allow for those directly affected by such orders to appeal to the state seeking reconsideration of the ban order in question.[39]

As the Court declared, the 'absence of these safeguards . . . *clearly makes its provisions unreasonable* and the learned Solicitor-General *obviously felt some difficulty* in supporting the validity of this section.'[40]

Viewed counterfactually, if the Supreme Court decided this case in the absence of the phrase 'reasonable restrictions' being part of Article 19(2), then once it was shown that the law was made to preserve public order it would have been the end of the matter. The Court could not have examined the reasonableness of the law itself. The most perverse law harming free speech could not be questioned once it was shown that the law traced its roots to an enumerated ground in Article 19(2).

There is another interesting aspect to this case. On finding the law constitutionally infirm, the Supreme Court did not embark on an expedition to rework the law and engage in a form of judicial legislation to somehow save it. This was despite the fact that there was an earlier provision in the same law, which authorized the state to prohibit the circulation of newspapers.

This other provision was upheld by Chief Justice Das, since it contained inbuilt safeguards.[41] Yet, despite this, the Court did not attempt to rework the provision which contravened the freedom of speech. The offending provision of law was declared wholly unconstitutional.

In recent years, another arrow has been added to the quiver of constitutional remedies available for protecting fundamental rights. It is the doctrine of manifest arbitrariness.

Manifest arbitrariness denotes that a law can be declared invalid if it is not guided by any rational purpose, if it is contrary to all canons of justice, and if it perpetuates an order which grates against all notions of constitutional morality. For many years, there was a lingering uncertainty over whether the doctrine of manifest arbitrariness could be used to test the validity of laws. These doubts were put to rest in 2019 by the decision of a Constitution Bench of five justices of the Supreme Court in the *Triple Talaq* case.[42]

Justice Nariman, speaking for the majority, declared that when it comes to the judicial review of fundamental rights, courts could use the doctrine of manifest arbitrariness to see whether a law measured up to a high constitutional standard. As he declared:

Manifest arbitrariness, therefore, must be something done by the legislature capriciously, irrationally and/or without adequate determining principle. Also, when something is done which is excessive and disproportionate, such legislation would be manifestly arbitrary. We are, therefore, of the view that arbitrariness in the sense of manifest arbitrariness as pointed out by us above would apply to negate legislation as well under Article 14.[43]

Justice Nariman observed that after the decision of the Supreme Court in the *R.C. Cooper* case, the fundamental rights enumerated in Articles 14, 19 and 21 had to be read together. As a result, the principle of 'reasonable restrictions' in Article 19 would inform the broad outlook of both Article 14 and Article 21. Tying these fundamental rights together established the idea that the principle of reasonableness was ingrained in the chapter on fundamental rights. As Justice Nariman declared:

> The thread of reasonableness runs through the entire fundamental rights chapter. What is manifestly arbitrary is obviously unreasonable and being contrary to the rule of law, would violate Article 14.[44]

In the *Triple Talaq* case, the doctrine of manifest arbitrariness was used to declare the practice of triple talaq unconstitutional.[45] Since then, the doctrine of manifest arbitrariness has been applied to invalidate several legislations and to further the cause of fundamental rights. The decisions which led to the decriminalization of homosexuality and the invalidation of the law concerning adultery in the IPC, to take a few instances, were possible by treating them as being manifestly arbitrary.[46]

The Power of Reason

The decisions in the *Virendra* as well as *Sakal Papers* cases open up an interesting point on whether the decision of the Supreme Court in the *Thappar–Bhushan* cases decided in 1950 continues to hold the field after the First Amendment.

As we saw, one of the main reasons behind the restructuring of Article 19(2) was to ensure that the freedom of speech and expression could be restricted on additional grounds, including public order.

During the debates in Parliament, the government seemed to have in mind the retrospective validation of laws of the kind which were declared unconstitutional in the *Romesh Thappar* case by the Supreme Court. However, Jawaharlal Nehru and Dr Ambedkar assured Parliament that the revival of these laws would be conditional, that if the laws could not be saved by the new Article 19(2), they would remain unconstitutional.

The *Romesh Thappar* case involved a challenge to Section 9(1-A) of the Madras Maintenance of Public Order Act, 1949. Acting under that law, the Governor of Madras passed an order banning the circulation of the journal *Cross Roads* in the state of Madras. That law had been struck down by the Supreme Court since 'public order' was not part of Article 19(2) and hence the law could not trace its provenance to it.

Yet, despite the addition of 'public order' in Article 19(2), the law involved in the *Romesh Thappar* case would continue to remain unconstitutional, even after the First Amendment. This is because the law would not be a reasonable restriction on free speech, even though it may be guided by a public order interest. The law directly prevented the circulation of newspapers and journals and gave too much discretion to the State to interfere with the freedom of the press.

Even after the First Amendment to the Constitution, the Supreme Court through the decades reaffirmed the principle, that laws which seek to regulate the content of newspapers as well as their circulation can never be sustained under Article 19(2). In 1959, a Constitution Bench of five judges in *Express Newspaper*[47] declared:

> While therefore no such immunity from the general laws can be claimed by the press *it would certainly not be legitimate* to subject the press to laws which take away or abridge the freedom of speech and expression or which would *curtail circulation and thereby narrow the scope of dissemination of information, or fetter its freedom to choose its means of exercising the right* or would undermine its independence by driving it to seek Government aid.[48]

The Court added:

> Laws which single out the press for laying upon it excessive and prohibitive burdens which would restrict the circulation, impose a penalty on its right to choose the instruments for its exercise or to seek an alternative media, prevent newspapers from being started and ultimately drive the press to seek Government aid in order to survive, would, therefore, be struck down as unconstitutional.[49]

This trend continued in famous decisions handed down by the Supreme Court in the 1960s, 1970s and 1980s. In 1961, a Constitution Bench of five judges in *Sakal Papers* declared that prime importance to be conferred on the fundamental right of the press to have complete freedom when it came to circulation of newspapers.

As the Supreme Court saw it, the Newspaper (Price and Page) Act, 1956 which was at issue, was viewed as directly controlling the 'circulation of a newspaper' which is integral to the 'right of freedom of speech'.[50] Controlling circulation, in the opinion of the Court, 'would necessarily undermine their power to influence public opinion'.[51] And if this is the final result of a law which affects the freedom of speech, then such a law would become a 'dangerous weapon which is capable of being used against democracy itself'.[52]

In *Bennett Coleman* (1972),[53] a Constitution Bench of five judges, by majority, reaffirmed the importance of ensuring that restrictions on the freedom of speech be viewed with rigorous scrutiny.

The State was prohibited from affecting free speech under the garb of imposing regulations. The Court reasserted the ideal that within the scheme of Article 19(1)(a), so far as the freedom of the press is concerned, the ability to circulate newspapers without hindrance was the only way the freedom of speech and expression could survive. As the Court declared:

> *Publication means dissemination and circulation*. . . . The law which lays excessive and prohibitive burden which would restrict the circulation of a newspaper will not be saved by Article 19(2). . . . *The freedom of a newspaper to publish any number of pages or to circulate it to any number of persons* has been held by this Court to be an *integral part* of the freedom of speech and expression. This freedom is *violated by placing restraints upon it or by placing restraints upon something which is an essential part of that freedom*. A restraint on the number of pages, a restraint on circulation and a restraint on advertisements

would affect the fundamental rights under Article 19(1)(a) on the *aspects of propagation, publication and circulation*.[54]

The Court also declared:

> *The faith of a citizen is that political wisdom and virtue will sustain themselves in the free market of ideas so long as the channels of communication are left open.* The faith in the popular Government rests on the old dictum, 'let the people have the truth and the freedom to discuss it and all will go well.' The liberty of the press remains an 'Ark of the Covenant' in every democracy. Steel will yield products of steel. Newsprint will manifest whatever is thought of by man. The newspapers give ideas. The newspapers give the people the freedom to find out what ideas are correct. . . . Newspapers have to be left free to determine their pages, their circulation and their new editions within their quota that has been fixed fairly.[55]

In *Bennett Coleman*, the Court used these principles of free speech to declare that the Newsprint Import Policy in question unconstitutionally sought to control the number of copies of a newspaper which could be circulated, the number of pages that could be printed in a newspaper, and how much space could be dedicated for advertisements.[56] These restrictions were declared unconstitutional, for nothing in Article 19(2) could help sustain them.[57]

In 1985, in *Indian Express Newspapers*,[58] the Supreme Court once again reaffirmed the principle that the freedom of the press, the freedom to ensure the circulation of newspapers and the freedom to determine the content of newspapers could not be subjected to onerous regulations. Indeed, this would be impermissible under the scheme of Article 19(1)(a) and Article 19(2). As the Court saw it, 'Freedom of [the] press . . . means freedom from interference from authority which would have the effect of interference with the content and circulation of newspapers.'[59]

Through these decisions, the Supreme Court reaffirmed the idea that when it came to the freedom of speech and expression and particularly the freedom of the press, the right to ensure the circulation of newspapers was a core part of Article 19(1)(a). Indeed, the ability of the press to make choices about its newspapers is firmly protected by the Constitution and is a right which the State cannot easily infringe.[60]

A ban on circulation, the Supreme Court had declared in *Romesh Thappar*, went to the heart of free speech and the ability of the press to disseminate information. Indeed, as the Supreme Court announced in *Virendra*, in respect of a law whose impact on the press was broadly similar to the law involved in *Romesh Thappar*, granting such powers to the State without any safeguards in favour of the press rendered the law unreasonable.

With the phrase 'reasonable restrictions' becoming part of Article 19(2) and in light of the series of decisions from the 1950s till the 1980s, it is unlikely that the laws involved in the *Thappar–Bhushan* cases would have revived even after the First Amendment.

11

The Value of Political Speech

SECTION 124A CANNOT BE TREATED AS A REASONABLE RESTRICTION ON the freedom of speech because of the serious harm it inflicts on the ability of people to engage in free political speech. We have seen the importance of elevating political speech to a higher pedestal of constitutional justice. But that elevation will be unhelpful if the ability of the State to regulate political speech is not sufficiently hedged.

When it comes to political speech directed against the government, such speech has to be understood in an absolute sense. In the paradigm of the Constitution, 'absolute' must mean that political speech is immune from all forms of regulation. In other words, laws cannot be made to curtail it. In the discussion and advocacy of political interests, political ideals, political critique, government officials, holders of public office and the development of politically transformative ideas, the freedom of speech must always remain unabridged.

Regulations can only be formulated to deal with those narrow sets of situations in which political speech is 'brigaded' with the spectre of an assault on the security of the State. If political speech is used only for the purposes of bringing about an imminently inevitable assault on State security, the brigading of speech with such violent actions can be the subject matter of regulation. However, any regulation that is framed must be reasonable, and the simple invocation of State security—or for that matter public order—must not give the State a free pass to defeat all forms of political speech.

There is also the important issue of the form that political speech takes. It is naïve to believe that people will only engage in political speech which is sober, sophisticated, and has all the trappings of what one may believe are the markers of civility.

Political speech involves criticism and implicitly demands change and transformation, and that demand can result in speech and writings often being vituperative, offensive and insulting. As the US Supreme Court put it, 'one man's vulgarity is another's lyric.' As a result, the Constitution does not allow the government to decide how a message is to be conveyed; that decision is left within the sole domain 'of taste and style so largely to the individual.'[1]

In India, early on in 1951, the Supreme Court struck a note of caution in alerting the government against overreacting to expressions which were vituperative in nature. The idea was that the tone and choice of words in and of itself cannot make the suppression of free speech constitutionally permissible. As the Court put it, if a person were to write calling for a 'bloody revolution' and 'total annihilation', writings containing a 'good deal of demagogic claptrap,' the State should ideally not act upon it unless there is a compelling justification.[2]

To be sure, when political speech is involved, the principle is clear. Since the Constitution has secured liberties for the people, the discussion of political affairs is not to be unduly fettered.

Consider, for instance, the decision of the US Supreme Court in *New York Times v. Sullivan*. It was recognized that the moment political speech is involved, it is but an inevitability that the tenor of the critique may take varying forms:

> Thus we consider this case against the background of a profound national commitment to the principle that debate on public issues should be uninhibited, robust, and wide-open, and that it may well include vehement, caustic, and sometimes unpleasantly sharp attacks on government and public officials. [3]

Building on this, the US Supreme Court in 1969 declared, '[t]he language of the political arena,' where speech targets political officials, including the head of State, can 'often be vituperative, abusive and inexact.'[4]

Personal preferences cannot control constitutional choices, much less the enforcement of the freedom of speech. The ideal to be achieved is complete freedom in the sphere of political speech. Outlawing speech only on the basis of how it has been projected is impermissible.[5]

From a constitutional perspective, the form that political speech takes must not be the controlling factor which justifies its suppression. Rather, what is paramount is the content of the speech. Even though a person may use words which from one view may seem revolting if not outright worthy of condemnation, what must be taken into account is the political content of the speech.

It is well-nigh impossible to regulate each person's choice of language; it is certainly not the business of the law to do so when it comes to political speech. The desire of the State to control the method in which political speech is conveyed will almost certainly sound the death knell of political speech altogether.

At any rate, as a general matter, political speech should be beyond the reach of ordinary methods of regulation. The State ought not to engage in tempering speech in which the State itself is at the receiving end.

Whatever regulation is imposed on core political speech must be treated as valid only if it draws a proportional balance between the speech and certain consequences affecting State security. People must have the full freedom—and more importantly, have the sense of complete freedom—of expressing their views and opinions on political matters.

The justification for thinking along these lines is the democratic interest. To ensure the survival of Indian democracy, to guarantee the success of the Indian republic, and to maintain the continued vitality of Indian political thought, it is critical that people are constitutionally empowered to engage in political speech which touches on matters of democracy and governance, without the slightest fear that a jail cell awaits them at the end of their exposition.

In *Kedar Nath Singh*, the Supreme Court upheld Section 124A on the ground that speech and expression which has the tendency to affect public order has validly been rendered an offence. This chapter explores the working framework which must be adopted in judging the constitutionality of a law such as sedition. We shall see that this 'tendency' test, as it is known, has a dubious history and is thoroughly discredited today.

The idea that speech and expression can be banned by merely alleging that it has a tendency to cause harm took birth in the US during World War I. This principle was crafted to quell speeches and writings which were critical of the American war efforts. Since then, in the US, constitutional thought has undergone a progressive transformation which is protective of free speech, including the right to dissent and disagree with the government.

Within the scheme of Article 19(2) it is possible to imagine a framework where speech which involves the discussion and advocacy of political ideas, which includes critical assessment of the government as well as its activities, is completely immune from regulation.

Only such speech which is 'brigaded' with imminent and inevitable violent reactions affecting State security can be the subject matter of regulations. Brigading means there must be a direct connection between the speech and the constitutionally proscribed events it seeks to bring about; events which are inevitable, if not preordained.

As we shall see, granting absolute protection to political speech in the realm of discussion and advocacy is entirely consistent with Article 19(2). This line of thinking has also been developed in Indian constitutional thought both before and after the decision in *Kedar Nath Singh*. Since the 1950s, the Indian Supreme Court has adhered to the idea that only the need to prevent an imminent and serious harm can furnish the basis to regulate the freedom of speech and expression.

Article 19(2) must be understood as containing the governing constitutional principle that political speech and expression cannot be regulated unless the law clearly demonstrates that it serves to tackle only those situations in which the speech results in imminent and inevitable harm to the security of the State. Otherwise, it is an unreasonable restriction on free speech.

It is not enough for courts to constantly reinterpret laws such as Section 124A as containing a higher threshold that needs to be crossed, before the law is triggered. Constitutional reason demands that rather than lingering in the domain of statutory interpretation and reinterpretation, where we are only concerned with how the law must operate, we must see whether the law itself is constitutionally defensible.[6]

As we shall see, the project of reading additional requirements into Section 124A in the hope of saving citizens from unmerited prosecutions has had calamitous consequences for the freedom of speech and expression.

The Need to Overhaul Constitutional Protection for Political Speech

Free speech, it is believed, can never be absolute, and none of the decisions of the Supreme Court on free speech will ever say that political speech is above and beyond the reach of any regulation. What these decisions stipulate, rather, is that the nature of the regulation has to be narrow in its scope to regulate exceptional situations, such as when political speech spills over into calls for violence and public disorder. But there is a dissonance in this line of thinking.

Consider the decision in *Kedar Nath Singh*, in which the Supreme Court saved Section 124A by declaring that it applies to cases where there is likelihood of something untoward occurring:

> The provisions of the sections read as a whole, along with the explanations, make it reasonably clear that the

sections aim at rendering penal only such activities as would be intended, or have a tendency, to create disorder or disturbance of public peace by resort to violence. . . . It is only when the words, written or spoken, etc. which have the pernicious tendency or intention of creating public disorder or disturbance of law and order that the law steps in to prevent such activities in the interest of public order. So construed, the section, in our opinion, strikes the correct balance between individual fundamental rights and the interest of public order.[7]

Here the Supreme Court glossed over the distinction between something positively occurring as opposed to something that could potentially occur. The former denotes a quality of certainty and inevitability. The latter denotes only a mere possibility of a development, which may or may not happen. From the perspective of regulating free speech, particularly political speech, respecting this distinction is important.

Phrases such as 'likely to create,' and 'likely to promote' are problematic because they introduce subjectivity and leave it to the government to decide what kind of speech is problematic. Further, 'likely' does not denote a level of certainty or inevitability which a word such as 'creates' indicates. The adoption of this 'likelihood standard' is nothing but an open invitation to the State to deploy the law on sedition against political speech and expression, which otherwise would not raise much concern.

The acceptance of the 'likelihood standard' also erodes the important concept that the State ought not to pervasively regulate free political speech, the subject of which is almost always the government. The 'likelihood standard' creates not a window but a sizeable back door for the State to deploy the law on sedition against any sort of speech by treating it as 'likely to create' disorder.[8]

Kedar Nath Singh's message resonates even today. In *Amish Devgan* (2021),[9] the Supreme Court secured the importance of free political speech, but then made a reference to *Kedar Nath Singh* and held that for the purposes of Article 19(2), only such 'anti-democratic speech in general and political extremist speech in particular, which has no useful purpose, *if and only when* in the nature of incitement to violence that "creates," or is "likely to create" or "promotes" or is "likely to promote" public disorder, would not be protected.'[10]

Avowedly, the Supreme Court in *Kedar Nath Singh* saved Section 124A from unconstitutionality and thought that it would build a safeguard in Section 124A by holding that no one could ever be prosecuted for sedition unless what they said threatened public order. But we now have the lessons of history and the benefit of hindsight to say with certainty that these safeguards have been nothing but a monumentally abysmal failure.[11]

Consider the decision of the Supreme Court in *Balwant Singh* (1995).[12] That was a decision in which the Court had to decide whether the offence of sedition was committed when a person engaged in sloganeering, which had the tinge of separatism, but which made no impact whatsoever on the listeners.[13] The Court declared that empty sloganeering against the State which did not evoke any reaction from the public could not be treated as sedition or as an act which affected the orderly life of the public.[14]

However, the problem that this decision brought to the fore was that since the prevailing standard is the 'likelihood test,' it is the State which decides the type of expression that should be punished. That person then has to fight a seemingly insurmountable battle to clear their name. Eventually, a court may conclude that the speech in question had no likelihood of causing any harm, but by then the damage is done because the person has been imprisoned, if not wrongly convicted, only for exercising the freedom of speech and expression.

Countervailing Considerations and Constitutional Reason

Having seen the salience of ensuring that any reasonable assessment of the free speech right in the Indian Constitution must emphasize the value of political speech being assured of top-tier protection, how do we determine which kind of regulation of political speech the Constitution contemplates as constitutionally tolerable.

Articles 19(1)(a) and 19(2) create a unique constitutional compact for the Constitution, specifically articulating the grounds on which restrictions can be imposed and when they will be deemed to be reasonable. In the context of sedition, countervailing considerations of securing State security and ensuring that the entire State is not destabilized are important interests which allow for the regulation of free speech.

Nonetheless, considering how valuable political speech is to democracy and its capabilities in generating change at a fundamentally political level, coupled with the fact that political speech is directed against the government, any restriction on political speech is only reasonable when it deals with narrow and exceptional situations.

Put differently, any regulation of political speech is unreasonable if it is broadly worded and does not properly account for the diversity of political speech. If the regulation in question is narrowly tailored and deals with specific instances in which the violent outcome of political speech will directly hurt State security, then the regulation may be tolerable. Political speech in which such an outcome is an inevitability, if not preordained, may properly fall within the remit of reasonable regulation.

Moreover, to regulate political speech the State must adopt an objective assessment in which the speech is regulated only because there is a larger and very real threat of consequences ensuing which directly and visibly harm the foundation of the State. Importantly, no law can ever be made which simply criminalizes messages conveyed against the State.

Bringing governmental conduct under the spotlight; building public support and consensus to critique governmental policy; and directing the attention of public consciousness against State activity in the hope of bringing about positive transformation which is consistent with the principle of constitutional morality are the shining hallmarks of political speech. Acknowledging how crucial political speech is to the future of Indian democracy helps in establishing that the regulation of political speech itself has to be held to a higher standard.

Political speech must never be subject to routine and standardized forms of legal control. The State cannot make a law which makes political speech a crime by simply invoking a State security interest without properly accounting for whether legitimate political speech is injured in the process. Open-ended regulations, especially in the realm of criminal law, which take within their sweep every single form of political speech, are unreasonable.

The pre-eminent justification for narrowing the bounds of state regulation springs directly from treating political speech as high-value speech. The constitutional scholar Cass Sunstein proposes that once political speech is treated as high value and as part of the first tier of free speech, its regulation is permissible only in a set of exceptional situations, where the deleterious consequences outweigh the advantages of political speech. For all other forms of speech which fall in the second tier, the regulation may need to meet a less onerous burden.[15] Once the focus of inquiry is the 'value' of speech, it is undeniable that a standardized or a one-size-fits-all approach to the regulation of free speech is untenable.

The arguments made in favour of standardized regulation is that the focus must lie only on preventing the 'harm' that the speech causes. Viewing the regulation of all speech from this perspective furnishes a strong justification for treating all instances of free speech on the same footing, rather than treating political speech as high value.[16] Sunstein acknowledges that although a tempting proposition in itself, there are two major constitutional concerns in treating all forms of speech on the same footing.

As a primary concern, such a conception renders the value of free speech irrelevant. Political speech on an issue of governance, and defamatory speech between two individuals will be one and the same in the eyes of the law for the purposes of regulation, when in reality they are not. If the focus is solely on preventing some harm caused by speech, then the government will find it easy to regulate all speech, including political speech, by invoking the idea that the harm caused by political speech must be prevented.

What follows is a dysfunctional system in which the government can designate political speech as causing enormous harm and curtail it, effectively leading to a 'high threat of censorship.'[17] If the yardstick by which political speech is to be regulated is the same as the standard by which obscene speech and defamation is regulated, then the government need not show any special reason for regulating political speech; there will be no necessity of meeting any higher threshold.[18]

Sunstein takes the example of 'misleading' and 'false' political speech. Political speech may contain inaccuracies or even untruths, but since political speech is crucial to democratic governance there must be a higher level of tolerance for citizens who make misleading political claims. If the principle of harm is employed, then the government has an easy handle with which to clamp down on all political speech by asserting that misleading political speech is harmful. The result of such an approach is that it will 'provide far too little breathing space for important speech.'[19]

On the other hand, applying the principle of harm and saying that the government must meet an exceedingly high standard to regulate any type of speech would also be problematic.

Although in this paradigm political speech may be free of much regulation, other types of speech such as obscenity and defamation will be next to impossible to regulate. Many types of speech inflict serious harm, and if the system prohibits their regulation unless the state can establish that it inflicts a high level of harm, they may well be rendered as matters outside of regulation.[20]

If in regulating speech the focus is on the prevention of harm without regard to the value of the speech, then all speech can be easily curbed, leading to political speech suffering serious injury. Conversely, if the threshold of what constitutes as harm is raised, then no type of speech can be easily regulated.

This may protect political speech, but end up allowing other forms of harmful speech, like hate speech and obscenity, to be immune from legal regulation.[21] Focusing on the 'value' of speech presents a way out of these two extreme positions. This is the reason why the only feasible alternative is to look at speech from the point of view of 'value' and create different sets of regulations for different types of speech.[22] And it is in this framework that political speech can justifiably be granted a higher level of protection.[23]

12

Beware the Ides of March

IN UPHOLDING SECTION 124A, THE SUPREME COURT IN *KEDAR NATH Singh* relied on the legal test that the speech in question must have the tendency to disturb public order.[1]

The regulation of speech, particularly political speech on a showing of a bad tendency of some harm being caused by it, originated in the jurisprudence of the US Supreme Court in the 1920s.[2] But in the US itself, this legal standard has been discarded in favour of a narrower and more stringent test to regulate free speech. If the bad tendency test has been done away with in the country of its birth, then it is high time India too does away with it.

The 1st Amendment to the US Constitution was present in the original Bill of Rights which became part of the US Constitution in 1791. However, for over a century thereafter, the 1st Amendment virtually lay dormant. In 1914, hostilities began between the Axis and the Allied Powers in World War I, which lasted till 1918.

The US entered the war in 1917 and its entry brought with it a new vigour in curbing speech and expression which opposed American efforts in the war. That led to the enactment of the Espionage Act in 1917 and the Sedition Act in 1918.[3] The clash of these two laws with the freedom of speech led to momentous judicial battles in 1919.

Between 3 and 10 March 1919, the US Supreme Court handed down three important decisions on the scope of free speech containing anti-war rhetoric. All three decisions involved the Espionage Act, which was signed into law by President Woodrow Wilson in June 1917, three years after World War I started.

One of its main provisions punished those who 'obstruct the recruiting or enlistment' of personnel into the military forces.[4] Although the Espionage Act allowed debates over state policies, 'its doubletalk concealed a singleness of purpose.'[5] And the purpose was to crush those who engaged in anti-war rhetoric.[6]

On 3 March 1919, the US Supreme Court handed down its decision in *Schenck v. United States*.[7] The major charge against Charles Schenck, who was the Socialist Party's general secretary, was that he had violated the Espionage Act because in August 1917 he had sought to dissuade the recruitment of troops into the US Army by circulating pamphlets and written material which asked those who had been recruited to the military to not join the war. The criminal charge was disputed on the grounds that a restraint on communication of such a nature was protected by the 1st Amendment.[8]

Writing for a unanimous Court, Justice Oliver Wendell Holmes evolved several legal tests and coined memorable phrases for each of them. One of them was the 'tendency' test, according to which circulation of the pamphlets in question possessed the tendency of convincing those who agreed to join the military, to withdraw.⁹ Justice Holmes acknowledged that although opposing the recruitment of soldiers for a war would otherwise be a permissible expression of free speech,[10] it was perfectly valid to prohibit such speech during wartime:

> The most stringent protection of free speech would not protect a man in *falsely shouting fire in a theatre* and causing a panic. It does not even protect a man from an injunction against uttering words that may have all the effect of force. The question in every case is whether the words used are used in such circumstances and are of such a nature as to create a *clear and present danger* that they will bring about the substantive evils that Congress has a right to prevent. ... If the act, (speaking, or circulating a paper,) *its tendency and the intent* with which it is done are the same, we perceive no ground for saying that success alone warrants making the act a crime.[11]

Schenck's conviction was upheld. But there was a flaw in the court's reasoning. Justice Holmes observed that once a court viewed the speech in question as possessing the tendency of resulting in something, there was no 'ground for saying that success alone warrants making the act a crime.'[12] But, Justice Holmes had used language which suggested that 1st Amendment protection would not apply when the act posed a clear and present danger to a particular goal which the State sought to achieve.

Clear and present danger denotes a degree of inevitability in the consequences ensuing after the speech or writings. This standard was not followed faithfully by Justice Holmes, who chose rather to judge the speech in question only from the point of view of the negative or bad 'tendency,' which is just another word for probability. If something is probable, then the bounds of human imagination can conjure up infinite possibilities, even though none may actually materialize. Although articulated, the 'clear and present danger' test ceded ground to a more open-ended 'tendency' test.

The other standard, the 'shouting fire' test, was certainly appealing. Yet, despite its appeal, as Howard Zinn wrote in *A People's History of the United States*, this particular aphorism was itself capable of generating innumerable variants:

> Holmes's analogy was clever and attractive. Few people would think free speech should be conferred on someone shouting fire in a theater and causing panic. But did that example fit criticism of war? Zechariah Chafee, a Harvard law school professor, wrote later (*Free Speech in the United States*) that a more apt analogy for Schenck was someone getting up between the acts at a theater and declaring that there were not enough fire exits. To play further with the example: was not Schenck's act more like someone shouting, not falsely, but truly, to people about to buy tickets and enter a theater, that there was a fire raging inside?[13]

Zinn proposed that 'shouting fire' in the context of the *Schenck* decision could also be treated as being protective of free speech by protecting the expression of opinion to those about to join the military to not participate in a war. Undeniably, a judgment of what was meant by 'fire' depended on the context and, ultimately, the person asserting the interest. Seen in this light, Zinn suggests:

> Did citizens not have a right to object to war, a right to be a danger to dangerous policies? The 'fire' in question could

be the war and the 'shout' could be a proactive warning to those about to enter it.[14]

In the week following the *Schenck* decision came the decisions of the US Supreme Court in *Frohwerk* and *Debs*. Both were announced on the same day—10 March 1919.

At issue in *Frohwerk*[15] was the allegation that between June and December 1917, Jacob Frohwerk was responsible for publishing and circulating a newspaper, *Missouri Statts Zeitung*, which contained twelve articles opposing American intervention in World War I.[16]

He was convicted under the Espionage Act for stirring 'disloyalty' and 'mutiny' in the armed forces. One article spoke of the foolishness of deploying American troops in France, while another deplored the tragedy of packing off youthful men to far-off lands to fight battles for a cause which was hopeless.[17]

Once again, Justice Holmes authored the decision for a unanimous Court and held that the articles in question conveyed the same message as the anti-war expressions in *Schenck's* case.

Applying the 'shouting fire in a theatre' and the 'clear and present danger' tests, Justice Holmes reasoned that a newspaper which criticized the World War, if regularly circulated in 'quarters where a little breath would be enough to kindle a flame.'[18] It would cause incalculable injury to the State. A conviction for violating the Espionage Act had to follow.[19] However, here too Justice Holmes's reasoning was faulty.

He realized that the articles in question spoke on a theme which would otherwise enjoy 1st Amendment protection in peaceful times. 'We do not lose our right to condemn either measures or men,' Justice Holmes wrote, 'because the country is at war.'[20] He even accepted that the defendants had not made any 'special effort' to ensure that the newspaper reached those who were to become soldiers in the military.[21]

Had the newspapers reached those in the military, there perhaps may have been a clear and present danger. Even so, Justice Holmes presumed that the newspaper posed an inherent danger. This presumption, and not actual proof of a clear and present danger occurring, led to the conviction.[22]

Debs v. United States[23] was the other case decided on the same day. Eugene Debs, a known socialist and a towering figure in the field of labour welfare,[24] was convicted under the Espionage Act. Sometime in June 1918 he had given orations in the town of Canton, Ohio, in which he praised socialism and trenchantly criticized the American war efforts.

During the speech, Debs praised the courage shown by women and men who had been jailed for opposing the recruitment of personnel into the military, including Rose Pastor Stokes, who was jailed for a decade for attempting to stall the recruitment of soldiers; a conviction based solely on an anti-war speech she had delivered.[25] Indeed, during his trial, Debs had openly said, 'I have been accused of obstructing the war. I admit it. Gentlemen, I abhor war. I would oppose the war if I stood alone.'[26]

In a short decision, Justice Holmes, once again writing for a unanimous Court, found no particular problems in convicting Debs under the Espionage Act, for his anti-war speeches.[27] He simply declared that the charges sufficiently established that Debs was guilty of both 'obstructing' and 'attempting to obstruct the recruiting service of the United States.'[28] There was neither a 1st Amendment analysis nor a discussion of whether the clear and present danger standard was fulfilled.

This was only worsened by the fact that when Justice Holmes applied the decision in *Schenck's* case in the *Debs's* case, he did not consider a vital point of distinction: in *Debs*, the anti-war rhetoric was aimed at the general population; in *Schenck*, the literature that was circulated was apparently directed towards those awaiting military recruitment. Surely, the difference in circumstances ought to have made a difference in how the 'clear and present danger' test was applied.[29] Not drawing this distinction has been criticized as showing 'no sensitivity to accommodating a tradition of political dissent ... and makes no effort to suggest the parameters for improper criticism of the war.'[30]

The 'bad tendency' test, the 'shouting fire in a theatre' analogy and the 'clear and present danger' standard were clearly creaking, because the suppression of political speech against war efforts was permitted by the US Supreme Court, on the assumption that something untoward may happen, as a result of people airing their opposition to World War I.

The assumption of guilt occurred even though Justice Holmes was at pains to state in *Schenk*[31] and in *Frohwerk* that if not for the World War, all the speeches and writings in question which attacked the US government and encouraged people to not join the war efforts would have received core 1st Amendment protection.

Indeed, the thread which connects Justice Holmes's decisions in *Schenk*, *Debs* and *Frohwerk* is that convictions followed without the US Supreme Court having any real proof before it of the actual effects of the speeches and writings. This development was possible only because of Justice Holmes's articulation, that it is the tendency of something possibly occurring because of the speech and writing that must guide the imposition of regulations which suppress the freedom of speech.

Correcting the Ides of March

In modern times, Justice Holmes's decision in *Debs* has been found so faulty for its curt treatment of free speech that it is no longer considered a worthy judgment. In *Debs*, Justice Holmes saw no reason to think of the case in terms of interpreting the freedom of speech; he spent not a moment considering whether attacking war efforts was protected by the 1st Amendment.[32]

Justice Holmes treated the *Debs*'s case not as a constitutional one, but as a 'routine criminal appeal.'[33] But the decision in *Debs* caught the attention of an academic, and with that the jurisprudence on the 1st Amendment was destined for a course correction.[34]

Soon after the decision in *Debs*, Ernst Freund, a law professor at the University of Chicago, authored a powerful piece in the *New Republic*. Freund excoriated the US Supreme Court's decision for basing the conviction on principles such as 'tendency' and 'intent' in respect of Debs's anti-war speech, even when there was not a sliver of proof that 'actual obstruction' occurred.[35] Applying a legal standard such as 'tendency' to freedom of speech is to apply, Freund wrote, 'loose common law doctrines of conspiracy and incitement to offense of a political character.'[36]

Freund then turned to French law to highlight the high level of sophistication it had reached. In France, Royer-Collard had advocated for a system of regulation in which for the press and 'political offenses,' the only acceptable standard of proof was 'direct provocation,' in the sense that the writings in question must have some relation to a 'definite criminal act.'[37]

Freund took Justice Holmes to task for formulating the 'shouting fire in a crowded theatre' test. According to Freund, this test was the equivalent of 'implied provocation,' which is the most 'unsafe doctrine' in the context of 'political offenses.'[38] Moreover, the distinction drawn in *Debs*, that World War I granted greater authority to the US Congress to suppress speech, was pulled out of thin air. As Freund wrote:

> It is well known that the Constitution in guaranteeing free speech *makes no difference* between peace and war time; if it did it would still be enormously difficult to formulate war time restraint as rules of law.[39]

Freund was searing in his critique that the nature of political speech involved in *Debs* was to remind the people of how a war can turn into a catastrophic misadventure, and of how acceptance of a principle to achieve complete cohesion in thought through the might of the State was anathema to the Constitution. As Freund saw it:

> A country can ill spare the men who when the waves of militant nationalism run high do not lose the courage of their convictions. . . . The peril resulting to the national cause from toleration of adverse opinion is largely imaginary; in any event it is slight as compared with the permanent danger of intolerance to free institutions.[40]

Freund's critique of Justice Holmes's decision in the *Debs* case changed the course of how the 1st Amendment to the US Constitution treated political speech and anti-war efforts. Justice Holmes had read the article, and that he was presented with a litany of reasons of just how wrong his decisions were, proved impactful. It marked a transition in his thinking, which culminated in his famous dissent in *Abrams* (1919).[41]

In *Abrams*,[42] Justice Holmes hoped to modulate and reform the constitutional tests he had previously formulated, such as 'shouting fire in a crowded theatre.' He hoped to craft a new doctrine in which political speech, including anti-war efforts, would enjoy full constitutional protection.

Abrams was charged with publishing material which used vile language against the US government, including the President, and opposed American war efforts.[43] All this had been done between July and August 1917.[44] In the US Supreme Court, Justice Clarke speaking for the majority convicted Abrams for violating the Espionage Act, but not Justice Holmes.

In dissent, he observed that political speech which attacked the head of government, as well as war efforts could not be punished unless the motivating purpose for the speech was to bring about a violent consequence. Here, Justice Holmes moved to the other end of the spectrum.

He articulated the premise that when political speech is involved, it is not sufficient to curb it by simply saying it has the 'tendency' of some harm ensuing or that public peace or a state interest will possibly be harmed. Political speech could only be curbed when the desire to bring about certain violent and dramatic developments was the principal motivating cause for the speech or expression in question. Otherwise, political speech could not be curbed.[45]

Justice Holmes observed that the Espionage Act had to be understood in a 'strict and accurate sense' and that routine criticism of governmental conduct could not always furnish a criminal charge.[46] He declared that a war did not give too great a power to the government to put curbs on free speech, for 'Congress certainly cannot forbid all efforts to change the mind of the country.'[47]

Justice Holmes was a master in coining timeless aphorisms, and in a 'burst of eloquence'[48] he did so too in his dissent:

> *Persecution for the expression of opinions* seems to me perfectly logical. If you have no doubt of your premises or

your power and want a certain result with all your heart you naturally express your wishes in law and *sweep away all opposition*. . . . But when men have realized that *time has upset many fighting faiths*, they may come to *believe* even more than they believe the *very foundations of their own conduct that the ultimate good desired is better reached by free trade in ideas*—that the *best test of truth* is the *power of the thought* to get itself *accepted* in the *competition of the market*, and that truth is the only ground upon which their wishes safely can be carried out. That at any rate is the theory of our Constitution. It is an experiment, as all life is an experiment.⁴⁹

Justice Holmes added:

Every year if not every day we have to wager our salvation upon some prophecy based upon imperfect knowledge. While that experiment is part of our system I think that *we should be eternally vigilant against attempts to check the expression of opinions that we loathe and believe to be fraught with death*, unless they so *imminently threaten* immediate interference with the lawful and pressing purposes of the law that an immediate check is required *to save the country.*⁵⁰

Although in his dissent Justice Holmes had observed that *Schenck, Frohwerk* and *Debs* were correctly decided,⁵¹ he had in reality abandoned those decisions. Justice Holmes had crafted a new constitutional vision for free speech. It was essential that each person's thoughts were allowed to compete in the 'marketplace of ideas,' for people could only hope to seek a higher truth by engaging in the 'free trade of ideas.'

Moreover, since the foundation of society rests upon the people having the ability to express their inner feelings about the state of their being, a curb on speech cannot be imposed unless it is meant to prevent an 'imminent threat' against the country itself. No other form of regulation was envisaged from the perspective of the 1st Amendment to the US Constitution.

After reading Professor Freund's article, Justice Holmes had gone to some lengths to dispute Freund's critique of his decision in *Debs*. On 22 June 1918, Justice Holmes wrote a letter to Harold Laski, the political theorist who wrote the famous book *A Grammar of Politics*. In that letter, Justice Holmes stridently defended his judgments:

> Freund's objection to a jury "guessing at motive, tendency and possible effect" is an objection to pretty much the whole body of the law, which for thirty years I have made my brethren smile by insisting to be everywhere a matter of degree.[52]

Yet, as Douglas H. Ginsburg notes, it is clear that it was Freund's article which changed how Justice Holmes came to view the importance of the freedom of speech, and particularly political speech:

> It is both plausible and intriguing to think that the criticism of *Debs* in the Freund article and in Hand's correspondence with Justice Holmes throughout the period between *Debs* and *Abrams* compelled Holmes to recognize the dangers

of *Debs's* casual approach and influenced his thinking about the value of political speech, even in time of war.⁵³

In *Abrams,* Justice Brandeis joined Justice Holmes's dissent. Eight years later, in 1927, Justice Brandeis further elaborated on the scope of granting proper protection to political speech in his concurring opinion in *Whitney,*⁵⁴ an opinion in which Justice Holmes supported Justice Brandeis. In this opinion, Justice Brandeis examined the 'clear and present danger' test and elaborated on the true scope of regulation of political speech.

Reading the *Abrams* dissent and the decision in *Schenck* together, as if *Abrams* only explained the meaning of *Schenck,*⁵⁵ Justice Brandeis reasoned that the particular history of the 1st Amendment to the US Constitution showed that those who fought for independence 'were not cowards. They did not fear political change. They did not exalt order at the cost of liberty.'⁵⁶

Justice Brandeis rejected the idea that political speech and expression can be curbed by pleading that a harm must be prevented. 'Fear of serious injury cannot alone justify suppression of free speech and assembly,' he wrote.⁵⁷ As he saw it, it is only through speech and expression that the people can escape the 'bondage of irrational fears.'⁵⁸

Justice Brandeis's most important contribution came in fusing the 'imminence' or 'inevitability' of a 'dangerous harm' standard with the 'clear and present danger' standard. Prior to this, the only issue for decision was whether the speech in question had the probability of causing harm. The fusion of these ideas created a new constitutional standard by which the measure affecting free speech had to be judged:

> There must be reasonable ground to believe that the danger apprehended is imminent. There must be reasonable ground to believe that the evil to be prevented is a serious one. . . . But even advocacy of violation, however reprehensible morally, is not a justification for denying free speech where the advocacy falls short of incitement and there is nothing to indicate that the advocacy would be immediately acted on. . . . In order to support a finding of clear and present danger it must be shown either that immediate serious violence was to be expected or was advocated, or that the past conduct furnished reason to believe that such advocacy was then contemplated.[59]

In Justice Brandeis's view, clear and present danger did not mean that any plea of harm was sufficient to curb speech. The animating principle for drawing this standard was the idea that more speech counters what has already been said:

> . . . [N]o danger flowing from speech can be deemed clear and present, unless the incidence of the evil apprehended *is so imminent* that it may befall before there is opportunity for full discussion. If there be time to expose through discussion the falsehood and fallacies, to avert the evil by the processes of education, the remedy to be applied is more speech, not enforced silence.[60]

Justice Brandeis was careful to note that the prevention of imminent harm must not become a bogey to suppress free speech. He realized that the government could invoke the need to prevent a harm and then use that as a ruse to suppress speech, especially the kind which discussed matters of national importance. To ensure the continuance of 'effective democracy', it was crucial for the government to demonstrate that 'serious injury to the State' would result due to the particular speech and expression which the government sought to prohibit. The avoidance of 'trivial harm to society' could never justify a curb on free speech.[61]

In any case, the suppression of speech was never to be the default response. It was to be a choice of last resort. Justice Brandeis believed that the prevention of harm was better achieved through 'education and punishment for violations of the law; not abridgment of the rights of free speech and assembly.'[62]

However, Justice Brandeis entered an important caveat as to how the principle of preventing imminent harm was to be applied by the State, since this standard should not become a ruse to quell speech and rights of assembly which were 'essential to effective democracy.'[63]

Justice Brandeis took the example of trespass laws. He concluded that the State may make laws which prohibited people from entering someone else's property. If people were to assemble on public property to express their grievances, their rights could be curtailed by the State saying that there was an imminent harm that the protestors will be guilty of trespass.

Justice Brandeis reasoned that such a law would be patently unconstitutional because the supposed harm suffered was not so significant. Since free speech, and particularly political speech, was at stake, it was essential that the only condition under which such speech could be curbed would be when the State itself was shown to suffer injury. Short of that, invoking the principle of prevention of imminent harm to impose restraint on free speech by itself would not be a constitutionally sound approach:

Thus, a state might, in the exercise of its police power, make any trespass upon the land of another a crime, regardless of the results or of the intent or purpose of the trespasser. . . . *But it is hardly conceivable* that this court would hold constitutional a statute which punished as a felony the mere voluntary assembly with a society formed to teach that pedestrians had the moral right to cross unenclosed, unposted, waste lands and to advocate their doing so, even if there was imminent danger that advocacy would lead to a trespass. *The fact that speech is likely to result in some violence or in destruction of property is not enough to justify its suppression. There must be the probability of serious injury to the State.*[64]

Alexander Bickel lauded this particular formulation of Justice Brandeis as granting two levels of protection to free speech—that of requiring the regulation to deal only with the prevention of imminent harm and, that the harm in question must be something that seriously affects the State.[65] In other words, trivial harm, no matter how imminent and inevitable, should not be the basis for curbing free speech.

Bickel noted that Justice Brandeis's formulation in *Whitney*, which required some evidence of 'proximity and degree,' directly led to the growth in jurisprudence, particularly in the decisions of the US Supreme Court in *Schneider*[66] and *Dennis*,[67] which required that '[t]he nature and gravity of the evil, its gravity as well as its proximity, thus form part of the judicial judgment.'[68] As Bickel put it, this is the 'ultimate formulation of the clear-and-present danger test.'[69]

One may of course ask, as Bickel suggested, a pertinent question: on what objective basis is it decided that a law deals with a serious harm as opposed to a harm of a lesser nature? Bickel proposed that if free speech is involved, and particularly if such speech is essential to matters of governance, then there has to be a need to decide which measure deals with a serious interest. Or else, there will be a regime where 'utterly trivial public interest' can trump free speech rights altogether.

What Bickel suggested was that there is an important value that must be ascribed to free speech involving governance as well as matters concerning the expression of dissent and protests. As he saw it, nurturing of free speech which related to matters of governance was fully compatible with the scheme of the US Constitution. The free speech right '*built into the system a kind of domesticated form of civil disobedience*'.[70]

The Turn to Freedom

The constitutional principle that free speech can be regulated only on showing that an imminent and serious threat affecting an interest had entered free speech jurisprudence, but it had not yet been elevated to the position of being the controlling standard for judging regulations on free speech. That happened in 1969,[71] and with it the 'shouting fire in a theatre' and the 'clear and present danger' standards were done away with.[72]

In *Brandenburg v. Ohio*[73] (1969), the US Supreme Court had to decide whether a person could be convicted and jailed for ten years for advocating 'crime, sabotage, violence, or unlawful methods of terrorism' in order to achieve 'industrial or political reform.'[74]

The US Court noted that the statute in question was a law found in several states where similar laws punished the advocacy of non-peaceful methods to attain change at a macro level. They were rendered constitutional because of the US Supreme Court's decision in *Whitney* (1927), where a similar law enacted in California was upheld. But, as the Court noted, since *Whitney*, the jurisprudence on free speech had changed considerably.

Between 1951 and 1964, at least a dozen decisions of the US Supreme Court had firmly established the principle that the State could use its law making powers only to check the occurrence of inevitable violent consequences:

> These later decisions have fashioned the principle that the constitutional guarantees of free speech and free press *do not permit* a State to *forbid or proscribe* advocacy of the use of force or of law violation *except* where such advocacy is *directed to* inciting or producing imminent lawless action *and is likely* to incite or produce such action.[75]

Although the US Supreme Court had now crafted a new principle by which free speech concerning advocacy and discussion of ideas could be regulated, the *Whitney* decision had not yet been overruled. To that end, the Court in *Brandenburg* overruled *Whitney*,[76] and re-emphasized that a statute which punished the advocacy of ideas to achieve 'industrial or political reform' was an unconstitutional regulation of free speech. The regulation of speech was permissible only to check the occurrence of 'incitement to imminent lawless action.'[77]

In his concurring opinion in *Brandenburg*, Justice William Douglas offered a different perspective for the reason why advocacy of ideas could not be regulated under the 1st Amendment. Justice Douglas remarked that although Justice Holmes had crafted the 'clear and present danger' test in the *Schenck* case, he had begun to dissent from it, for instance in *Abrams*.

This showed that such a standard could be 'manipulated to crush' the very ability of the people to engage in any discussion by which a progressive transformation of the status quo could be achieved.[78]

Justice Douglas then dismantled the virtues of the 'clear and present danger' test. He noted that none of the decisions of the US Supreme Court could clearly enunciate how this standard was to be applied. Justice Douglas observed that in almost all the cases that came before the Court 'the threats were often loud but always puny and made serious only by judges so wedded to the status quo that critical analysis made them nervous.'[79]

The most striking condemnation of the 'clear and present danger' test, according to Justice Douglas, was the spectre when those supporting the communist cause were hounded and their case made a 'political trial' as part of the American standpoint in the Cold War. It had led to the destruction of 'substantial parts of the First Amendment.'[80]

Under the 1st Amendment, only a small set of cases could be regulated. Those set of cases related to situations in which the speech and the action causing the disturbance were intertwined. Justice Douglas introduced the concept of brigading.

In his opinion, this same principle was notably distilled in Justice Holmes's aphorism 'falsely shouting fire in a crowded theater' in his decision in the *Schenck* case. According to Justice Douglas, this was an instance where 'speech is brigaded with action.'[81]

Once it was demonstrated that the speech and the action that were sought to be produced are interconnected to a degree where they cannot be disentangled, a 'prosecution may be launched for the overt acts actually caused.'[82] Short of that, all of free speech, according to Justice Douglas, was beyond the realm of regulation:

> The line between what is permissible and not subject to control and what may be made impermissible and subject to regulation *is the line between ideas and overt acts.*[83]

Indeed, viewing speech as brigaded with action was something which even Justice Holmes had alluded to in his dissent in *Abrams*. He had observed that the only circumstance in which any curb can be imposed on free speech is when the desire to bring about violent consequences is the principal reason for the speech or writings..

At any rate, the conditions under which political speech could be limited had been narrowed substantially. The enduring influence of this idea meant that punishing people for simply expressing their thoughts and opinions on political issues was constitutionally impermissible. That is the modern, and indeed the governing principle in free speech rights.

13

Truly Free Political Speech

In the years which followed the First Amendment to the Indian Constitution, the Supreme Court was called upon to decide the yardstick by which a curb on free speech was to be judged as being reasonable.

In developing a workable judicial methodology for reviewing the validity of such regulations, the Supreme Court articulated the premise that it was not enough for the State to recite, for instance, a public order interest or a state security interest to justify the regulation.

What must be established with sufficient clarity was that, absent the regulation in question, a particular, identifiable and imminent harm would be inflicted. Article 19(2) demands that if the 'evil' in question will not imminently occur if the regulation in question is not formulated, then the State has no authority to curb free speech.

Judging Free Speech

The First Amendment to the Indian Constitution was passed by Parliament in June 1951. In May 1952, the Supreme Court announced its decision in the *Shailabala Devi* case, which was an appeal against the decision of the Patna High Court—the decision of Justice Sarjoo Prasad which had precipitated matters leading to the First Amendment.

In the Supreme Court, the *Shailabala Devi* case was heard by a Constitution Bench of five justices headed by Chief Justice Patanjali Sastri. Justice M.C. Mahajan (later he became Chief Justice of India on 4 January 1954) authored the decision.

The printed material in question had given a cry for a 'bloody revolution' by 'causing a total annihilation.'[1] Despite the use of this language, the Supreme Court was unimpressed and decided no legal action was called for. In so deciding, the Supreme Court laid the foundation of the ideal that speech and writings can only be curbed when the real possibility of a particular harm is demonstrated, and not otherwise.

As the Court saw it, despite all the cries for 'bloody revolution,' the State was unable to present any 'evidence whatsoever for connecting this pamphlet with any agitation or movement at the time it was written in that locality.'[2]

Justice Mahajan had laid the foundation for the idea that even after the First Amendment to the Constitution, the State still needed to establish a close link between the speech and the spectre of a disturbance occurring. This meant that speech could not be curbed simply because of its political content.

Justice Mahajan did observe that such hysterical cries for revolution may usually fall on deaf ears, and make the writer the 'laughing-stock of his readers.'[3] Nonetheless, Justice Mahajan declared that the controlling factor to determine the correct stage at which the State was justified in imposing legal control was the State's ability to demonstrate that something disturbing would surely result due to the speech or writing:

> Rhetoric of this kind might in conceivable circumstances inflame passions as, for example, *if addressed to an excited mob*, but if *such exceptional circumstances exist* it was *for the State to establish* the fact. In the absence of any such proof, we must assume that the pamphlet would be read by educated persons in the quietness of their home or in other places where the atmosphere is normal.[4]

The Supreme Court was careful to also note that when dealing with speech and writings containing political content, it was essential that they must be 'considered as a whole and in a fair and free and liberal spirit, not dwelling too much upon isolated passages or upon a strong word here and there, and an endeavour should be made to gather the general effect which the whole composition would have on the mind of the public.'[5]

In 1952 itself, Justice Mahajan had established the fundamental framework which must guide any inquiry to determine whether the speech in question ought to be regulated. The form of the speech and writings ought not to be the only factor considered. Speech and writings containing political content may use wild rhetoric, sometimes bordering on language which one finds utterly distasteful.

Still, it is not enough for the State to assert a public order interest to curb speech without first proving that the speech in question will cause some level of harm which ought to be prevented. In determining whether the speech and writings ought to be regulated, what must be accounted for is the possibility of the speech directly and imminently resulting in an inevitable disturbance.

The enduring contribution of this decision is that it established, in the immediate aftermath of the First Amendment to the Indian Constitution, that despite the changes made to Article 19(2), constitutional courts must still ensure that tolerance for differing views is respected and that short of the speech or writing imminently and inevitably setting off a series of violent events, free speech cannot be subjected to onerous legal controls. When something said or written is incapable of producing the tendency to 'excite any person,' no purpose is served in triggering the imposition of legal controls.[6]

However, the 1950s was also a period of churning in Indian constitutional thought, and it appeared that free speech rights may face rough weather. In two decisions, the Supreme Court evidently loosened the strictness with which courts would review regulations affecting free speech. And this level of looseness entered Indian constitutional thought as a result of the First Amendment to the Indian Constitution.

As we saw, the new Article 19(2) announced that reasonable restrictions could be imposed on the freedom of speech and expression 'in the interests of' certain specified grounds such as 'security of the State' and 'public order.'

In *Ramji Lal Modi's* case decided in 1957,[7] the Supreme Court took this particular phrase—'in the interests of'—to mean that it was unnecessary for the State to show that a law on free speech was specifically designed to prevent public disorder from occurring. The law would be justified under Article 19(2) if the law was 'in the interests' of public order even though it did not actually seek to prevent public disorder.

This meant that if the State proclaimed that a general public order interest justified the law, it would be constitutional, even if in its core the law did not really deal with a specific 'public order' situation that had to be met. As the Supreme Court declared:

> It will be noticed that language employed in the amended clause is 'in the interests of' and not 'for the maintenance of.' . . . [T]he expression 'in the interests of' makes the ambit of the protection very wide. A law may not have been designed to directly maintain public order and yet it may be enacted in the interests of public order.[8]

The Court also added:

> If, therefore, certain activities have a tendency to cause public disorder, a law penalising such activities as an offence cannot but be held to be a law imposing reasonable restriction 'in the interests of public order' although in some cases those activities may not actually lead to a breach of public order.[9]

With this, the Court gave the State unshackled powers to impose curbs on free speech. It created a position under which the State could invoke public order to completely shut down free speech of all hues, even if the speech and expression did not, to use the Court's language, result in a 'breach of public disorder.' This declaration, and indeed this line of reasoning, did away even with the tendency test that we are familiar with.

Under this doctrine, there was no need for the State to justify actions which harmed free speech. All it had to do was claim that public order interests guided its actions. And that was sufficient for free speech to die a slow death. Whether there was a particular public order interest that was actually sought to be saved was inconsequential.

If the only thing that mattered was a simple declaration by the State that the law was made in the interests of public order and if this declaration by the State was enough to designate the law as a reasonable restriction, then it would be next to impossible to declare that the law violated free speech.

The 1957 decision was authored by Chief Justice S.R. Das and a year later he endeavoured to cement this line of thinking, as the only way in which free speech regulations ought to be reviewed. In *Virendra*, Chief Justice S.R. Das reaffirmed the decision in *Modi* and declared:

> The expression 'in the interest of' makes the ambit of the protection very wide, for a law may not have been designed to directly maintain the public order or to directly protect the general public against any particular evil and yet it may have been enacted 'in the interests of' the public order or the general public as the case may be.[10]

However, by the 1960s there was a perceptible shift. The Supreme Court developed the idea that speech causing imminent harm could be the only acceptable principle for regulating free speech. In developing this line of thinking, the decisions in *Modi* and *Virendra* were redefined.

In *Ram Manohar Lohia*, Justice Subba Rao, speaking for a Constitution Bench of five justices, observed that when a curb was imposed on free speech on the ground that the interest of public order demanded it, the central focus of the constitutional inquiry ought to be the discovery of whether the regulation in question possessed an 'intimate connection' between the law and the interest that it be protected.[11]

Such a regulation will not be counted as a reasonable restriction on free speech, for the absence of a 'proximate relationship' between the law and the preservation of public order renders the law constitutionally unreasonable.[12]

In *Lohia*, Justice Subba Rao was evidently disturbed by the line of thinking in the *Modi* and *Virendra* cases because they veritably removed all obstacles in the way of the State to curb free speech. Justice Subba Rao endeavoured to move away from them and towards a more workable and properly balanced model of constitutional review. The balance that was needed was to link Article 19(2) with a proximity test, in that a law can be compliant with Article 19(2) only if it seeks to avert an imminent harm.

After referring to the decisions in *Modi* and *Virendra*, Justice Subba Rao observed that Chief Justice Das's views in those two decisions could not possibly mean 'that any remote or fanciful connection between the impugned Act and the public order would be sufficient to sustain its validity.'[13]

A simple invocation of the grounds mentioned in Article 19(2) was not sufficient to confer validity on the law. The phrase 'in the interests of' in Article 19(2) nonetheless demanded that there be a direct link between the law and a particular harm that it sought to avert; a harm that could only be prevented by curbing free speech and not by other means. As Justice Subba Rao saw it:

> The learned Chief Justice was only making a distinction between an Act which expressly and directly purported to maintain public order and one which did not expressly state the said purpose but left it to be implied therefrom; and between an Act that directly maintained public

order and that indirectly brought about the same result. *The distinction does not ignore the necessity for intimate connection between the Act and the public order sought to be maintained by the Act.*[14]

Justice Subba Rao treated that nebulous phrase 'in the interests of' contained in Article 19(2) as stipulating an outer limit when it came to lawmaking. And that outer limit was the requirement of sufficient proximity between laws which were justified under Article 19(2), such as public order and security of the state which curtain speech, and the recognition of a specific harm which were sought to be averted through these laws; a harm which will inevitably follow if the speech is not regulated. Simply saying a law is in the interest of public order was not enough to confer constitutional validity on the law in question.

Justice Subba Rao then made a second move. He took the phrase 'reasonable restrictions' in Article 19(2) to also incorporate the requirement that the law must have a proximate connection with the grounds enumerated in Article 19(2). This Justice Subba Rao called the 'proximate relationship' test.

In other words, a law may be in the 'interests of' public order but it will not count as a reasonable restriction on free speech, if it is not aimed at preventing a direct and immediate harm; that is, a harm that will inevitably ensue if the law curbing free speech is not in place. As Justice Subba Rao saw it:

> The word 'reasonable' has been defined by this Court in more than one decision. It has been held that in order to be reasonable, 'restrictions must have reasonable relation to the object which the legislation seeks to achieve and must not go in excess of that object.' *The restriction made*

> *'in the interests of public order' must also have reasonable relation to the object to be achieved i.e. the public order. If the restriction has no proximate relationship to the achievement of public order, it cannot be said that the restriction is a reasonable restriction within the meaning of the said clause.*[15]

The State may have the authority to make the law. It may even have particular public order interests in mind that need to be protected. But if the law cannot draw any connect with what it seeks to ultimately achieve, the law is constitutionally unsustainable. As Justice Subba Rao declared:

> The limitation imposed in the interests of public order to be a reasonable restriction, should be one which has a *proximate connection or nexus* with public order, but not one *far-fetched, hypothetical or problematical* or too *remote* in the chain of its relation with public order.[16]

Justice Subba Rao was careful to acknowledge that the freedom of speech was critically important for democracy since it played a vital role in ensuring the continuity of Indian democratic thought;. The State should not have the power to easily quell free speech and chill the entire process of free exchange of ideas.

If free speech is critical to the functioning of democracy, then it is logical that laws affecting free speech have to meet a strict standard of proximity and close connection with preventing disturbing instances of public disorder. Simply saying public order justifies the law would not make the law in question a reasonable restriction:

> It is said that in a democratic set-up there is no scope for agitational approach and that if a law is bad the only course is to get it modified by democratic process and that any instigation to break the law is in itself a disturbance of the public order. *If this argument without obvious limitations be accepted, it would destroy the right to freedom of speech which is the very foundation of democratic way of life. Unless there is a proximate connection between the instigation and the public order, the restriction, in our view, is neither reasonable nor is it in the interest of public order.*[17]

The decision in *Lohia* has been praised because it marked a shift in constitutional thought, in that courts were supposed to be tentative of any regulation which affected free speech and not take governmental justifications at face value.[18] Indeed, this was also the message which the Full Bench of the Allahabad High Court had projected in 1958 in the *Ram Nandan* case.

After discussing the decision of the Supreme Court in *Ramji Lal Modi*, the Allahabad High Court had declared that although the First Amendment, by employing the phrase 'in the interests of,' had widened the powers of the State to impose restrictions, it still had to be shown that Section 124A had 'some nexus with public disorder.'[19]

For the High Court, even if the test in the *Ramji Lal Modi* case was applied, Section 124A was not in the interests of preserving public order, simply because the excitement of disaffection harming public order was not a constitutive element of the offence of sedition.[20]

Unfortunately, in *Kedar Nath Singh*, the Supreme Court did not take notice of Justice Subba Rao's decision in *Lohia*, and it overruled the decision in *Ram Nandan* without even discussing the judgment of the Full Bench.

In *Kedar Nath Singh*, Chief Justice Sinha took note only of the *Modi* case and held that sedition was in the interests of public order and hence a reasonable restriction on free speech. There was no analysis of whether sedition had a proximate connection with the prevention of public disorder or with acts which harmed the security of the State.

The Supreme Court entirely ignored *Lohia* and the fact that Justice Subba Rao had brought together the decisions in *Modi* and *Virendra* and given them proper shape by incorporating the proximity test and the prevention of imminent harm test into Article 19(2).[21]

The Proximity Test

The understanding that Article 19(2) required a close link between the end that is to be achieved and the means of achieving it was followed in many decisions. In 1962, a Constitution Bench of the Supreme Court in the *Kameshwar Prasad*[22] case applied this principle of imminent harm to invalidate a regulation which affected free speech and expression.

At issue was a service rule which barred governmental employees from engaging in any 'demonstration' or 'strike' in relation to any of their 'conditions of service'.[23] This was a rule which imposed a blanket embargo on the ability of such employees to agitate their cause.

Justice Ayyangar, speaking for the Constitution Bench, recognized almost immediately that the constitutional question involved was of 'considerable public importance' and 'great constitutional significance'.[24] As the Court saw it, 'serving the government' could never mean that the employee forgoes all the fundamental rights guaranteed by the Constitution.[25]

Justice Ayyangar acknowledged that demonstrations and shows of protest may be 'noisy and disorderly' or 'peaceful and orderly'.[26] The aim of preventing disorderly gatherings which disrupted public order did not justify a regulation which, although neutrally worded, brought within its sweeping condemnation every sort of show of protest.

The regulation banned *all* demonstrations. The absence of this close proximity between the regulation and the supposed interest that was to be secured was fatal and rendered the regulation unconstitutional.[27] Justice Ayyangar found that the regulation in question did not have any proximate connection with preventing a public order disturbance.

Though, the Court did not use phrases such as 'imminence' to make its point, the same meaning obtained in the word 'proximity'. The Court essentially sought to ensure that there had to be a closely built link between any regulation of free speech and the interest that it sought to achieve.

In 1989, a three-judge bench of the Supreme Court in *S. Rangarajan v. P. Jagjivan Ram*[28] presented a sophisticated analysis of the central importance of free speech in promoting democracy. 'In democracy it is not necessary,' the Court declared, 'that everyone should sing the same song.'[29] The Court reasoned that a democratic system is by its very nature polyvocal and it is impossible to demand standardization in thoughts and beliefs:

> Freedom of expression is the rule and it is generally taken for granted. Everyone has a fundamental right to form his own opinion on any issue of general concern. He can form and inform by any legitimate means.[30]

From here the Court went on to establish that the key justification for imagining a system in which the people had the greatest freedom to express their thoughts on their state of being was the idea of democracy. The democratic process encouraged change, it demanded regeneration, and above all its continuity depended on the people contributing to political discourse in order to achieve certain progressive ends. As the Court reasoned:

> The democracy is a Government by the people via open discussion. The democratic form of Government itself demands [from] its citizens an active and intelligent participation in the affairs of the community. *The public discussion with people's participation is a basic feature and a rational process of democracy which distinguishes it from all other forms of Government. The democracy can neither work nor prosper unless people go out to share their views.* The truth is that public discussion on issues relating to administration has positive value.[31]

The Supreme Court then crafted a second principle to strengthen the proposition that the survival of democracy hinged on the freedom of speech. Drawing on the work of Alexander Meiklejohn, the Court observed that in a democratic set-up there would always be 'proponents' and 'opponents' of any governmental measure. Yet, the idea of ensuring that both sides were able to air their views was 'because there is freedom in this country for expressing even differing views on any issue.'[32]

Interestingly, in *Rangarajan*, the Supreme Court marshalled a welter of judicial decisions from pre-independent India to demonstrate that there were many colonial judges who were keen to ensure that free speech was provided adequate breathing space.

For instance, the Supreme Court took the example of the case of *Kamal Krishna Sircar* decided by the Calcutta High Court in 1935.

In that case, Sircar had been convicted for demanding that the British government in India be replaced with a 'Bolshevik'-style government. This was nothing short of calling for total revolution. But the Calcutta High Court overturned the conviction for sedition by declaring that demanding a new form of government was not tantamount to exciting disaffection against the British government.[33] A colonial-era judge upheld the right of Indians to engage in vituperative political speech.

Rangarajan's greatest contribution came in locating the exact relationship between free speech, democracy and the frontiers of crafting reasonable restrictions. The Supreme Court noted that within the scheme of Article 19(2), the State was empowered to enact laws which curbed free speech.

The scheme of Article 19(2) thus demanded that although restrictions can be imposed, they must be of such nature that they attach only to those parts of speech and expressions which imminently and inevitably seek the achievement of ends which grievously harm the interests mentioned in Article 19(2). The regulation must have a proximate link with the interest that it seeks to achieve:

> The problem of defining the area of freedom of expression when it appears to conflict with the various social interests enumerated under Article 19(2) may briefly be touched upon here. There does indeed have to be a compromise between the interest of freedom of expression and special interests. *But we cannot simply balance the two interests as if they are of equal weight.*[34]

The Court then added:

> Our commitment of freedom of expression demands that it cannot be suppressed unless the situations created by allowing the freedom are pressing and the community interest is endangered. *The anticipated danger should not be remote, conjectural or far-fetched. It should have proximate and direct nexus with the expression. The expression of thought should be intrinsically dangerous to the public interest. In other words, the expression should be inseparably locked up with the action contemplated like the equivalent of a 'spark in a powder keg'.*[35]

In *Rangarajan*, the Supreme Court introduced the concept of 'brigading' free speech with action. This declaration has also been seen as embodying the 'spark in a powder keg' test, which is that for speech to be curbed the State must demonstrate that an imminent and disastrous harm will follow if the speech is not regulated.[36]

Only when free speech borders on expression which seeks to bring about dangerous consequences which are imminent and inevitable can that narrow category of speech be regulated. In other words, all speech cannot be swept aside by regulations which purport to deal with the preservation of State security or public order but do not do so in actuality.

In this framework, the Supreme Court carefully calibrated the freedom of speech with the need to control such speech which is deemed constitutionally dangerous, in an effort to ensure that such speech and expression which cannot be 'brigaded' with action receive constitutional protection and were not nefariously rendered effete rights. To draw from *Rangarajan*, if the speech is not the kind which immediately and inevitably results in dangerous consequences affecting State security, the State has no constitutional jurisdiction to regulate the speech in any manner.[37]

In 2015, the Supreme Court in *Shreya Singhal* emphatically announced that embedded in Article 19(2) is the idea of granting complete freedom to the 'discussion' and advocacy of ideas. The only circumstance in which the State can regulate free speech is when the 'incitement' of particular harms is to be dealt with. As Justice Nariman declared:

> There are three concepts which are fundamental in understanding the reach of this most basic of human rights. The first is discussion, the second is advocacy, and the third is incitement. Mere discussion or even advocacy of a particular cause howsoever unpopular is at the heart of Article 19(1)(a). It is only when such discussion or advocacy reaches the level of incitement that Article 19(2) kicks in.[38]

The decision in *Shreya Singhal* has been praised because it demonstrated fidelity to the constitutional principle carved out by Justice Subba Rao in *Ram Manohar Lohia,* that when it comes to the regulation of the freedom of speech, what is at stake is the larger interest of society and not the narrow preferences of an individual. As a result, when speech does not have any effect on the larger question of the security of the State, or for that matter public order, then a curb on free speech cannot be defended under Article 19(2).[39]

All this demonstrates that Indian jurisprudence has organically developed the idea that there is only a narrow set of situations for which the State can enact regulations which impose curbs on the freedom of speech and expression, particularly in the context of political speech.[40]

It is a different matter altogether that within Indian jurisprudence, the *Brandenburg* decision of the US Supreme Court has often been a point of discussion. In recent years, the Indian Supreme Court has discussed the salience of using the *Brandenburg* standard when judging the validity of regulations imposed under Article 19(2).

In *Anuradha Bhasin* (2020), the Supreme Court observed that during the Vietnam War, the US Supreme Court had crafted a new standard in *Brandenburg* where 'advocacy' and 'unlawful conduct' were generally beyond the reach of regulation 'unless it is intended to incite and is likely to incite "imminent lawless action."'[41]

The Supreme Court was also careful to note that the American understanding of curbing the expression of dissent during war had undergone a dramatic transformation, and that the singular principle which emerged from this transformation was the ideal that only such 'speech which incites imminent violence does not enjoy constitutional protection.'[42]

The same point can be put differently: every single form of speech and expression involving political speech, before it reaches the level where it 'incites imminent violence,' enjoys core and absolute constitutional protection.

Two decisions in 2021 once again reiterated the importance of the *Brandenburg* standard in protecting free speech from onerous regulations. In *Amish Devgan*, the Supreme Court restated the importance of the *Brandenburg* standard to reinforce the need for its observance in Indian constitutional jurisprudence.[43] *Amish Devgan* dealt with the correct manner in which laws concerning hate speech should be interpreted. In the course of its decision, the Supreme Court commented on the advantages of adhering to the *Brandenburg* standard.

The Court, speaking through Justice Sanjiv Khanna, noted that the acceptance of the 'imminent lawless action' standard was a repudiation of both the 'bad tendency' test and the 'clear and present danger' test. It was a repudiation because this new standard stepped out of the shadows of probability, in order to judge whether the speech in question had any direct consequences, as opposed to determining whether the speech possessed some potential of causing something destructive.[44]

Essentially, this new standard was much more protective of free speech rights. It was this which led the Supreme Court to announce that 'advocacy' as well as 'discussion', properly speaking, 'fall within the domain of freedom to express and convey one's thoughts and ideas.'[45] Only when it reaches the level of incitement which can imminently cause some destruction can the law step in to regulate free speech.[46]

Moreover, even in *Brandenburg*, the 'clear and present danger' test applied only to such events which were imminently lawless. Taking note of this, the Indian Supreme Court declared that in the context of the First Amendment to the US Constitution, 'The State cannot restrict and limit the First Amendment protection by forbidding or proscribing advocacy by use of force or law, except when the speaker intends to incite a violation of the law—that is both imminent and likely.'[47]

Focusing on the meaning of 'imminent,' Justice Khanna declared that it partakes of the character of inevitability, which is that deleterious consequences will undoubtedly follow. Moreover, the speech or writings must be of the nature of 'active incitement,' for mere discussion can never be proscribed:

'Promote' does not imply mere describing and narrating a fact, or giving opinion criticising the point of view or actions of another person—it requires that the speaker should actively incite the audience to cause public disorder. However, in case the speaker does not actively incite the descent into public disorder, and is merely pointing out why a certain person or group is behaving in a particular manner, what are their demands and their point of view, or when the speaker interviews such person or group, it would be a passive delivery of facts and opinions which may not amount to promotion.[48]

In May 2020, a First Information Report was filed in the northern state of Himachal Pradesh against Vinod Dua, a veteran journalist, for creating web-based video content in which he criticized the government's efforts in combating the COVID-19 pandemic raging across India. For speaking on State action during the time of the pandemic, Dua was booked for sedition. He swiftly took his case to the Supreme Court, challenging the charge of sedition.

The Supreme Court's 2021 decision in *Vinod Dua v. Union of India*[49] is important because it involved a direct clash between journalistic investigation into the state of the nation, which involved all the trappings of political speech, and the crime of sedition.

In an elaborate decision, Justice U.U. Lalit (he became Chief Justice of India on 27 August 2022) overturned the charges against Dua. Justice Lalit began by invoking the judgment in the *Romesh Thappar* case, and was swift to restate that when a citizen's fundamental rights are impacted in the most unwholesome manner, the only remedy available is to knock on the doors of the highest court of the land. And when that citizen knocks, the doors must be opened.[50] He also observed that the Supreme Court had, through a series of decisions, laid the bedrock for recognizing that the freedom of the press will always involve a critique of the state of the nation and the method of governance as well as a critical assessment of political affairs.[51]

Justice Lalit reasoned that in the facts of the case before the Supreme Court, not a single ingredient of the offence of sedition was established. Dua was a journalist, and in his journalistic pursuit he endeavoured to uncover the shortcomings in the way the government dealt with the pandemic. At the highest, Dua's journalistic critique could only count as 'disapprobation' of governmental measures. There was no question of sedition having been committed.[52] To think otherwise, said Justice Lalit, would be 'unjust.'[53]

In reaching this conclusion, Justice Lalit alluded to the fact that the news reports in question were 'certainly not made with the *intent to incite* people' to harm public order and cause violence.[54] The Court did not rely on the *Brandenburg* standard, yet the fact that the Court employed a phrase such as 'intent to incite' shows that in the view of the Supreme Court, a person cannot be guilty of sedition on the pure basis that their speeches and writings had some tendency to hurt public peace. Something much more serious has to be established—an intention to incite others to embark on actions to achieve disturbing outcomes.

Unshackling Freedom

We are now able to clearly gauge the importance of recalibrating the constitutional approach when determining the reasonableness of a regulation which affects the freedom of speech and expression, particularly political speech. It is beyond dispute that Indian jurisprudence firmly recognizes the principle that a regulation curbing free speech is consistent with the Constitution only if it aims to avert an imminent harm.

Yet, the simple invocation of avoiding some imminent harm itself may prove harmful to free speech, for the State may seek to base its claims on specious grounds. That is the reason why, when political speech is involved, the only 'harm' that can influence the framing of regulations for political speech is the interest of preventing harm to the State itself, and nothing short of that.

This is a principle which was passionately affirmed in the Constituent Assembly by the likes of K.M. Munshi, assiduously implemented by the Supreme Court in the *Romesh Thappar* case and in the carefully developed American jurisprudence on the 1st Amendment concerning political speech, which has great value for India in terms of determining the best course for unshackling political speech. There is no room whatsoever to even momentarily doubt its central place in Indian juristic thought.

Taking the entire body of jurisprudence together, coupled with the idea that the free speech right at its core ought to protect political speech in a near-absolute manner, it is impossible to draw any other conclusion but that Section 124A is an unreasonable restriction on the freedom of speech and expression and patently unconstitutional.

It is a law which brings within its tentacles, and criminalizes, every form of political speech, regardless of all considerations. It is not a law which deals with a narrow set of situations in which speech must result in imminent and inevitable harm to the State in order for it to be the subject matter of regulation. But, above all, it is a law which directly targets the ability of the people to use the power of their thoughts to engage in free political discussions and hold the government accountable.

There is nothing in Section 124A which has any redeeming value. It is unreasonable, manifestly arbitrary, and violates the civil liberty rights of citizens in the most deleterious sense. It is unconstitutional.

14

Avoiding a Pyrrhic Victory

In May 2022, the Supreme Court suspended the operation of Section 124A of the IPC pending a final decision on whether the law on sedition is consistent with the Constitution. But even if Section 124A is ultimately done away with, sedition will still be a crime in India because it is treated as an offence under the Unlawful Activities (Prevention) Act (UAPA).

To be sure, the Supreme Court in suspending Section 124A has not commented on the UAPA's sedition provision and has not suspended its operation, even though both these laws are substantially the same. It thus becomes important to examine whether the UAPA's version of sedition is consistent with the Constitution. If the provision for sedition in the UAPA continues to operate, doing away with Section 124A will only be a pyrrhic victory.

The Sixteenth Amendment

On 5 October 1963, the Sixteenth Amendment of the Constitution came into force.[1] By this amendment, Parliament introduced a new ground in Article 19(2) by which the State could impose reasonable restrictions on the freedom of speech and expression—'the sovereignty and integrity of India.'[2]

The Sixteenth Amendment also ordained that the fundamental right to assemble peacefully without arms guaranteed by Article 19(1)(b), as well as the fundamental right to form associations and unions, which is guaranteed by Article 19(1)(c), could also be curbed in the interests of the 'sovereignty and integrity of India.' As a result, Article 19(3) and Article 19(4) were also amended to give effect to this.[3]

The Sixteenth Amendment also amended the constitutional provisions concerning the oath of office which elected members of Parliament and the state legislatures, as well as the judges of the constitutional courts, including those of the Supreme Court, are to take. They are required to swear their allegiance to 'uphold the sovereignty and integrity of India.'[4]

In the years immediately preceding the Sixteenth Amendment, in several states such as Tamil Nadu in the south, Punjab in the north and Nagaland in the east, calls had been made for secession from India. The Sixteenth Amendment was enacted to ensure that the State was given adequate powers to deal with calls for secession.[5] For this reason, the bill for the Sixteenth Amendment was termed the 'Anti-Secession Bill.'[6]

One of the major legislative steps undertaken pursuant to the Sixteenth Amendment was the enactment of the UAPA in 1967.[7] The UAPA aims to 'provide for the more effective prevention of certain unlawful activities of individuals and associations.'[8] In 2004, the ambit of the Act was widened, and it was amended so that it could also deal with 'terrorist activities.'[9] In recent years the UAPA has undergone several revisions which have come under critical gaze and has also become the subject matter of a constitutional challenge in the Supreme Court of India.

Section 2(1)(o) of the UAPA defines an 'unlawful activity,'[10] and Section 2(1)(o)(iii) deals with sedition. It is an 'unlawful activity' for any person or an association to use the freedom of speech and expression in a manner which 'causes or is intended to cause disaffection against India.' Functionally, Section 2(1)(o)(iii) in the UAPA is the equivalent of sedition as defined in Section 124A of the IPC.[11] Under Section 13, the punishment for committing an unlawful activity is imprisonment for seven years. Further, under Section 43D(4), a person accused of committing an offence under the UAPA does not have the right to apply for anticipatory bail.

Absence of Balance

When compared with Section 124A, the provision on sedition and disaffection in the UAPA raises many troubling questions.[12]

For a law to be sustained under Article 19(2), it must satisfy three requirements. It must be traceable to an enumerated restriction in Article 19(2). It must be 'in the interests of' the particular ground in Article 19(2). This means that the law must have a proximate and direct connection with preserving the interest in Article 19(2), under which the law is sought to be sustained. Finally, the law must be a reasonable restriction in that the restriction must not be excessive and disproportionate. Section 2(1)(o)(iii) does not satisfy any of these requirements.

As a starting matter, it is noticeable that 2(1)(o)(iii) perniciously harms the freedom of speech and expression. This particular definition of sedition in the UAPA does not make any allowance for critical speech directed against the

State. This is because the UAPA does not contain any of the Explanations of the kind found in Section 124A. In other words, even critical speech against the State, which is the expression of disapprobation against State activity falls within the sweep of sedition in the UAPA.

Section 124A is accompanied by three Explanations. The critical provisions are Explanations 2 and 3.

Explanation 2 provides that 'Comments expressing disapprobation of the measures of the Government with a view to obtain their alteration by lawful means, without exciting or attempting to excite hatred, contempt or disaffection, do not constitute an offence under this section [Section 124A].' Explanation 3 lays down that 'Comments expressing disapprobation of the administrative or other action of the Government without exciting or attempting to excite hatred, contempt or disaffection, do not constitute an offence under this section [Section 124A].'

Expression of disapprobation against the State—that is, expression of critical thought about State activities—will not be treated as sedition. To be sure, Explanations 2 and 3 in themselves do not render Section 124A constitutional and, as we have seen, there are numerous problems which have arisen when it comes to the interpretation of these particular provisions.

In the UAPA, however, critical assessment of State activities, expression of disapprobation against the measures adopted by the State and the desire to bring about a transformation in the conduct of the State, are not mentioned as specific situations which will not be treated as causing disaffection against India.

The absence of these limiting qualities in the UAPA is a major flaw, because in their absence the expression of disapprobation against governmental measures is treated as causing disaffection against India. On the other hand, for Section 124A, the expression of disapprobation can never be treated as sedition.

Section 2(1)(o)(iii) is manifestly arbitrary and is a law which is contrary to Articles 14, 19 and 21 of the Constitution of India. The law is manifestly arbitrary because there is no justifiable reason as to why the expression of disapprobation against State conduct is treated as the high crime of sedition.

As we have seen, the judgments on free speech rights had clearly enunciated the position that the expression of dissent and disagreement is a fundamental facet of the freedom of speech and expression. Indeed, the singular purpose which guided the crafting of this particular fundamental right was to secure democratic interests in allowing citizens to ventilate their grievances against the State.

The expression of disapprobation against State activity is intimately connected with the democratic project of ushering in transformation and change by the citizens engaging with the State, through the power of the freedom of speech and expression. As early as 1950, the Supreme Court declared in the *Romesh Thappar* case that '*without free political discussion no public education, so essential for the proper functioning of the processes of popular Government, is possible.*'[13] This meant that the constitutionality of any restriction on this particular aspect of the freedom of speech and expression is doubtful.

The declaration in *Romesh Thappar* is by no means an isolated example. The decisions of the Supreme Court in *Sakal Papers, Ram Manohar Lohia, S.P. Rangarajan* and *Shreya Singhal*, to take a few examples, reaffirm this central principle. It is the foundational concept for the freedom of speech and expression.

They established the principle that at the core of Article 19(1)(a) lies the right of the citizens to use their rights and liberties to question State activity and bring about progressive transformation. The exercise of this right will undoubtedly involve critical thought. This is universally accepted. But Section 2(1)(o)(iii) enacts a dogma—that the activities of the State ought never to be questioned.

Any law which speaks of disaffection is speaking the language of sedition. When it comes to the Constitution, a sedition law must be narrowly tailored so that it is only concerned with that set of activities where the foundations of the country are truly threatened. It cannot be a catch-all provision of law which punishes citizens simply for speaking in less than affectionate terms against the State.[14]

The categorical principle of constitutional reason synthesized in Article 19(1)(a) and Article 19(2) is that speech concerning the State, the government as well as political affairs has to be given the maximum breathing space, and that a very high bar has to be crossed before speech on political questions is curbed.

A law which wholly bars the expression of disapprobation against State activity and the discussion of political affairs is manifestly arbitrary and entirely unreasonable. Is it possible to think that the Constitution bars citizens from expressing even a whisper of their true feelings against the State? Is it permissible, in the eyes of the Constitution, that those who wish to give vent to their grievances must do so at the risk of severe punishment? These are the questions which will naturally arise when the provision of sedition in the UAPA is viewed with a degree of careful attention.

We have seen the specific reasons why Section 124A is an unreasonable restriction on the freedom of speech and expression as well as manifestly arbitrary. The same arguments apply to Section 2(1)(o)(iii) with equal, if not greater, force. It renders this provision in the UAPA constitutionally unsustainable.

Absence of Proximity

One view on Section 2(1)(o)(iii) is that it may be saved by the Sixteenth Amendment to the Constitution, since it is a law in the interests of preserving the sovereignty and integrity of India. This may be because Section 2(1)(o)(iii) is differently worded from Section 124A, and refers to 'India' when it speaks of the entity against which disaffection is raised.

The Sixteenth Amendment did amend Article 19(2) and the UAPA was enacted soon after the amendment was approved by Parliament. However, the fact remains that Section 2(1)(o)(iii) does not have any proximate link with preserving the sovereignty and integrity of India.

We have seen in the previous chapters that raising disaffection alone can never be treated as threatening public order, State security or even the State itself. Applying this to Section 2(1)(o)(iii), it is clear that causing disaffection in itself has no relation with protecting the sovereignty and integrity of India.

Within the UAPA, there are some clues as to the kind of offences which aim to preserve the sovereignty and integrity of India.

Section 2(1)(o)(i) treats as unlawful activity any expression, 'which is intended, or supports any claim, to bring about, on any ground whatsoever, the cession of a part of the territory of India or the secession of a part of the territory of India from the Union, or which incites any individual or group of individuals to bring about such cession or secession.'

Likewise, Section 2(1)(o)(ii) treats as unlawful activity any expression 'which disclaims, questions, disrupts or is intended to disrupt the sovereignty and territorial integrity of India.'

Unlike these two provisions, Section 2(1)(o)(iii) does not contain anything which suggests that it is meant to curb such disaffection which directly and dangerously harms the sovereignty and integrity of India.

Within the broad heading of 'unlawful activity' in Section 2(1)(o), it is the provision on sedition which is unconcerned and unconnected with protecting the sovereignty and integrity of India. It is only concerned with punishing those who use the freedom of speech and expression to question State activity. Section 2(1)(o)(iii) is not saved by Article 19(2).

In view of this, it might be tempting to read into 2(1)(o)(iii) the requirement that the disaffection in question must affect the sovereignty and integrity of India, before it is treated as an offence under the UAPA. After all, in the *Kedar Nath Singh* case, once the Supreme Court found that on a plain reading Section 124A was not saved by Article 19(2), it redefined its meaning to somehow render it consistent with Article 19(2).

That approach is constitutionally wrong, and such a view is unwarranted. Indeed, the structure of the UAPA and the well-recognized principles of constitutional interpretation caution against adopting this approach in respect of the provision on sedition in the UAPA.

The UAPA is a penal statute which aims at rendering certain kinds of expressions and actions criminally culpable. If a criminal statute is involved, it must be viewed strictly, and its meaning must not be unduly expanded.

When judged from the perspective of Article 19, the point of critical inquiry is the text of the law as it stands. Section 2(1)(o)(iii) makes no mention of the fact that the expression of disaffection becomes an unlawful activity only when it immediately, directly and imminently harms the sovereignty and integrity of India.

The important fact is that in the structure of the UAPA itself sufficient references have been made to the preservation of India's sovereignty and integrity in each of the sub-provisions to Section 2(1)(o) which define 'unlawful activity'. For Section 2(1)(o)(iii), the question of disaffection alone is relevant and not whether it has any effect on the sovereignty and integrity of India.

In other words, Section 2(1)(o)(iii) criminalizes only the causing of disaffection without there being a need to examine as to whether the sovereignty and integrity of India has been affected. The absence of this requirement makes it difficult to sustain any claim that the Sixteenth Amendment to the Constitution and the addition of 'sovereignty and integrity of India' in Article 19(2) save this particular provision in the UAPA.

The decision of the Supreme Court in *Shreya Singhal* is a direct source of authority which states that if a provision of law is unconnected to Article 19(2), then the law is unconstitutional.

In *Shreya Singhal*, the Supreme Court reasoned that there was nothing in Section 66A of the IT Act which remotely dealt with the preservation of public order. It simply criminalized the dissemination of messages through electronic means, without concern for what followed thereafter.

As the Court saw it, nothing in that provision stipulated that action would be taken if the messages in question had the tendency of causing some harm to public order. To impose criminal sanctions on the freedom of speech and expression without the law drawing any link with the enumerated grounds in Article 19(2) was held to be unconstitutional.[15]

The UAPA categorizes distinct and separate actions and conducts which constitute an 'unlawful activity'. And each of the offences is clearly demarcated from the other. Further, when it comes to 2(1)(o)(iii), not a single word is used relating to either the sovereignty or the integrity of India, and this absence makes it difficult to draw any proximate link between the Sixteenth Amendment to the Constitution and the sedition provision in the UAPA.

When judged from the perspective of the Constitution, it must be shown that despite everything, the law in question can establish a link with the enumerated grounds in Article 19(2). But nothing in 2(1)(o)(iii) traces any link to Article 19(2) and, as a result, the UAPA's provision on sedition cannot seek any protection from Article 19(2).

Article 19(2), Sedition and the UAPA

We have seen how the law on sedition contained in Section 124A of the IPC was not saved by Article 19(2) because it could not proximately be linked to any of the enumerated grounds. In the case of Section 2(1)(o)(iii) in the UAPA, too, this provision is not saved by any of the grounds in Article 19(2).

Very clearly, Section 2(1)(o)(iii) does not create any relationship between the expression of disaffection and the consequences which follow. In fact, from the words of Section 2(1)(o)(iii) it is clear that consequences are irrelevant for the purposes of treating disaffection as an unlawful activity.

The constitutional issue at stake is that it is paramount that the law is indeed directed towards one of the interests enumerated in Article 19(2). In the case of Section 124A, we have seen that by its own words the law is unconcerned with consequences. Whether public disorder ensues or whether the security of the State is harmed because of what is said or expressed is not the concern of Section 124A.

As a result, Section 124A punishes the expression of less than favourable opinion about the government and governmental affairs. As we saw, this can never furnish a sure basis for imposing criminal sanctions on the people who exercise their freedom of speech and expression to discuss governmental and State affairs.

All that has been said about Section 124A also applies to Section 2(1)(o)(iii) in the UAPA. Just like Section 124A, the UAPA's sedition provision is unconcerned with the after effects, or the lack of them, of the speech and expressions in question.

Just like Section 124A, the UAPA's sedition provision punishes the causing of disaffection without taking regard of the fact as to whether disaffection against the State has actually stirred anyone to do anything which poses great harm. Indeed, the use of the phrase 'causing disaffection' in the UAPA connotes the same meaning as 'excitement of disaffection' does under Section 124A.

The most glaring problem with Section 2(1)(o)(iii) is that it does not state that the coercive arm of the State's machinery will be triggered only when the disaffection reaches a level which harms public order or the security of the State. Just like Section 124A, Section 2(1)(o)(iii) of the UAPA punishes the expression of disaffection and thus impermissibly restricts the freedom of speech and expression.

There is nothing which suggests that the law requires an objective assessment of whether the speech and expression in question has wider ramifications affecting the State. Further, the sedition provision makes it an unlawful activity to cause disaffection, without stipulating whether the success or failure of this attempt makes any difference to the outcome of the particular case at hand. These are the same flaws which Section 124A is also riddled with. And just as with Section 124A, these flaws render Section 2(1)(o)(iii) of the UAPA unconstitutional.

The UAPA, Sedition and the Imminent Harm Standard

As we saw, internationally as well as within Indian jurisprudence, the standard by which curbs on free speech are to be judged is whether they are designed to deal with the occurrence of an imminent harm. We also saw that the principle of 'imminent harm' was preferred to other constitutional tests, such as 'intent' and 'tendency to cause harm' tests, for in these kinds of inquiries the nature of review is not sufficiently objective.

The focus lies on deciphering the mental make-up of the person involved, and there is no justification for curbing the freedom of speech and expression without the State showing that something perceivably dangerous has to be avoided through the medium of restricting free speech.

Like in Section 124A, the sedition provision in the UAPA does not deal with the prevention of imminent harm. It simply makes it an unlawful activity for a person or an association to cause or intend to cause disaffection against India.

Contrast this with the other descriptions used in Section 2(1)(o) which define unlawful activity, which have specific references to actions which result in demands for secession, or which disrupt the sovereignty and territorial integrity of India. In respect of these, there is at least an objective criterion available in the law to determine the kind of consequences which are to be taken note of.

The decision of the Supreme Court in *Ram Manohar Lohia* is important. Justice Subba Rao, speaking for a Constitution Bench of five judges, carefully weaved together the decisions of the

Supreme Court in *Ramji Lal Modi* and *Virendra* to hold that a law must have an 'intimate connection' with the particular ground in Article 19(2) which is presented as the proffered justification for the law itself.

According to Justice Subba Rao, the absence of such a 'proximate relationship' rendered the law unreasonable, apart from the fact that the law could not be treated as being in the interests of the particular ground in question in Article 19(2).[16]

Further, Justice Subba Rao also declared that there had to be a close connection between the law and Article 19(2), and the simple invocation of Article 19(2) is not sufficient to sustain the validity of the law. As Justice Subba Rao declared:

> The word 'reasonable' has been defined by this Court in more than one decision. It has been held that in order to be reasonable, 'restrictions must have reasonable relation to the object which the legislation seeks to achieve and must not go in excess of that object.' ... The limitation imposed in the interests of public order to be a reasonable restriction, should be one which has a *proximate connection or nexus* with public order, but not one *far-fetched, hypothetical or problematical* or too *remote* in the chain of its relation with public order.[17]

Nothing in Section 2(1)(o)(iii) ventures to suggest that there is a specific and particular harm that is to be prevented. Indeed, the provision only deals with the expression of disaffection, The decisions of the Supreme Court in *Ram Manohar Lohia* as well as in *S.P. Rangarajan* are directly applicable.

As such, this provision falls foul of the Constitution because it is not directed at averting an imminent incitement of action affecting the sovereignty and integrity of India. As such, Section 2(1)(o)(iii) is also not in the interests of the sovereignty and integrity of India. All that has been said so far in respect of Section 124A, the *Brandenburg* standard, and the constitutional standards enunciated in a plethora of decisions of the Indian Supreme Court applies to the provision of sedition in the UAPA to render it unconstitutional.

Background Factors and the Endurance of Free Speech

The preamble of the Sixteenth Amendment to the Constitution which amended Article 19(2) states that this particular amendment was framed to give effect to the recommendations of the Committee on National Integration and Regionalism. A key recommendation was that Article 19 be amended to allow the State to preserve the sovereignty and integrity of India. The Preamble states:

> The Committee on National Integration and Regionalism appointed by the National Integration Council recommended that article 19 of the Constitution be so amended that adequate powers become available for the preservation and maintenance of the integrity, and sovereignty of the Union.[18]

From the perspective of Article 19, it is immaterial how the law in question is formulated. Whether it is the result of a detailed study or whether it has been crafted on the recommendation of a high-ranking committee is beside the point. What is critical is that in the ultimate analysis, the law must be consistent with Article 19(2) for it to be judged a reasonable restriction on free speech.

This proposition flows directly from the famous decision of the Supreme Court in *Sakal Papers*. In that case, the Court had to decide whether the Newspaper (Price and Page) Act, 1956 and the Daily Newspaper (Price and Page) Order, 1960 were constitutional.

The newspapers had complained that in effect the law allowed the State to directly control how many pages a newspaper could print.[19] The first ground which the government enlisted in its defence was that the law had been made because the Press Commission appointed in 1952 had in its report recommended that such a law should be made in order to regulate the activities of the press.[20]

After a thorough analysis, the Court held that the law was unconstitutional. In dealing with the objection that the law had been made pursuant to important recommendations by the Press Commission, the Court held:

> Its object thus is to regulate something which, as already stated, is directly related to the circulation of a newspaper. Since circulation of a newspaper is a part of the right of freedom of speech the Act must be regarded as one directed against the freedom of speech. . . . *Such a course is not permissible and the courts must be ever vigilant in guarding perhaps the most precious of all the freedoms guaranteed by our Constitution.* The reason for this is obvious. *The freedom of speech and expression of opinion is of paramount importance under a democratic Constitution which envisages changes in the composition of legislatures and governments and must be preserved.*[21]

The Court then declared:

> *No doubt, the law in question was made upon the recommendation of the Press Commission but since its object is to affect directly the right of circulation of newspapers which would necessarily undermine their power to influence public opinion it cannot but be regarded as a dangerous weapon which is capable of being used against democracy itself.*[22]

Sakal Papers, which is a decision of a Constitution Bench of five judges, declared in no uncertain terms that the background of how the law was enacted and the recommendations which led to its creation could not, in the final analysis, confer constitutionality on the law. To ensure its survival, the law must succeed in demonstrating that Article 19(2) sustained it.

Applying this to Section 2(1)(o)(iii), what matters is whether the grounds enumerated in Article 19(2) help to confer constitutionality on the law. Once it is shown that the sedition provision in the UAPA is contrary to the freedom of speech and expression and that nothing in Article 19(2) can come to its rescue, then the circumstances of its enactment and the reasons which led to its crafting cannot assume much significance.

Epilogue

The Future of Free Speech

———◆———

FOR ANY RATIONAL PERSON INTERESTED IN THE PROCESS OF PROGRESSIVE change, it is undeniable that political speech plays a central if not a defining role, in achieving that constitutional ideal. Political speech involves a critique of our state of being. It implicates matters of governance and issues concerning policies affecting the lives of the people. It assuredly seeks to achieve a transformation of the status quo, in that the people must be invigorated and empowered to direct their deeply held opinions and firm beliefs against those they have installed in office—the government.[1]

A democracy built on the idea of constant regeneration and political change demands a robust constitutional architecture, for creating pathways for the people to use the power of political speech to achieve transformation with some hope of reaching that higher mountain of justice.

To craft laws which seek to filter political opinions on the proffered justification that the purity of the political process, and indeed of society, ought to be maintained is to permit a regime of regulation in which the lawmakers invest in the coercive machinery of the State, the awesome power of laying waste to all that is held sacrosanct under our constitutional schema—the power to articulate our premise on matters concerning the political system itself.

If at all our constitutional history teaches us anything, it is that the people are not to be afraid. Our jurisprudence affirms this cardinal value and our Constitution firmly secures it. At the heart of the Indian Constitution lies the individual and their fundamental rights. Within reason, no law can take it away; not even an amendment to the Constitution. To believe that a law on sedition such as Section 124A can exist in a democratic republic and a system of enterprise which nurtures political speech is to speak at cross purposes.

Generations of Indians have been reminded that sedition allows political critique, but not the excitement of disaffection. This duality is presented as the unimpeachable defence to the charge of sedition being an insidious restriction on free speech. Yet, any law which stifles political speech dogmatically treats this duality as its saving grace.

Consider the experience of a country such as the US with the Espionage Act, a law which recited this duality to plead that it was a proper legislation which balanced free speech with national interest. 'But its double-talk,' Howard Zinn had presciently warned, 'concealed a singleness of purpose.'[2] And the purpose was to imprison those who engaged in political speech to oppose World War I.

The 'singleness of purpose' which invigorates Section 124A is the attainment of the ideal of imprisoning freethinking Indians, both within and without, in the pursuit of preventing the government from acquiring any disrepute. And this is despite the fact that much has been made about Section 124A permitting reasonable critical thinking about State affairs.[3]

One need not look further than the honest testimonials of James Fitzjames Stephen, the father of sedition in India, in 1870, and of M.D. Chalmers, the father of the reconstructed version of sedition, in 1898, whose only hope was to use sedition as a weapon to maintain obedience and the pristine image of the British colonial government.

Yet, how utterly wrong the Supreme Court was in *Kedar Nath Singh*. It deliberately wrote into the Indian Constitution and into the hallowed chapter of fundamental rights, the discredited theory that the people must blindly obey the government and say nothing against it. Even though the Court declared that giving voice to 'criticism or comment so long as he does not incite people to violence against the Government established by the law'[4] was something which Section 124A permitted, the Court unforgivably blundered.

It prefaced this observation, this tempering of the law on sedition, as it were, with an audacious declaration. The Supreme Court announced for all times to come that bringing the government into 'contempt or hatred, or creating disaffection against it would be within the penal statute because the feeling of disloyalty to the Government established by law or enmity to it *imports the idea of tendency* to public disorder by the use of actual violence or incitement for violence.'[5]

This was a daring leap of faith into an abyss. *Kedar Nath Singh* sanctified, as a constitutional principle, the continuation of the old idea—an idea developed by the colonial masters—that to speak against the government was itself an act of sedition. That implicit in the critique of government was the bad tendency to cause upheaval.

Kedar Nath Singh did not even make a pretence of testing this audacious declaration on the anvil of the freedom of speech. In one fell swoop the ghosts of the past came to life and the Supreme Court buried political speech by treating it as being per se illegal and seditious. The disastrous effects of this declaration play out even today.

One may imagine a whole range of situations where contempt and disaffection for the government are unaccompanied by anything more. One may express criticism for a government but still remain loyal to the State and not engage in acts of disobedience. One may have no particular affection whatsoever for the government but still retain one's instinct to remain a law-abiding citizen.

Yet again, one may express strong disaffection against the government, even contempt, in seeking to bring about a change in a particular measure; here the line between disapprobation and disaffection gets blurred if not crossed, but without a message of violence. As far as all these forms of expressions are concerned, they properly fall within the domain of political speech. But they will be punished for sedition.[6]

One need only to recall the dictum of the Supreme Court in *Shreya Singhal* when declaring Section 66A of the IT Act (a law which in large part mimicked Section 124A) unconstitutional. Justice Nariman observed that 'Section 66A is cast so widely that virtually any opinion on any subject would be covered by it, as any serious opinion dissenting with the mores of the day would be caught within its net.'[7] This is the same problem that afflicts

Section 124A. It punishes peaceful speech and has the power to liken such speech to be the crime of sedition.

The moment the ability of the people to draw their collective ire on the government is put in harm's way, the fundamental right to free speech and expression must come to the rescue. After all, the State cannot decide the way the people are to give vent to their grievances. Some may do it by expressing disapprobation in sober language. Other may not. Expression of disaffection may have the veneer of civility, or may use vituperative language.

However, if the person, is only guilty of choosing the wrong words to express themselves, then that cannot mean that the crime of sedition has been committed. After all, as Justice Robert Jackson, the undisputed poet laureate of the US Supreme Court who 'made [US] Supreme Court opinions sing,'[8] famously put it in a 1934 decision:

> If there is any fixed star in our constitutional constellation, it is that no official, high or petty, can prescribe what shall be orthodox in politics, nationalism, religion, or other matters of opinion or force citizens to confess by word or act their faith therein.[9]

If the expression of both disapprobation as well as disaffection is unaccompanied by any call to cause any sort of mass disturbance affecting State security, then to single out only the excitement of disaffection and treat it as sedition is unconstitutional and an injuriously arbitrary method of determining the manner in which people can give vent to their thoughts and opinions. What the decision in *Kedar Nath Singh* achieved directly was to proscribe all expression of criticism against the government. There was no act of balancing in the decision; there was only a pretence of doing it.

Fundamentally, the judgment in *Kedar Nath Singh* outlawed all political speech. Seen today with the benefit of constitutional history and the evolution of Indian jurisprudence, the decision in *Kedar Nath Singh* makes little constitutional sense. It is rife with discredited ideas and antiquated notions about the powers of the State to regulate free speech, particularly political speech.

Indian jurisprudence now stands at a crossroads and it must take the decisive turn towards constitutional progress. The old idea propounded by the Supreme Court in *Kedar Nath Singh*, that sedition occurs when speeches or writings have a tendency to disturb public order, is now part of the *ancien regime* of free speech jurisprudence. If the bad tendency standard is used to measure the full potential of free speech, then history teaches us that much of political thought will be swept away.

The modern conception of free speech demands the achievement of two ideals. The advocacy and discussion of an idea which falls within the category of political speech ought to be protected and generally be immune from regulation. Relatedly, only when the speech and writing in question has the imminent and inevitable effect of bringing about an outcome which directly harms State security, in a manner where the State is left without the ability to counteract it, may the State regulate such speech.

Importantly, an imminent threat to 'public order' can never be the justification for a law on sedition. Nor can the mechanical incantation of preserving obscure interests be the basis to quell political speech. In the scheme of the Indian Constitution, as noted by its framers, sedition is to be treated as something which affects State security. Since for the purposes of Article 19(2) public order is unrelated to State security, protection of public order is not a ground which can give a lease of life, or rather a new lease of life, to a law on sedition.

Seen thus, Section 124A is unconstitutional. It is not a reasonable restriction on free speech and expression. It directly punishes political discussion and the advocacy of political issues. We know only too well that political speech includes a panoply of varied opinions, political discussion and advocacy of political critique. Section 124A has no concern whatsoever with dealing with the situation of whether the political speech imminently leads to any disruption which affects the security of the State.

It is purely and only a criminal sanction on political speech concerning the discussion and advocacy of political ideas, without any proximate connection with preventing any perceivable harm.

Under the *Ram Manohar Lohia* standard articulated by Justice Subba Rao as well as the *Brandenburg* standard enunciated by the US Supreme Court, which Indian jurisprudence has now adopted, Section 124A is unconstitutional.

It is vitally important to remember that in numerous decisions of the Indian Supreme Court which are part of the constitutional canon—starting from *Romesh Thappar*, *Brij Bhushan* and *Virendra* from the 1950s, *Lohia* and *Kameshwar Prasad* from the 1960s, to *Shreya Singhal* in the twenty-first century—once the statute in question was found to be unconstitutional because it criminalized the advocacy and promotion of political ideas and ideals, the law was declared unconstitutional.

More importantly, in none of these decisions was an effort made to somehow save the law in question by (mis)reading it as containing implicit standards for dealing with the imminent incitement of lawless action. Much of Indian jurisprudence stands as a torchbearer to how the highest court of the land emphatically responds to and invalidates laws and regulations which offend political speech.

To remain faithful to the Constitution, once it is demonstrated that Section 124A directly affects the discussion and advocacy of political speech and expression, and that nothing in Section 124A contains any standard dealing with the occurrence of imminent disturbances affecting State security, Section 124A cannot enlist a single defence in its favour.

When confronted with the weight of history and the experience of Indian and global jurisprudence, Section 124A is crying out to be declared unconstitutional. When charged with unconstitutionality, the natural instinct must never be to preserve sedition. It deserves no degree of special respect; it is unworthy of it.

To quell the voice of the people using the hammer of sedition ought to be treated as a constitutional sin. And each day that sedition remains on the statute book is a day when the freedom of speech and expression, and indeed the state of Indian democracy, suffers the unkindest unconstitutional cut of all.

Notes

Prologue

1 Pankaj Butalia, 'Sedition law has no place in a modern democracy,' *The Indian Express*, 10 July 2021.
2 A.G. Noorani, 'The Plague of Sedition,' *Frontline*, 13 March 2021 (available at https://frontline.thehindu.com/the-nation/the-plague-of-sedition/article30913046.ece).
3 Special Correspondent, 'Parliament Proceedings Minister, Congress MPs trade charges over misuse of sedition law,' *The Hindu*, 16 March 2021.
4 Arshad Afzaal Khan, 'Ayodhya police drop sedition charge against students, say no evidence found,' *The Times of India*, 28 December 2020 (available at https://timesofindia.indiatimes.com/city/lucknow/ayodhya-police-drops-sedition-charge-against-students-says-no-evidence-found/articleshow/79995383.cms).
5 Krishandas Rajagopal, 'Republic Day violence: Supreme Court protects Shashi Tharoor, Rajdeep Sardesai and five journalists from arrest,' *The Hindu*, 9 February 2021 (available at https://www.thehindu.com/news/national/republic-day-violence-sc-stays-arrest-of-shashi-tharoor-rajdeep-sardesai-and-five-journalists/article33789972.ece).

6   Namrata Biji Ahuja, 'Sedition law: SC order raises more questions than answers,' *The Week*, 29 May 2022 (available at https://www.theweek.in/theweek/current/2022/05/20/sedition-law-sc-order-raises-more-questions-than-answers.html).

7   Saadhya Mohan and Meghnad Bose, 'Protests, Cricket Matches, COVID-19: How Sedition Law Has Been Used Since 2010,' *The Quint*, 13 May 2022 (available at https://www.thequint.com/news/law/protests-cricket-matches-covid-19-how-sedition-law-has-been-used-since-2010-supreme-court#read-more).

8   Jason Burke, 'Indian cartoonist Aseem Trivedi jailed after arrest on sedition charges,' *The Guardian*, 10 September 2012 (available at https://www.theguardian.com/world/2012/sep/10/indian-cartoonist-jailed-sedition).

9   Ramakrishna Badseshi, 'Nothing seditious in play staged at Bidar school: Court,' *The New Indian Express*, 7 March 2020 (available at https://www.newindianexpress.com/states/karnataka/2020/mar/07/nothing-seditious-in-play-staged-at-bidar-school-court-2113387.html).

10 Abhishek Chakraborty, 'Hanuman Chalisa Row: No Ground for Sedition against MP–MLA Couple, says Court,' *NDTV*, 6 May 2022 (available at https://www.ndtv.com/india-news/hanuman-chalisa-row-no-ground-for-sedition-against-mp-mla-couple-says-court-2950670).

11 Ajay Sura, 'Faridabad Court raps use of sedition law in hoax call,' *The Times of India*, 14 January 2022 (available at https://timesofindia.indiatimes.com/city/faridabad/fbd-court-raps-use-of-sedition-law-in-hoax-call/articleshow/88886851.cms).

12 Nida Najar and Swati Gupta, 'Sedition Arrests in India Inflame Old Free Speech Tensions,' *The New York Times*, 24 February 2016 (available at https://www.nytimes.com/2016/02/25/world/asia/with-sedition-arrests-india-continues-to-wrestle-with-free-speech.html).

13 Express News Service, 'Strike down sedition law, former judge Rohinton Nariman urges Supreme Court,' *The New Indian Express*, 11 October 2021 (available at https://www.newindianexpress.com/nation/2021/oct/11/strike-down-sedition-law-former-judge-rohinton-nariman-urges-supreme-court-2370163.html); Fali S. Nariman, 'A Dispiriting Law,' *The Indian Express*, 1 June 2022.

14 Lubhyathi Rangarajan, 'A Decade in Darkness: Our New Database Reveals How a Law Discarded by Most Democracies Is Misused in India,' *Article 14*, 4 February 2022 (available at https://article-14.com/

post/a-decade-of-darkness-our-new-database-reveals-how-a-law-discarded-by-most-democracies-is-misused-in-india-61fcb8768d15c).

15 Section 124A. Sedition: Whoever, by words, either spoken or written, or by signs, or by visible representation, or otherwise, brings or attempts to bring into hatred or contempt, or excites or attempts to excite disaffection towards the Government established by law in India, shall be punished with imprisonment for life, to which fine may be added, or with imprisonment which may extend to three years, to which fine may be added, or with fine.
Explanation 1. The expression 'disaffection' includes disloyalty and all feelings of enmity.
Explanation 2. Comments expressing disapprobation of the measures of the Government with a view to obtain their alteration by lawful means, without exciting or attempting to excite hatred, contempt or disaffection, do not constitute an offence under this section.
Explanation 3. Comments expressing disapprobation of the administrative or other action of the Government without exciting or attempting to excite hatred, contempt or disaffection, do not constitute an offence under this section.

16 Express News Service, 'Supreme Court issues notice to Centre on plea challenging sedition law,' *The Indian Express*, 1 May 2021 (https://indianexpress.com/article/india/sc-seeks-response-from-centre-on-plea-challenging-sedition-law-7297159/). Also see, Samanwaya Rautray, 'Misuse of sedition laws breaches functioning of institutions says Chief Justice,' *The Economic Times*, 16 July 2021 (available at https://economictimes.indiatimes.com/news/india/misuse-of-sedition-laws-breaches-functioning-of-institutions-says-chief-justice/articleshow/84453904.cms).

17 PTI, 'SC to examine interpretation of sedition law over right of press, free speech,' *The Economic Times*, 31 May 2021 (https://economictimes.indiatimes.com/news/politics-and-nation/sc-restrains-andhra-pradesh-police-from-coercive-action-against-news-channels-in-sedition-case/articleshow/83110263.cms?from=mdr).

18 *S.G. Vombatkere v. Union of India,* (2022) 7 SCC 433 [hereinafter *Vombatkere*]. In the interest of full disclosure, I must state that I was part of the legal team led by Arvind Datar, Senior Advocate, who presented arguments in the Supreme Court on why Section 124A was unconstitutional. However, the project of writing this book commenced much before I was asked by Arvind Datar to assist him in the Supreme Court.

19 'Minute by Hon'ble T.B. Macaulay dated the 2nd February 1835' (available at http://www.columbia.edu/itc/mealac/pritchett/00generallinks/macaulay/txt_minute_education_1835.html).
20 Bibek Debroy, 'The Macaulay we don't know,' *The Indian Express*, 7 September 2017 (available at https://indianexpress.com/article/opinion/columns/the-macaulay-we-dont-know-ipc-macaulay-indian-penal-code-law-commission-4831988/).
21 See Chapter 3.
22 Chitranshul Sinha, *The Great Repression: The Story of Sedition in India* (India: Penguin Random House India, 2019) pp. 144–149 [hereinafter Sinha, *Repression*].
23 Areeb Uddin Ahmed, Afreen Alam, 'International Women's Day 2022: Eight Indian women who broke the legal profession's glass ceiling,' *Bar and Bench*, 8 March 2022 (available at https://www.barandbench.com/columns/indias-first-women-who-broke-social-barriers-in-the-legal-field). (Violet Alva was an Indian lawyer, journalist and politician. She was married to Joachim Alva, who was also a politician, lawyer, journalist and Parliamentarian. The couple is fondly remembered as the first Parliamentarian couple of India. In 1944, Alva became the first woman advocate in India to have argued a case before a full high court bench. In the same year, she started a women's magazine called *The Begum* (later *Indian Women*). In 1947, Alva served as an Honorary Magistrate in Bombay, and from 1948–1954 she served as president of the Juvenile Court. She was also the first woman to be elected to the Standing Committee of the All India Newspaper Editors Conference in 1952. In 1952, Alva was elected to the Rajya Sabha, where she made major contributions to family planning, animal rights in research and defence strategy, notably in the naval sector. In 1957, she was made the Deputy Minister of State for Home Affairs. Alva was appointed Deputy Chairman of the Rajya Sabha in 1962, making her the first female to preside over the Rajya Sabha in its history. She held the office for two consecutive terms.)
24 Joachim Alva, 'Member's Profile', Third Lok Sabha, Parliament of India (available at http://loksabhaph.nic.in/writereaddata/biodata_1_12/588.htm).
25 In 1952, Joachim and Violet Alva entered Parliament and they hold the record for being the first couple to be elected to Parliament—Joachim Alva to the Lok Sabha and Violet Alva to the Rajya Sabha. Violet Alva became the Deputy Chairman of the Rajya Sabha in 1962. Their portrait now hangs in the Central Hall of Parliament and they

have been immortalized in a commemorative stamp released in 2008 by India Post in their honour.

26　See Anushka Singh, *Sedition in Liberal Democracies* (New Delhi: Oxford University Press, 2018), p. 148 [hereinafter Singh, *Sedition*]. ('By equating disaffection as disloyalty to the government, the offence of sedition had been equated with betrayal and unfaithfulness to one's rulers. The British government, however, constantly emphasized on disapprobation as an accepted mode of expressing criticism of the government in all trials of sedition which rhetorically was a reiteration of the 'liberal' nature of British colonialism. In reality, however, any expression critical of the government or of its policies or measures that could have possibly hinted at the nature of British rule as anything but benevolent and developmental, was penalized.')

27　Gopalkrishna Gandhi, '100 years ago, a movement of Hindu–Muslim oneness', *Hindustan Times*, 8 April 2022.

28　The debates of the Constituent Assembly are contained in the Constituent Assembly Debates (New Delhi: Lok Sabha Secretariat, Sixth Reprint, 2014) [hereinafter CAD].

29　Tripurdaman Singh, *Sixteen Stormy Days: The Story of the First Amendment to the Constitution of India* (India: Penguin Random House India, 2020), pp. xiii, xix–xx, 192, 195, 199 [hereinafter Singh, *Sixteen*]; Abhinav Chandrachud, *Republic of Rhetoric: Free Speech and the Constitution of India* (India: Penguin Random House India, 2017), p. 5 [hereinafter Chandrachud, *Rhetoric*]. *Per contra* see, Gautam Bhatia, *Offend, Shock, or Disturb: Free Speech under the Indian Constitution* (New Delhi: Oxford University Press, 2018 paperback edition), p. 92 [hereinafter Bhatia, *Offend*].

30　The theoretical framework for developing ideas about the importance of political speech and its place of high importance in a Constitution is in large measure inspired from Cass R. Sunstein, *Democracy and the Problem of Free Speech* (New York: The Free Press, 1995) [hereinafter Sunstein, *Democracy*].

31　*Sakal Papers v. Union of India*, (1962) 3 SCR 842 [hereinafter *Sakal Papers*]. See p. 866.

32　H.M. Seervai, *Constitutional Law of India*, vol. 1 (Delhi: Universal Traders, 4th edition, 1999), pp. 702–703 [hereinafter Seervai, *Constitutional Law*].

33　*Vombatkere*, para. 5

34　Seervai, *Constitutional Law*, p. 711.

1: Disaffectionately Yours, Sedition

1. Courtney Ilbert, *The Government of India Being a Digest of the Statute Law Relating Thereto with Historical Introduction and Explanatory Matter* (London: Oxford University Press, 1907), pp. 1–2 [hereinafter Ilbert, *Government of India*].
2. Id., pp. 77–78.
3. Id., pp. 81.
4. Id., p. 82.
5. Id., pp. 82–83.
6. Id., p. 84.
7. Elizabeth Kolsky, 'Codification and the Rule of Colonial Difference: Criminal Procedure in British India,' *Law and History Review*, vol. 23 (2005): pp. 631–632 [hereinafter Kolsky, 'Codification']; Ilbert, *Government of India*, p. 85.
8. Ilbert, *Government of India*, p. 86.
9. Ibid.
10. Ibid.
11. Ibid.
12. Id., pp. 86–87.
13. M.C. Setalvad, *The Common Law in India* (London: Stevens & Sons Ltd, 1960), p. 123 [hereinafter Setalvad, *Common Law*].
14. *Navtej Singh Johar v. Union of India*, (2018) 10 SCC 1, para 279 (per R.F. Nariman, J.).
15. Eric Stokes, *The English Utilitarians in India* (Clarendon: Oxford University Press, 1959), p. 179 [hereinafter Stokes, *Utilitarians*].
16. Id., pp. 196, 221–222.
17. James Fitzjames Stephen, *A History of the Criminal Law of England*, vol. III (London: Macmillan and Co., 1883), pp. 297–299 [hereinafter Stephen, *History*, vol. III]; Stokes, *Utilitarians*, pp. 219, 224.
18. Stephen, *History*, vol. III, p. 299; Stokes, *Utilitarians*, p. 191; Setalvad, *Common Law*, pp. 123–124.
19. *The Indian Penal Code as Originally Framed in 1837 with Notes by T.B. Macaulay, J.M. Macleod, G.W. Anderson, and F. Millet and the First and Second Reports Thereon Dated 23rd July 1846 and 24th June 1847 by C.H. Cameron and D. Elliot Indian Law Commissioners* (Madras: Higginbotham and Co., 1888) [hereinafter *ILC's Penal Code*].
20. Id., pp. viii–xiv.
21. Id., pp. viii–ix.

22 David Skuy, 'Macaulay and the Indian Penal Code of 1862: The Myth of the Inherent Superiority and Modernity of the English Legal System Compared to India's Legal System in the Nineteenth Century,' *Modern Asian Studies*, vol. 32 (1998): p. 525 [hereinafter Skuy, 'Macaulay'].
23 Id., pp. 525–527.
24 Id., pp. 528–529.
25 Id., pp. 529.
26 Id., pp. 530–532.
27 Id., pp. 532–534.
28 Id., pp. 534–537.
29 Id., p. 538.
30 Id., pp. 538, 554.
31 Id., p. 517.
32 Stephen, *History*, vol. III, pp. 313–314.
33 *Mohd Rafiq @ Kallu v. The State of Madhya Pradesh*, (2021) 10 SCC 706, para. 11 (per S. Ravindra Bhat, J.) (internal citations omitted).
34 Stephen, *History*, vol. III, p. 315. One of the most infamous duels in history is the Burr–Hamilton duel which occurred between Alexander Burr Vice-President of the United States) and Alexander Hamilton on 11 July 1804 in New Jersey, USA. Hamilton was grievously injured and died the next day. See Jeff Wallenfeldt, 'Burr–Hamilton duel', *Encyclopaedia Britannica*, 4 July 2020 (available at https://www.britannica.com/event/Burr-Hamilton-duel).
35 Stokes, *Utilitarians*, p. 51.
36 Ibid., pp. 220, 225, 231–233; Skuy, 'Macaulay,' p. 524.
37 Ibid., p. 226. (Emphasis added.)
38 *ILC's Penal Code*, p. 198 (Ref. First Report on the Penal Code by the Indian Law Commissioners, 23 July 1846). Also see Skuy, 'Macaulay,' pp. 542–543.
39 Ibid., p. xiii. (Emphasis added.)
40 Id., pp. xiii–xiv (internal citation omitted). (Emphasis added.) Also see Setalvad, *Common Law*, p. 126.
41 Kolsky, 'Codification,' pp. 632–633.
42 Id., p. 633 (quoting from George O. Trevelyan, *The Life and Letters of Lord Macaulay*, 387 [London: Lowe and Brydone, 1959]).
43 *ILC's Penal Code*, p. xiv.
44 Id., p. xvi.
45 Ibid.
46 Id., pp. xviii–xx.
47 Skuy, 'Macaulay,' p. 540.

48 *ILC's Penal Code*, pp. 21–24.
49 Stokes, *Utilitarians*, p. 228.
50 Clause 113. Whoever, by words, either written or spoken or intended to be read, or by signs, or by visible representations, attempts to excite feelings of disaffection to the Government established by law in the territories of the East India Company, among any class of people who live under that Government, shall be punished with banishment for life or for any term from the territories of the East India Company, to which a fine may be added, or with simple imprisonment for a term which may extend to three years, to which a fine may be added, or with fine.
Explanation: Such a disapprobation of the measures of the Government as is compatible with a disposition to render obedience to the lawful authority of the Government, and to support lawful authority of the Government against unlawful attempts to subvert or resist that authority, is not disaffection. Therefore the making of comments on the measures of the Government, with the intention of exciting only this species of disapprobation, is not an offence within this clause.
51 Stokes, *Utilitarians*, pp. 219–220. (Emphasis added.)
52 Setalvad, *Common Law*, p. 185.
53 *ILC's Penal Code*, p. xvi.
54 See Chandrachud, *Rhetoric*, pp. 22–23. For a history on how the law on sedition developed in England, see Singh, *Sedition*, pp. 74–89.
55 James Fitzjames Stephen, *A History of the Criminal Law in England*, vol. II (London: Macmillan and Co., 1883), pp. 373–374 [hereinafter Stephen, *History*, vol. II].
56 Id., p. 377.
57 Id., pp. 373–376.
58 Id., p. 373.
59 Justice Deepak Gupta, 'Law of Sedition in India and Freedom of Expression' (2020) 4 *SCC (Journal)*, pp. 14–27.
60 Stephen, *History*, vol. II, p. 373.
61 Id., p. 375. (Emphasis added.)
62 Skuy, 'Macaulay,' pp. 543–545.
63 Stephens, *History*, vol. II, p. 298. (Emphasis added.)
64 Singh, *Sedition*, p. 75.
65 Stokes, *Utilitarians*, p. 219.
66 *ILC's Penal Code*, Appendix, Note R (On the Chapter on Defamation), p. 185. (Emphasis added.)
67 Id., pp. 189–328.

68 Id., pp. 338–497.
69 Id., p. 345.
70 Id., pp. 345–346.
71 Id., p. 346.
72 Ibid.
73 Ibid. (Emphasis added.)
74 Id., pp. 346–347.
75 K.N. Pannikar, 'The First Major Challenge: The Revolt of 1857' in *India's Struggle for Independence*, eds Bipin Chandra, Mridula Mukherjee, Aditya Mukherjee, K.N. Pannikar and Sucheta Mahajan (India: Penguin Books, 1989), pp. 31–40.
76 Proclamation by the Queen in Council to the Princes, Chiefs and People of India (published by the Governor-General at Allahabad), 1 November 1858 (available at https://www.bl.uk/collection-items/proclamation-by-the-queen-in-council-to-the-princes-chiefs-and-people-of-india#).
77 See Stephen, *History*, vol. III, p. 299. ('The suppression of the mutiny and the transfer of the government from the Company to the Crown made a great change and gave an extraordinary impetus to legislation. Amongst other measures, the Penal Code was passed into law as Act XLV of 1860 and was followed a year afterwards by Act XXV of 1861—the first of three successive versions of the Code of Criminal Procedure.')
78 Henry Mead, *The Sepoy Revolt: Its Causes and Consequences* (London: John Murray, 1857), pp. 184–197 [hereinafter Mead, *Sepoy Revolt*].
79 Id., pp. 377–379.
80 Id., p. 380. (Emphasis added.)
81 Id., pp. 381–385, 392–396.
82 Id., p. 379.
83 Id., p. 196.
84 Abstracts of the Proceedings of the Council of the Governor General of India Assembled for the Purpose of Making Laws and Regulations 1870, vol. XI (Calcutta: Office of the Superintendent of Government Printing India, 1906) [hereinafter Abstracts, 1870].
85 Id., p. 371.
86 Id., pp. 373–374.
87 Id., p. 374.
88 Ibid.
89 Ibid.
90 Ibid.

91 Ibid. Also see pp. 440–441.
92 Id., p. 374
93 Bhatia, *Offend*, p. 84.
94 Ibid.
95 Abstracts, 1870, p. 438.
96 Ibid.
97 Id., pp. 445–446.
98 Id., p. 446.
99 Id., pp. 445–446.
100 Arun K. Thiruvengadam, 'The Evolution of the Constitutional Right to Free Speech in India (1800–1950): The Interplay of Universal and Particular Rationales,' 1 December 2013, University of Washington Trans-Pacific Comparative Constitutional Roundtable on 6 December 2013, Centre for Asian Legal Studies, National University of Singapore, Working Paper Series, p. 11 (available at https://papers.ssrn.com/sol3/papers.cfm?abstract_id=2470905).
101 Abstracts, 1870, p. 446. (Emphasis added.)
102 See Singh, *Sedition*, pp. 137–138.
103 Abstracts, 1870, p. 449.
104 Id., p. 450.
105 Id., p. 441.
106 Id., p. 452.
107 Id., p. 454.
108 Gideon Colquhoun Sconce, *The Legislative Acts of the Governor-General of India in Council of 1870* (Calcutta: Thacker, Spink and Co., 1871), pp. 229–230.
Section 124A read as follows:
Whoever, by words, either written or spoken or intended to be read, or by signs, or by visible representations, attempts to excite feelings of disaffection to the Government established by law in British India, shall be punished with transportation for life or for any term, to which a fine may be added, or with imprisonment for a term which may extend to three years, to which a fine may be added, or with fine.
Explanation: Such a disapprobation of the measures of the Government as is compatible with a disposition to render obedience to the lawful authority of the Government, and to support lawful authority of the Government against unlawful attempts to subvert or resist that authority, is not disaffection. Therefore the making of comments on the measures of the Government, with the intention of exciting only this species of disapprobation, is not an offence within this clause.

109 See Jayant Sriram, 'Should the sedition law be scrapped?' *The Hindu*, 6 March 2020 (available at https://www.thehindu.com/opinion/op-ed/should-the-sedition-law-be-scrapped/article62108419.ece).
110 Julia Stephens, 'The Phantom Wahabi,' *Modern Asian Studies*, vol. 47 (2013): p. 22 [hereinafter Stephens, 'Phantom'].
111 Id., pp. 31–36.
112 Id., p. 37.
113 Id., pp. 38–45.
114 Id., p. 42.
115 Id., p. 46.

2: Half a League, Half a League, Half a League Onward

1 See Chapter 1.
2 Present-day Kolkata.
3 *Queen-Empress v. Jogendra Chunder Bose and others*, ILR 19 Cal 36 (Calcutta High Court), (1891) [hereinafter *Bose*].
4 Id., pp. 36–37.
5 Tanika Sarkar, 'A Prehistory of Rights: The Age of Consent Debate in Colonial Bengal,' *Feminist Studies*, vol. 26 (2000): p. 601.
6 Special Correspondent, 'Notes from India,' *The Lancet*, no. 4050 (13 April 1901): pp. 1107–1108 (available at https://archive.org/details/dli.ernet.67347/page/1107/mode/2up).
7 See, generally, Barbara D. Metcalf and Thomas R. Metcalf, *A Concise History of Modern India* (New York: Cambridge University Press, 2nd edition, 2006), pp. 154–155 [hereinafter Metcalf, *Concise History*].
8 *Bose*, pp. 39–40.
9 Id., p. 40.
10 Id., p. 44.
11 Ibid.
12 Ibid.
13 Id., p. 45.
14 Id., p. 47.
15 Walter Russel Donogh, *A Treatise on the Law of Sedition and Cognate Offences in British India* (Calcutta: Thacker, Spink & Co., 1911), p. 41. Donogh's book was a sympathetic assessment of the law on sedition and justified why it was necessary for the British administration to prosecute a large number of cases under Section 124A of the IPC.
16 Present-day Mumbai.

17 Bipin Chandra, 'The Fight to Secure Press Freedom,' in *India's Struggle for Independence*, eds Bipin Chandra, Mridula Mukherjee, Aditya Mukherjee, K.N. Pannikar and Sucheta Mahajan (India: Penguin Books, 1989), p. 109 [hereinafter Chandra, 'Press Freedom'].
18 *Queen-Empress v. Bal Gangadhar Tilak and Keshav Mahadev Bal*, ILR vol. XXII, p. 112 (Bombay High Court), (1897) [hereinafter *Tilak*, 1897].
19 A.G. Noorani, *Indian Political Trials 1775–1947* (New Delhi: Oxford University Press, 2005), pp. 115–116 [hereinafter Noorani, *Political Trials*]. Also see Abhinav Chandrachud, 'Plague of 1896 redefined sedition. Coronavirus mustn't bring in laws that outlives crisis,' *The Print*, 24 March 2020 (available at https://theprint.in/opinion/plague-1896-sedition-covid-19-mustnt-set-laws-outlive-crisis/386552/).
20 *Tilak*, 1897, p. 121.
21 Chandra, 'Press Freedom,' pp. 108–109.
22 See Metcalf, *Concise History*, p. 150.
23 House of Commons Debate, 5 August 1897, vol. 52, cc 435–504 (available at https://api.parliament.uk/historic-hansard/commons/1897/aug/05/british-rule).
24 Ibid.
25 Sinha, *Repression*, pp. 63–64.
26 *Tilak*, 1897, p. 129.
27 Id., p. 134. (Emphasis added.)
28 Ibid. (Emphasis added.)
29 Id., p. 135. (Emphasis added.)
30 Id., p. 136.
31 Ibid.
32 Id., p. 137.
33 Id., p. 138.
34 Id., p. 145.
35 Noorani, *Political Trials*, p. 117.
36 Chandrachud, *Rhetoric*, p. 31.
37 Chandra, 'Press Freedom,' p. 110.
38 Id., pp. 146–148.
39 Id., p. 148. (Emphasis added.)
40 Id., p. 145.
41 Id., pp. 149–152.
42 P.B. Vacha, *Famous Judges, Lawyers and Cases of Bombay: A Judicial History of Bombay During the British Period* (Bombay: N.M. Tripathi

Pvt. Ltd, 1962), p. 264 [hereinafter Vacha, *Famous Judges*]; Noorani, *Political Trials*, p. 122.
43 *Bal Gangadhar Tilak v. The Queen-Empress*, in the Privy Council, Council Chamber, Whitehall, Friday, 19 November 1897 (transcript from the Shorthand Notes of Messers. Marten, Meredith and Henderson, 13, New Inn, Strand, WC), available in the British Library.
44 Id., p. 6.
45 Id., p. 12.
46 Ibid.
47 Id., p. 20.
48 Id., p. 21.
49 Id., pp. 21–23.
50 Id., p. 22.
51 Ibid.
52 Id., pp. 22–23.
53 Id., p. 26; *Gangadhar Tilak v. Queen-Empress*, (1897) SCC OnLine PC 23 (Privy Council) (SCC OnLine version).
54 *Queen-Empress v. Amba Prasad*, (1897) ILR 20 All 55; MANU/UP/0084/1897 [hereinafter *Prasad*].
55 *Prasad*, para. 1. The High Court's decision only notes the title of the offending article but does not contain a description of the article, which became the basis of the case.
56 Id., para. 2.
57 Id., para. 5.
58 Ibid.
59 Id., paras. 5–12.
60 Id., para. 12.
61 Id., para. 13.
62 Id., para. 14. (Emphasis added.)
63 John Bruce Norton, *The Rebellion in India and How to Prevent Another* (London: Richardson and Brothers, 1857), p. viii.
64 Bhagwat Prasad Singh, 'Censorship and the Indian Press between 1857 and 1945,' Master of Arts Thesis, State University of Iowa (1949), pp. 19–20 [hereinafter Singh, 'Censorship'].
65 Id., p. 21.
66 Id., pp. 24–25.
67 Id., p. 34.
68 Ibid.
69 Id., p. 35.
70 Ibid.

71 Ibid.
72 Id., p. 36.
73 Id., pp. 37–38.
74 Id., p. 39–40.
75 Metcalf, *A Concise History*, p. 120.
76 Singh, 'Censorship', p. 51.
77 Id., pp. 57–62.
78 Singh, *Sedition*, pp. 143–146.
79 Abstracts of the Proceedings of the Council of the Governor-General of India, vol. XXXVI, Jan.–Dec., 1897 (Calcutta: Printed by the Superintendent of Government Printing, India, 1898) (available at https://eparlib.nic.in/bitstream/123456789/783719/1/ilcd_21-december-1897.pdf) [hereinafter Abstracts, December 1897].
80 Id., p. 380.
81 Ibid.
82 Ibid.
83 Id., p. 381.
84 Ibid.
85 Id., p. 379.
86 Ibid.
87 Id., p. 380.
88 Ibid.
89 Abstracts of the Proceedings of the Council of the Governor-General of India, vol. XXXVII, January–December., 1898 (Calcutta: Printed by the Superintendent of Government Printing, India, 1899) (available at https://eparlib.nic.in/bitstream/123456789/784022/1/ilcd_18-february-1898.pdf) [hereinafter Abstracts, February 1898].
90 Id., p. 32.
91 Id., p. 34.
92 Id., p. 37.
93 Id., p. 38.
94 Id., p. 120.
95 Id., pp. 33–34. Chalmers's illustration was as follows: 'If I smoke a cigar on the *maidan*, it pleases me, and hurts no one else. If I smoke a cigar in the powder magazine of the Fort, I endanger the lives of many and do an act well deserving punishment.' This illustration has been likened to anticipating Justice Oliver Wendell Holmes's formulation of 'shouting fire in a theater' test. See Chandrachud, *Rhetoric*, p. 34.
96 Abstracts, February 1898, p. 34.
97 Id., p. 63.

98 Ibid.
99 Id., p. 152.
100 '124A. Sedition:
Whoever by words, either spoken or written, or by signs or by visible representation, or otherwise, brings or attempts to bring into hatred or contempt, or excites or attempts to excite disaffection towards Her Majesty or the Government established by law in British India, shall be punished with transportation for life or any shorter term, to which fine may be added, or with imprisonment which may extend to three years, to which fine may be added, or with fine.
Explanation 1. The expression "disaffection" includes disloyalty and all feelings of enmity.
Explanation 2. Comments expressing disapprobation of the measures of the Government with a view to obtain their alteration by lawful means, without exciting or attempting to excite hatred, contempt or disaffection, do not constitute an offence under this section.
Explanation 3. Comments expressing disapprobation of the administrative or other action of the Government without exciting or attempting to excite hatred, contempt or disaffection do not constitute an offence under this section.'

3: Wounded Vanity

1 See Bhatia, *Offend*, p. 88; Singh, *Sedition*, pp. 161–162.
2 MANU/MH/0064/1906 [hereinafter *Bhopatkar*].
3 *Bhopatkar*, paras. 2, 16.
4 Id., para. 6.
5 Id., para. 7.
6 Id., para. 3.
7 Id., paras. 12, 16.
8 *Emperor v. Bal Gangadhar Tilak*, vol. X BLR 848, (1908) (Bombay High Court) [hereinafter *Tilak*, 1908].
9 Id., p. 851.
10 In present-day Bihar.
11 *Tilak*, 1908, pp. 849–855; Sinha, *Repression*, pp. 91–93.
12 *Tilak*, 1908, p. 888.
13 Ibid.
14 Ibid.
15 Id., pp. 888–889.

16 Id., p. 889.
17 Id., p. 851.
18 *Tilak*, 1897, p. 113.
19 Metcalf, *Concise History*, p. 150.
20 *Tilak*, 1908, pp. 889–890.
21 Id., p. 900. Also see Noorani, *Political Trials*, p. 124.
22 *Tilak*, 1908, p. 900.
23 Id., p. 902.
24 Ibid.
25 Id., p. 903.
26 Metcalf, *A Concise History*, p. 159.
27 *Tilak*, 1908, p. 902.
28 Id., p. 903.
29 Ibid.
30 Vacha, *Famous Judges*, pp. 268–269.
31 Id., pp. 269–270. Vacha himself is critical of the unveiling of this tablet because he viewed it as an act of condemning past decisions and judgments, which would perhaps influence future justices to decide cases with one eye on how history would judge them. Id., pp. 270–271.
32 'Gandhi Arrested on Charge of Sedition; London Reports India Quiet Thus Far; Lord Derby to Take Montagu's Place', *The New York Times*, 11 March 1922.
33 Ibid.
34 Rajmohan Gandhi, *Mohandas: A True Story of a Man, His People and an Empire* (New Delhi: Penguin, 2006), p. 269 [hereinafter Gandhi, *Mohandas*].
35 M.K. Gandhi, *The Law and the Lawyers* (Ahmedabad: Navajivan Trust, 1962), pp. 104–105 [hereinafter Gandhi, *The Law*].
36 Id., p. 105.
37 Id., p. 106.
38 Ibid.
39 Noorani, *Political Trials*, p. 229.
40 Id., p. 108.
41 Id., pp. 108–109.
42 Id., p. 109.
43 Even after Judge Broomfield made it clear that there was no need for a trial, Strangman kept pressing for it. He raised the spectre of Gandhi's writings having resulted in the violent outbreak at Chauri Chaura and that because of it there was a serious need for the court to undertake a detailed examination of Gandhi's writings. See Id., pp. 110–112.

44 Id., p. 112.
45 Id., pp. 118–119; Noorani, *Political Trials*, p. 235. (Emphasis added).
46 Gandhi, *The Law*, p. 120.
47 Id., p. 121.
48 Gandhi, *Mohandas*, p. 270–271.
49 Gandhi, *The Law*, pp. 121–122.
50 Gandhi, *Mohandas*, p. 270; Gandhi, *The Law*, p. 122.
51 Noorani, *Political Trials*, pp. 236–237.
52 Gandhi, *The Law*, p. 122.
53 Ibid.
54 In re *India in Bondage* (1929) vol. LVII ILR (Calcutta) 1217 [hereinafter In re *India*].
55 Id., pp. 1217–1220.
56 Dadabhai Naoroji, *Poverty and Un-British Rule in India* (London: Swan Sonnenschein & Co., 1901), p. v.
57 Id., p. ix.
58 Id., p. x.
59 Id., p. viii (quoting from James Mill, *History of India*, vol. VI, p. 671).
60 In re *India*, p. 1219.
61 Id., pp. 1220–1221.
62 Id., pp. 1221–1226.
63 Id., pp. 1218–1221.
64 Id., pp. 1225–1227.
65 *Emperor v. Narayan Vasudev Phadke*, (1940) vol. XLII, Bombay Law Reporter 861 [hereinafter *Phadke*].
66 Id., p. 862.
67 Id., p. 864.
68 Metcalf, *Concise History*, p. 159.
69 Id., pp. 160–161.
70 *Manmohan Ghose v. Emperor*, (1910) vol. XXXVIII ILR (Calcutta) 253 [hereinafter *Ghose*].
71 Id., pp. 254–258.
72 Id., p. 263.
73 Ibid.
74 Id., p. 265.
75 Id., p. 264.
76 Id., pp. 265–267.
77 *Emperor v. Bal Gangadhar Tilak*, (1916) vol. XIX, Bombay Law Reporter 211 [hereinafter *Tilak*, 1916].
78 *Tilak*, 1916, pp. 212–213.

79 Id., p. 264.
80 Id., p. 265.
81 Id., p. 269.
82 Ibid.
83 Ibid.
84 Id., p. 268.
85 Id., p. 264.
86 *Niharendu Dutt Majumdar v. The King Emperor*, (1942) FCR 38 [hereinafter *Majumdar*].
87 See Sections 205, 207 and 208 of the Government of India Act, 1935 (available at https://www.legislation.gov.uk/ukpga/1935/2/pdfs/ukpga_19350002_en.pdf).
88 Section 212, Government of India Act, 1935.
89 *Majumdar*, pp. 38–39.
90 Id., pp. 50–51.
91 The other two justices were Justices Srinivas Varadachariar and Muhammad Zafrulla Khan.
92 Seervai, *Constitutional Law*, p. 717.
93 *Majumdar*, p. 48.
94 Metcalf, *Concise History*, p. 206. For a more detailed assessment of the Quit India Movement, see Gandhi, *Mohandas*, pp. 447–519.
95 *Majumdar*, p. 48.
96 Ibid.
97 Ibid.
98 Id., pp. 48–49.
99 Id., p. 49.
100 Id., p. 50. (Emphasis added.)
101 Ibid.
102 Bhatia, *Offend*, p. 88. ('Suddenly, sedition was no longer about alienation of allegiances, imputation of base and immoral motives to the government, or feelings of enmity: the test had been radically altered to inciting disorder, or intending to do so.')
103 *Majumdar*, p. 51.
104 *Majumdar*, p. 52.
105 Stephen, *History*, vol. II, p. 374.
106 Ibid.
107 Id., pp. 374–375.
108 *Majumdar*, p. 51.
109 Ibid.
110 Id., p. 52.

111 Id., p. 50.
112 Ibid. (Emphasis added.)
113 *Wallace-Johnson v. The King*, (1940) AC 231.
114 *Emperor v. Sadashiv Narayan Bhalerao*, (1947) PC 18 (Privy Council) [hereinafter *Bhalerao*].
115 Id., pp. 20–21.
116 Section 212, Government of India Act, 1935: 'The law declared by the Federal Court and by any judgment of the Privy Council shall, so far as applicable, be recognised as binding on, and shall be followed by all courts in British India, and, so far as respects the application and interpretation of this Act or any Order in Council thereunder or any matter with respect to which the Federal Legislature has power to make laws in relation to the State, in any Federated State.'

4: The Many Lives of the Prince

1 B. Shiva Rao, *The Framing of India's Constitution: Select Documents*, vol. I (New Delhi: Indian Institute of Public Administration, 1966), p. 213 [hereinafter B. Shiva Rao, *Framing*, vol. I].
2 Id., p. 214.
3 Granville Austin, *The Indian Constitution: Cornerstone of a Nation* (New Delhi: Oxford University Press, 32nd edition, 2018), p. 12 [hereinafter Austin, *The Indian Constitution*].
4 B. Shiva Rao, *Framing*, vol. I, p. 214.
5 Id., p. 216.
6 CAD, vol. II, pp. 328–333.
7 Id., pp. 347–349.
8 B. Shiva Rao, *The Framing of India's Constitution: Select Documents*, vol. II (New Delhi: Indian Institute of Public Administration, 1967), pp. 65–67 [hereinafter B. Shiva Rao, *Framing*, vol. II], Minutes of the first meeting of the Advisory Committee, 27 February 1947.
9 Id., p. 65.
10 Id., pp. 65–66.
11 Id., p. 114, Minutes of the Meeting of the Sub-Committee, 27 February 1947.
12 Id., p. 115.
13 Ibid.
14 Id., pp. 115–116.
15 Id., pp. 115–116.

16 Id., pp. 67–114.
17 Id., pp. 114–137. The Fundamental Rights Sub-Committee met for the first time on 24 February 1947 and then reconvened on 24 March 1947, after which it met almost every day.
18 Id., p. 116.
19 Id., pp. 137–143.
20 Id., p. 139. See Clause 9(a).
'9. There shall be liberty for the exercise of the following rights subject to public order and morality:
The right of every citizen to freedom of speech and expression.
The publication or utterance of seditious, obscene, slanderous, libellous or defamatory matter shall be actionable or punishable in accordance with law.'
21 Id., pp. 163–169, Minutes of the Meetings of the Sub-Committee, 14–15 April 1947.
22 Id., p. 163, Minutes of the Meetings of the Sub-Committee (14 April 1947).
23 Id., pp. 169–198.
24 Id., p. 172. See Clause 10(a).
'10. There shall be liberty for the exercise of the following rights subject to public order and morality or to the existence of grave emergency declared to be such by the Government of the Union or the unit concerned whereby the security of the Union or the unit, as the case may be, is threatened:
The right of every citizen to freedom of speech and expression.
The publication or utterance of seditious, obscene, slanderous, libellous or defamatory matter shall be actionable or punishable in accordance with law.'
25 Id., pp. 230–233.
26 CAD, vol. III, pp. 437–444. See Clause 8(a). Id., p. 441.
'8. There shall be liberty for the exercise of the following rights subject to public order and morality or to the existence of grave emergency declared to be such by the Government of the Union or the unit concerned whereby the security of the Union or the unit, as the case may be, is threatened:
The right of every citizen to freedom of speech and expression:
Provision may be made by law to make the publication or utterance of seditious, obscene, blasphemous, slanderous, or defamatory matter actionable or punishable.'
27 B. Shiva Rao, *Framing*, vol. II, p. 288.

28   CAD, vol. III, pp. 399–400.
29   Id., p. 457.
30   Ibid. (Emphasis added.)
31   Ibid.
32   Id., p. 458.
33   CAD, vol. I, p. 460. See speech of Somnath Lahiri, 30 April 1947.
34   Id., pp. 458–460.
35   Id., p. 458.
36   Id., p. 468.
37   B. Shiva Rao, *Framing*, vol. II, p. 301.
38   CAD, vol. V, pp. 293–294.
39   B. Shiva Rao, *The Framing of India's Constitution: Select Documents*, vol. III (New Delhi: Indian Institute of Public Administration, 1967), p. 315 [hereinafter B. Shiva Rao, *Framing*, vol. III].
40   CAD, vol. V, pp. 293–294. This Resolution was moved by Satyanarayan Sinha.
41   Id., pp. 294–295.
42   Speech of M. Ananthasayanam Ayyangar, Id., pp. 295–296; speech of Tajamul Hussain, Id., p. 303; speech of Jaipal Singh, Id., p. 306.
43   Id., p. 301.
44   Id., p. 309.
45   See Rohan J. Alva, *Liberty After Freedom: A History of Article 21, Due Process and the Constitution of India* (Gurugram: HarperCollins Publishers, 2022), Chapter 2.
46   CAD, vol. XI, p. 974.
47   B. Shiva Rao, *Framing*, vol. III, p. 8.
     '15. (1) There shall be liberty for the exercise of the following rights subject to public order and morality namely: the right of every citizen to freedom of speech and expression.'
48   Ibid.
49   B. Shiva Rao, *Framing*, vol. I, p. 59.
50   B. Shiva Rao, *Framing*, vol. III, p. 316.
51   Id., pp. 317–319.
52   Id., p. 329.
53   Ibid.
     '15(1) Subject to public, order and morality, every citizen shall have the right:
     to freedom of speech and expression;

[Provided that the publication or utterances of seditious, slanderous, libellous or defamatory matter shall be actionable and punishable in accordance with law:].' (Internal star footnote omitted.)

54 Id., p. 328. The minutes of the meeting only record: '*Clause 15*: It was decided that sub-clause (1) of this clause should be revised in the form shown in Appendix B to these minutes.' (Italics in the original.)

55 Id., pp. 329, 331, Meeting of the Drafting Committee (1 November 1947).

56 Id., p. 331. See Appendix A.
'Clause 15(3): Nothing in clause (a) of sub-section (1) shall prevent the State from making any law declaring the publication or utterances of seditious, slanderous, libellous or defamatory matters to be actionable or punishable.'

57 See Id., p. 329. '*Clause 15*: It was decided that sub-clause (1) of this clause should be revised in the form shown in Appendix B to these minutes.' (Italics in the original.)

58 Id., pp. 339–340, Meeting of the Drafting Committee (4 November 1947).
'(1) The committee accepted the suggestion of Shri Alladi Krishnaswami Ayyar that sub-clause (3) of clause 15 of the Draft Constitution should be so worded that the operation of existing law relating to libel, slander, defamation or sedition may not be affected by paragraph (a) of sub-clause (1) of that clause. The committee was of opinion that sub-clauses (4) and (5) of that clause should be also revised to save the operation of existing laws. It was accordingly decided that clause 15 should be revised as shown in Appendix A to these minutes.'

59 Id., pp. 509–675.

60 B. Shiva Rao, *The Framing of India's Constitution: Select Documents*, vol. IV (New Delhi: Indian Institute of Public Administration, 1968), pp. 415–416 [hereinafter B. Shiva Rao, *Framing*, vol. IV].

61 CAD, vol. VII, pp. 31–44.

62 See B. Shiva Rao, *Framing*, vol. III, p. 522; B. Shiva Rao, *Framing*, vol. IV, p. 39.

63 CAD, vol. V, p. 301. (Emphasis added.)

64 Ibid.

65 P.K. Tripathi, 'Perspectives on the American Constitutional Influence on the Constitution of India' in *Constitutionalism in Asia: Asian Views of the American Influence*, ed. Lawrence W. Beer (California: University of California, 1979), p. 72 [hereinafter Tripathi, 'Perspectives'].

66 CAD, vol. VII, pp. 31–44.

67 Id., p. 40.
68 Ibid.
69 Ibid.
70 Ibid.
71 Ibid.
72 Ibid.
73 Setalvad, *Common Law*, p. 205.
74 CAD, vol. VII, p. 40.
75 Id., pp. 40–41. For an assessment of the development of the police powers doctrine in India, see Arvind Datar and Shivprasad Swaminathan, 'Police Powers and the Constitution of India: The Inconspicuous Ascent of an Incongruous American Implant,' *Emory International Law Review*, vol. 28 (2014): p. 63.
76 CAD, vol. VIII, pp. 40–41.
77 Id., p. 41. Dr Ambedkar took the instance of the decision of the US Supreme Court in *Gitlow v. New York*, 268 US 652 (1925).
78 Tripathi, 'Perspectives,' pp. 72–74.
79 CAD, vol. VII, pp. 40–41.
80 Id., p. 41.
81 Ibid.
82 Id., p. 245.
83 Id., p. 256.
84 Ibid.
85 Id., p. 262.
86 Id., p. 331.
87 Id., p. 305. ('Sir, coming to the Fundamental Rights, I find that what has been given with one hand has been taken away by the other. Fundamental Rights should be such that they should not be liable to reservations and to changes by Acts of legislature. It is essential that at least some of the civil liberties of the citizen should be preserved by the Constitution and it should not be easy for the legislature to take them away. Instead of this, we find the provision relating to these Rights full of provisos and exceptions. This means that what has been given today could easily be changed tomorrow by an Act of the legislature.')
88 Id., p. 336. ('Criticism 5: The criticism regarding the fundamental rights was that they are hedged in by so many restrictions that no value can be attached to the rights guaranteed under the constitution. The great problem in providing for and guaranteeing fundamental rights in any constitution is where to draw the line between personal liberty and social control. True liberty can flourish only in a well ordered state

and when the foundations of the state are not imperilled. The Supreme Court of the U.S.A. in the course of its long history has read a number of restrictions and limitations based upon the above principle into the rights expressed in wide and general terms. The Draft Constitution, instead of leaving it to the courts to read the necessary limitations and exceptions, seeks to express in a compendious form the limitations and exceptions recognised in any well-ordered state. It cannot be denied that there is a danger in leaving the courts, by judicial legislations to speak, to read the necessary limitations, according to idiosyncrasies and prejudices it may be of individual judges.')

89 Id., p. 394.
90 Id., p. 398.
91 Id., p. 712.
92 Id., p. 720. Kamath's speech did not focus on sedition in particular but on the larger question of the freedom of speech being bound down by a litany of restrictions, which the Constituent Assembly had not approved when it deliberated on this particular right on 30 April 1947.
93 Ibid.
94 Id., p. 730.
95 See *Emperor v. Hari Moreshwar Joshi*, (1931) vol. LVI 61 ILR (Bombay).
96 CAD, vol. VII, p. 731.
97 Ibid.
98 Ibid.
99 Ibid.
100 Ibid.
101 Id., pp. 731–732.
102 Id., p. 732.
103 Id., pp. 737–738.
104 Id., p. 751.
105 Ibid.
106 Id., pp. 750–751.
107 Id., p. 762.
108 Id., p. 773.
109 Id., p. 779.
110 Id., p. 786.

5: Thunder and Lightning

1 CAD, vol. VII, pp. 755–756.

2   *Romesh Thappar v. State of Madras*, (1950) SCR 594 [hereinafter *Thappar*].
3   *Brij Bhushan v. The State of Delhi*, (1950) SCR 605 [hereinafter *Bhushan*].
4   The correct spelling of the name is Romesh Thapar. But since the decision of the Supreme Court used the spelling 'Romesh Thappar' instead, I will follow it in the book for the sake of continuity. Whenever the name is in italics, it is a reference to the judgment of the Supreme Court.
5   Singh, *Sixteen*, pp. 12–19.
6   Granville Austin, *Working a Democratic Constitution: The Indian Experience* (New Delhi: Oxford University Press, 1999), p. 40 [hereinafter Austin, *Democratic Constitution*]; Singh, *Sixteen*, pp. 12–15.
7   *Thappar*, pp. 595–596.
8   Id., pp. 596–597.
9   Nirmalendu Baksh Rakshit, 'Right to Constitutional Remedy: Significance of Article 32,' *Economic and Political Weekly* (21 August–3 September, 1999), vol. 34: p. 2379.
10 CAD, vol. VII, p. 953.
11 *Thappar*, p. 597.
12 Ibid.
13 Id., p. 599.
14 Id., pp. 600–601.
15 *Thappar*, pp. 602–603.
16 Article 372(1): Notwithstanding the repeal by this Constitution of the enactments referred to in Article 395 but subject to the other provisions of this Constitution, all the laws in force in the territory of India immediately before the commencement of this Constitution shall continue in force therein until altered or repealed or amended by a competent Legislature or other competent authority.
17 Article 366(10): 'existing law' means any law, Ordinance, order, bye-law, rule or regulation passed or made before the commencement of this Constitution by any Legislature, authority or person having power to make such a law, Ordinance, order, bye-law, rule or regulation.
18 Article 395: The Indian Independence Act, 1947 and the Government of India Act, 1935, together with all enactments amending or supplementing the latter Act, but not including the Abolition of Privy Council Jurisdiction Act, 1949 are hereby repealed.
19 Article 13(1): All laws in force in the territory of India immediately before the commencement of this Constitution, in so far as they are

inconsistent with the provisions of this Part, shall, to the extent of inconsistency, be void.
20 Thappar, p. 602. (Emphasis added.)
21 Ibid.
22 Id., pp. 599–603.
23 Id., p. 602. (Emphasis added.)
24 Id., p. 603.
25 Ibid.
26 Singh, *Sixteen*, p. 23 (quoting from a letter from Sardar Patel to Jawaharlal Nehru, 3 July 1950, Durga Das, ed., *Sardar Patel's Correspondence*, vol. X (Ahmedabad: Navjivan Publishing House, 1974), p. 358).
27 *Bhushan*, p. 607.
28 Id., pp. 607–608.
29 The decisions in *Romesh Thappar* and *Brij Bhushan* are slightly tricky to read. The majority authored a detailed judgment in the *Thappar* case and then applied it to the *Bhushan* case. On the other hand, Justice Fazl Ali authored a detailed dissent in the *Bhushan* case and then applied it to the *Thappar* case. For this reason, the judgments in the *Thappar* and *Bhushan* cases are always read together although they involved entirely different laws.
30 *Bhushan*, pp. 609–612.
31 Id., pp. 614–617.
32 Id., pp. 614–616.
33 Id., p. 616.
34 In 1978, the right to property was deleted by the Forty-Fourth Amendment to the Constitution. By the same constitutional amendment, a new Article 300A was introduced which was a watered-down version of the right to property.
35 See CAD, vol. VII, p. 783.
36 *Thappar*, p. 601.
37 *Indukumar Shankerlal Saherwalla v. State*, AIR 1950 Guj 9 (Gujarat High Court).
38 *Amar Nath Bali v. The State*, (1950) SCC OnLine P&H 74.
39 The Editors, Encyclopaedia Britannica, *Tara Singh*, 18 November 2020 (available at https://www.britannica.com/biography/Tara-Singh).
40 *Tara Singh v. The State*, AIR 1951 P&H 27.
41 Id., para. 13.
42 Ibid.

43 *Bharati Press v. CS Government of Bihar*, vol. XXX ILR (Patna) 31 (Full Bench) [hereinafter *Bharati Press*]. The case was heard by Justices Sarjoo Prasad, Ramaswami and Shearer. This decision is more popularly known as the *Shailabala* case.
44 Id., pp. 35–42.
45 Id., p. 41.
46 Id., pp. 49–59.
47 Id., p. 54.
48 Id., pp. 54–55.
49 Id., p. 59.
50 Id., p. 56.
51 Id., pp. 54–57.
52 Id., p. 58.
53 Ibid.

6: The Prince Is Dead, Long Live the King

1 1962 Supp (2) SCR 769 [hereinafter *Kedar Nath Singh*]. The five judges were Chief Justice B.P. Sinha, Justices S.K. Das, A.K. Sarkar, N. Rajagopala Ayyangar and J.R. Mudholkar.
2 *Kedar Nath Singh*, pp. 775–780.
3 Parliamentary Debates (Part-II Proceedings Other than Questions and Answers) Official Report, Third Session of Parliament, Saturday, 12 May 1951, column 8584 (available at https://eparlib.nic.in/bitstream/123456789/760585/1/ppd_12-05-1951.pdf) [hereinafter PD, 12 May 1951].
4 Parliamentary Debates (Part-II Proceedings Other than Questions and Answers) Official Report, Third Session of Parliament, Monday, 16 May 1951 (available at https://eparlib.nic.in/bitstream/123456789/760708/1/ppd_16-05-1951.pdf) [hereinafter PD, 16 May 1951].
5 Parliamentary Debates (Part-II Proceedings Other than Questions and Answers) Official Report, Third Session of Parliament, Friday, 18 May 1951, columns 9088–9089 (available at https://eparlib.nic.in/bitstream/123456789/760696/1/ppd_18-05-1951.pdf) [hereinafter PD, 18 May 1951].
6 The Constitution (First Amendment) Bill, 1951, Report of the Select Committee, 25 May 1951 (available at https://eparlib.nic.

in/bitstream/123456789/58338/1/jcb_1951_constitution_1st_amendment_bill.pdf) [hereinafter Select Committee Report].
7   Parliamentary Debates (Part-II Proceedings Other than Questions and Answers) Official Report, Third Session of Parliament, Friday, 25 May 1951, columns 9307–9308 (https://eparlib.nic.in/bitstream/123456789/760702/1/ppd_25-05-1951.pdf) [hereinafter PD, 25 May 1951].
8   The Constitution (First Amendment Act), 1951 published in the The Gazette of India, Extraordinary, Part II–Section 1, (New Delhi: 18 June 1951), pp. 203–206.
9   See the Constitution (First Amendment) Bill, 1951 (as amended by the Select Committee) annexed to the Select Committee Report, p. 19, line numbers 10–22.
10 Rohinton F. Nariman, *Discordant Notes: The Voice of Dissent in the Court of Last Resort*, vol. 1 (Gurugram: Penguin Random House India, 2021), pp. 241–243.
11 PD, 16 May 1951, columns 8827–8828.
12 PD, 18 May 1951, column 9075.
13 Id., columns 9007–9010. Speech of Dr B.R. Ambedkar.
14 Select Committee Report, pp. 1, 19.
15 PD, 18 May 1951, columns 9014–9015.
16 Id., column 9015.
17 Id., columns 9074–9075.
18 The Constitution (First Amendment) Bill, 1951 (as amended by the Select Committee) annexed to the Select Committee Report, p. 20, line numbers 1–9. The Explanation to this provision read: 'In this sub-section, the expression "law in force" has the same meaning as in clause (1) of article 13 of the Constitution.'
19 Singh, *Sixteen*, p. 25.
20 Austin, *Democratic Constitution*, pp. 78–80.
21 *Sir Kameshwar Singh v. The State of Bihar*, (1951) SCC OnLine Pat 56.
22 PD, 16 May 1951, column 8830.
23 The Constitution (First Amendment) Bill, 1951 (as amended by the Select Committee) annexed to the Select Committee Report, p. 20, line numbers 10–32.
24 Austin, *Democratic Constitution*, p. 85.
25 The Constitution (First Amendment) Bill, 1951 (as amended by the Select Committee) annexed to the Select Committee Report, p. 20, line numbers 33–43.
26 Id., p. 22, line numbers 10–11.

27 Id., p. 22, line numbers 12–33.
28 Article 13(1): All laws in force in the territory of India immediately before the commencement of this Constitution, in so far as they are inconsistent with the provisions of this Part, shall, to the extent of such inconsistency, be void.
Article 13(2): The State shall not make any law which takes away or abridges the rights conferred by this Part and any law made in contravention of this clause shall, to the extent of the contravention, be void.
29 *S.T. Sadiq v. State of Kerala*, (2015) 4 SCC 400.
30 *State of Bihar v. Kameshwar Singh*, (1952) SCR 889. See pp. 894–895.
31 In *I.R. Coelho v. State of Tamil Nadu*, (2007) 2 SCC 1, the Supreme Court watered down the extent to which the Ninth Schedule could prevent judicial review of laws. A nine-judge bench of the Supreme Court declared that any law added to the Ninth Schedule after 24 April 1973 would not receive the protection of Article 31B. The date of 24 April 1973 was chosen because that was the day on which the Supreme Court's decision in the *Kesavananda Bharati* case was announced—a decision which declared that Parliament could not use the powers of constitutional amendment to disturb the basic structure of the Constitution.
32 PD, 16 May 1951, column 8816.
33 Ibid.
34 Id., column 8820.
35 Id., column 8823.
36 Ibid.
37 Ibid.
38 PD, 16 May 1951, column 8828.
39 Id., columns 8828–8829.
40 PD, 16 May 1951, columns 8841–8842.
41 Id., columns 8873–8875.
42 Id., column 8875.
43 Id., columns 8868–8874.
44 Id., column 8871.
45 PD, 18 May 1951, column 9021.
46 Id., columns 9021–9022.
47 Id., columns 9021–9022.
48 Id., columns 9021–9022.
49 Id., column 9023.
50 Id., column 9028.

51 Ibid.
52 *Kesavananda Bharati v. State of Kerala*, (1973) 4 SCC 225.
53 PD, 18 May 1951, column 9021.
54 Id., column 9046.
55 Id., column 9056.
56 Id., column 9080.
57 Select Committee Report, p. 4.
58 Id., p. 17.
59 Parliamentary Debates (Part-II Proceedings Other than Questions and Answers), Saturday, 1 May 1951, column 9885 (available at https://eparlib.nic.in/bitstream/123456789/760814/1/ppd_01-06-1951.pdf).
60 *I.C. Golak Nath v. State of Punjab*, (1967) 2 SCR 762 [hereinafter *Golak Nath*].
61 Justice Hidayatullah has the rare distinction of being part of all three branches of the State as well as being the head of all three. He was appointed to the Supreme Court in 1958 and retired in 1970, thus serving in the three formative decades of the Supreme Court. He served as the Chief Justice of India from 25 February 1968 till 16 December 1970. During his tenure as the Chief Justice of India, the President of India, Zakir Husain, passed away on 3 May 1969. Since the Vice-President, V.V. Giri, decided to contest the presidential elections, he resigned from office. As a result, Chief Justice Hidayatullah was appointed acting President of India from 20 July 1969 till 23 August 1969. For this one-month period, he was the head of both the Executive as well as the Judiciary. From 31 August 1979 till 30 August 1984, Hidayatullah was the Vice–President of India and, as the ex-officio Chairman of the Rajya Sabha, he was also the head of the legislative branch of the State. See Profile of M. Hidayatullah, Rajya Sabha, Parliament of India (available at https://rajyasabha.nic.in/rsnew/picture_gallery/96mhidaya.asp).
62 *Golak Nath*, p. 881. (Emphasis added.)
63 *Kedar Nath Singh*, pp. 802–811.
64 PD, 18 May 1951, column 9080. (Emphasis added.)
65 Parliamentary Debates (Part-II Proceedings other than Questions and Answers) Official Report, Third Session of Parliament, Tuesday, 29 May 1951, columns 9620–9621 (available at https://eparlib.nic.in/bitstream/123456789/760712/1/ppd_29-05-1951.pdf). (Emphasis added) [hereinafter PD, 29 May, 1951].
66 Ibid. (Emphasis added.)

67 Ram Nandan v. State, (1958) SCC OnLine All 117 [hereinafter Ram Nandan].
68 Id., paras. 132, 137.
69 PD, 29 May 1951, columns 9619–9621.

7: The Decisive Distinction

1   CAD, vol. III, pp. 437–444. See Clause 8(a). Id., p 441.
    '8. There shall be liberty for the exercise of the following rights subject to public order and morality or to the existence of grave emergency declared to be such by the Government of the Union or the unit concerned whereby the security of the Union or the unit, as the case may be, is threatened:
    The right of every citizen to freedom of speech and expression:
    Provision may be made by law to make the publication or utterance of seditious, obscene, blasphemous, slanderous, or defamatory matter actionable or punishable.'
2   Id., p. 457.
3   CAD, vol. I, p. 468. Also see B. Shiva Rao, Framing, vol. II, p. 301.
4   B. Shiva Rao, Framing, vol. III, p. 8.
5   Article 40(6) 1, Constitution of Ireland: 'The State guarantees liberty for the exercise of the following rights, subject to public order and morality:
    i) The right of the citizens to express freely their convictions and opinions.
    The education of public opinion being, however, a matter of such grave import to the common good, the State shall endeavour to ensure that organs of public opinion, such as the radio, the press, the cinema, while preserving their rightful liberty of expression, including criticism of Government policy, shall not be used to undermine public order or morality or the authority of the State.
    The publication or utterance of seditious or indecent matter is an offence which shall be punishable in accordance with law.'
6   B. Shiva Rao, Framing, vol. III, p. 522.
7   CAD, vol. VII, p. 731.
8   Ibid.
9   Id., p. 712.
10 Id., p. 744.
11 Id., p. 788.

12 Id., p. 783.
13 *Ram Nandan*, para. 132.
14 B. Shiva Rao, *Framing*, vol. III, p. 522.
15 *The Superintendent, Central Prison Fategarh v. Ram Manohar Lohia*, (1960) 2 SCR 821[hereinafter *Lohia* (I)].
16 Id., p. 831.
17 Id., p. 833.
18 Ibid.
19 Ibid.
20 Id., pp. 833–834.
21 Id., p. 839.
22 *Ram Manohar Lohia v. State of Bihar*, (1966) 1 SCR 709. See p. 746. (Emphasis added.)
23 *Kedar Nath Singh*, pp. 803, 810–811.
24 See, generally, Singh, *Sedition*, p. 201.

8: Reinvention

1 *Kedar Nath Singh*, pp. 796–797.
2 Id., p. 797.
3 Id., p. 809.
4 Ibid. (Emphasis added.)
5 Ibid.
6 Article 246:
(1) Notwithstanding anything in clauses (2) and (3), Parliament has exclusive power to make laws with respect to any of the matters enumerated in List 1 in the Seventh Schedule (in this Constitution referred to as the 'Union List').
(2) Notwithstanding anything in clause (3), Parliament and subject to clause (1), the Legislature of any State also, have power to make laws with respect to any of the matters enumerated in List III in the Seventh Schedule (in this Constitution referred to as the 'Concurrent List').
(3) Subject to clauses (1) and (2), the Legislature of any State has exclusive power to make laws for such State or any part thereof with respect to any of the matters enumerated in List II in the Seventh Schedule (in this Constitution referred to as the 'State List').
(4) Parliament has power to make laws with respect to any matter for any part of the territory of India not included in a State notwithstanding that such matter is a matter enumerated in the State List.

7 Article 141: The law declared by the Supreme Court shall be binding on all courts within the territories of India.
8 *S.T. Sadiq v. State of Kerala*, (2015) 4 SCC 400; in re, *Punjab Termination of Agreement Act*, (2017) 1 SCC 121.
9 *Ram Jawaya Kapur v. State of Punjab*, (1955) 2 SCR 225. (Emphasis added.)
10 The preservation of the separation of powers is also a Directive Principle of State Policy.
   Article 38: The State shall take steps to separate the judiciary from the executive in the public services of the State.
11 *Central Bureau of Investigation v. Ramesh Gelli*, (2016) 3 SCC 788.
12 *Tarulata Shyam v. Commissioner of Income Tax, West Bengal*, (1977) 3 SCC 305, para. 34 ('There is no scope for importing into the statute words which are not there. Such importation would be, not to construe, but to amend the statute. Even if there be a casus omissus, the defect can be remedied only by legislation and not by judicial interpretation.')
13 *Eera v. State (NCT of Delhi)*, (2017) 15 SCC 133, para. 147 (per R.F. Nariman, J., concurring).
14 *S.S. Bola v. B.D. Sardana*, (1997) 8 SCC 522, paras. 108, 153; *Nikesh Tarachand Shah v. Union of India*, (2018) 11 SCC 1.
15 *Romesh Thappar*, p. 603.
16 Ibid.
17 Ibid.
18 *Behram Khursheed Pesikaka v. The State of Bombay*, (1955) 1 SCR 613, pp. 655–656. (Emphasis added.) The Constitution Bench comprised of five justices, and Chief Justice Mahajan spoke for a majority of four.
19 *Sakal Papers v. Union of India*, (1962) 3 SCR 842 [hereinafter *Sakal Papers*].
20 Id., p. 851.
21 Id., pp. 851–856.
22 Id., pp. 854–868.
23 Id., pp. 862–863.
24 Id., pp. 864–868.
25 Id., p. 866. (Emphasis added.)
26 Ibid. (Emphasis added.)
27 Id., pp. 867–868.
28 *Lohia* (I), p. 821. Section 3, UP Special Powers Act, 1932: Whoever, by word, either spoken or written, or by signs or by visible representations, or otherwise, instigates, expressly or by implication, any person or class of persons not to pay or to defer payment of any liability, and whoever

does any act, with intent or knowing it to be likely that any words, signs or visible representations containing such instigation shall thereby be communicated directly or indirectly to any person or class of persons, in any manner whatsoever, shall be punishable with imprisonment which may extend to six months, or with fine, extending to Rs 250, or with both.

29 Id., pp. 827–828
30 Id., p. 836
31 Id., pp. 836–837.
32 Id., p. 840.
33 Id., p. 837.
34 Id., p. 840.
35 Id., p. 839.
36 Id., p. 840.
37 Ibid.
38 Ibid.
39 Ibid.
40 *Shreya Singhal v. Union of India*, (2015) 2 SCC 1 [hereinafter *Shreya Singhal*].
41 Id., para. 51.
42 Ibid.
43 Id., para. 52.
44 *Kedar Nath Singh*, pp. 807–808.
45 Id., pp. 809–811.
46 *Ram Nandan*, para. 119.
47 Ibid.
48 *National Insurance Company v. Pranay Sethi*, (2017) 16 SCC 680.
49 See *Kaushal Kishore v. State of UP*, (2023) SCC OnLine SC 6, para. 38 [hereinafter *Kaushal Kishore*].
50 CAD, vol. III, p. 525. (Emphasis added.)
51 *State of Madras v. V.G. Row*, (1952) SCR 597.
52 Section 66-A: *Punishment for sending offensive messages through communication service, etc.*—Any person who sends, by means of a computer resource or a communication device—
    (*a*) any information that is grossly offensive or has menacing character; or
    (*b*) any information which he knows to be false, but for the purpose of causing annoyance, inconvenience, danger, obstruction, insult, injury, criminal intimidation, enmity, hatred or ill will, persistently by making use of such computer resource or a communication device; or

(c) any electronic mail or electronic mail message for the purpose of causing annoyance or inconvenience or to deceive or to mislead the addressee or recipient about the origin of such messages, shall be punishable with imprisonment for a term which may extend to three years and with fine.

Explanation: For the purposes of this section, terms 'electronic mail' and 'electronic mail message' means a message or information created or transmitted or received on a computer, computer system, computer resource or communication device including attachments in text, image, audio, video and any other electronic record, which may be transmitted with the message.

53 *Shreya Singhal*, para. 25 (citing *Supt., Central Prison v. Ram Manohar Lohia*, (1960) 2 SCR 821. See pp. 834–836).
54 Id., para. 38. (Emphasis added.)
55 Ibid. (Emphasis added.)
56 Id., para. 47.
57 Singh, *Sedition*, pp. 193–196.
58 *Ram Nandan*, paras. 27, 40, 47–50, 70, 78, 83, 137.
59 Id., para. 83.

9: Triumph of Democracy

1 See Singh, *Sedition*, p. 70.
2 Austin, *The Indian Constitution*, p. 58.
3 Stephen, *History*, vol. II, p. 299.
4 Ibid.
5 Ibid. (Emphasis added.)
6 Id., pp. 299–300. (Emphasis added.)
7 Id., p. 300. (Emphasis added.)
8 CAD, vol. VII, p. 731.
9 Ibid. (Emphasis added.)
10 CAD, vol. VII, p. 777.
11 Ibid. (Emphasis added.)
12 Ibid.
13 See CAD, vol. I, p. 4.
14 CAD, vol. VII, p. 41. Speech of 4 November 1948 of Dr B.R. Ambedkar introducing the Draft Constitution.
15 *Shreya Singhal*, paras. 18–20.

16 An Act in Addition to the Act, entitled 'An Act for the Punishment of Certain Crimes Against the United States' (available at https://avalon.law.yale.edu/18th_century/sedact.asp.).
'SEC. 2. *And be it farther enacted*, that if any person shall write, print, utter or publish, or shall cause or procure to be written, printed, uttered or published, or shall knowingly and willingly assist or aid in writing, printing, uttering or publishing any false, scandalous and malicious writing or writings against the government of the United States, or either house of the Congress of the United States, or the President of the United States, with intent to defame the said government, or either house of the said Congress, or the said President, or to bring them, or either of them, into contempt or disrepute; or to excite against them, or either or any of them, the hatred of the good people of the United States, or to stir up sedition within the United States, or to excite any unlawful combinations therein, for opposing or resisting any law of the United States, or any act of the President of the United States, done in pursuance of any such law, or of the powers in him vested by the Constitution of the United States, or to resist, oppose, or defeat any such law or act, or to aid, encourage or abet any hostile designs of any foreign nation against United States, their people or government, then such person, being thereof convicted before any court of the United States having jurisdiction thereof, shall be punished by a fine not exceeding two thousand dollars, and by imprisonment not exceeding two years.'

17 Britannica, The Editors of Encyclopedia, 'Virginia and Kentucky Resolutions,' *Encyclopedia Britannica*, 11 February 2020 (available at https://www.britannica.com/event/Virginia-and-Kentucky-Resolutions).

18 Virginia Resolution, 24 December 1798 (available at https://avalon.law.yale.edu/18th_century/virres.asp). (Emphasis added.)

19 *New York Times v. L.B. Sullivan*, 376 US 254 (1964) (SCC OnLine version) [hereinafter *New York Times*].

20 Id., para. 23. (Emphasis added.)

21 Id., para. 24 (Quoting from 4 Elliot Debates on the Federal Constitution (1876), p. 571).

22 Id., para. 27.

23 Id., para. 28. (Emphasis added.)

24 Id., para. 29.

25 Singh, *Sedition*, p. 99.

26 *New York Times*, para. 29.

27 Ibid.

28 Ibid. (Emphasis added.)
29 Christina L. Boyd, 'Sedition Act of 1918,' The First Amendment Encyclopedia (available at https://www.mtsu.edu/first-amendment/article/1239/sedition-act-of-1918).
30 See Coroners and Justice Act 2009 (available at https://www.legislation.gov.uk/ukpga/2009/25/pdfs/ukpga_20090025_en.pdf).
31 Section 73: Abolition of common law libel offences etc.
    The following offences under the common law of England and Wales and the common law of Northern Ireland are abolished—
    (a) the offences of sedition and seditious libel;
    (b) the offence of defamatory libel;
    (c) the offence of obscene libel.
32 Clare Feikert-Ahalt, 'Sedition in England: The Abolition of a Law from a Bygone Era,' Library of Congress, 2 October 2012 (available at https://blogs.loc.gov/law/2012/10/sedition-in-england-the-abolition-of-a-law-from-a-bygone-era/).
33 Ibid.
34 Hannah Arendt, *The Promise of Politics*, edited with an introduction by Jerome Kohn (New York: Schocken Books, 2005), pp. 129–130.
35 Id., p. 129.
36 Ernst Freund, 'The Debs Case and Freedom of Speech,' *The New Republic* (3 May 1919), reprinted in Harry Kalven Jr., 'Ernst Freund and the First Amendment Tradition—Professor Ernst Freund and Debs v. United States': *University of Chicago of Law Review*, vol. 40 (1973): p. 239 [hereinafter Freund, '*Debs* case'].
37 Id., p. 240. (Emphasis added.)
38 Id., p. 242. (Emphasis added.)
39 Alexander M. Bickel, *The Morality of Consent* (Delhi: Universal Law Publishing House), Chapter 3, 'Domesticated Civil Disobedience: The First Amendment, from *Sullivan* to the Pentagon Papers' [hereinafter Bickel, *Morality*].
40 Id., p. 62.
41 Ibid.
42 Id., p. 63.
43 Ibid.
44 Alexander Meiklejohn, 'The First Amendment Is an Absolute,' *Supreme Court Review*: p. 245 (1961) [hereinafter Meiklejohn, 'Absolute'].
45 Id., pp. 253–254.
46 Id., p. 255.
47 Id., pp. 252–255.

48 Id., p. 254.
49 Id., p. 255.
50 Ibid.
51 Id., p. 256.
52 Sunstein, *Democracy*, Chapter 5: 'Political Speech and the Two-Tier First Amendment.'
53 Id., p. xiv.
54 *Thappar*, p. 602
55 Ibid. (Emphasis added.)
56 *Ram Nandan*, paras. 88, 106, 107, 137.
57 *Lohia* (I), p. 837.
58 *Sakal Papers*, p. 866.
59 Ibid. (Emphasis added.)
60 Ibid.
61 (2021) 1 SCC 1.
62 Id., para. 78. (Emphasis added.)
63 Ibid. (Emphasis added.)
64 Seervai, *Constitutional Law*, p. 711.
65 Sunstein, *Democracy*, p. 121.
66 Id., p. 130. (Italics in the original.)
67 Id., p. 127.
68 Id., p. 123.
69 Id., p. 130.
70 Id., pp. 124–129.
71 Id., p. 132.
72 Id., p. 133.
73 Ibid.
74 Id., p. 135.
75 Id., p. 134 (internal citation omitted). (Emphasis added.)
76 Id., p. 136.
77 Id., pp. 136–137.
78 *Shreya Singhal*, para. 13.
79 Ibid. ('This leads us to a discussion of what is the content of the expression "freedom of speech and expression". There are three concepts which are fundamental in understanding the reach of this most basic of human rights. The first is discussion, the second is advocacy, and the third is incitement. Mere discussion or even advocacy of a particular cause howsoever unpopular is at the heart of Article 19(1)(a). It is only when such discussion or advocacy reaches the level of incitement that Article 19(2) kicks in. It is at this stage

that a law may be made curtailing the speech or expression that leads inexorably to or tends to cause public disorder or tends to cause or tends to affect the sovereignty and integrity of India, the security of the State, friendly relations with foreign States, etc. Why it is important to have these three concepts in mind is because most of the arguments of both petitioners and respondents tended to veer around the expression "public order."')

10: Putting the Soul in a Lifeless Article

1 PD, 17 May 1951, column 8888.
2 CAD, vol. VII, pp. 735–736.
3 Id., p. 739.
4 Ibid.
5 Id., pp. 739–740.
6 Id., p. 740.
7 Id., p. 787. Generally, see, Tripathi, 'Perspectives,' pp. 86–88.
8 Id., pp. 786–787.
9 CAD, vol. X, p. 397.
10 Ibid.
11 Ibid.
12 Ibid.
13 Id., p. 403.
14 Tripathi, 'Perspectives,' p. 74.
15 Ibid.
16 PD, 16 May 1951, columns 8879–8880.
17 Id., column 8880.
18 PD, 17 May 1951, column 8888. ('The proposed clause 19(2) is too narrow in one sense and too wide in another. This provision needs to be amended. The word "reasonable" should be put before "restrictions" and again in the later portion also, dealing with the making of laws relating to contempt of court, defamation or incitement to an offence. Reasonable restrictions have to be put on the exercise of the right to make the laws. Restrictions are put on individual rights of freedom of speech and expression in the interest of security of the State. There should be a balance of the two. Unless there is this balance it will be difficult to protect such fundamental rights as have been given to us by the Constitution.')
19 PD, 18 May 1951, column 9021.

20　Report of the Cabinet Committee: Amendment of the Constitution (9 April 1951), p. 3 (available at the National Archives, New Delhi).
21　The Constitution (First Amendment) Bill (Report of the Select Committee), p. 1. ('*Clause 3*. Our discussions centred mainly round the proposed clause (2) of article 19. After considering several alternative forms, we have come to the conclusion that the only substantial change required in the draft clause is the insertion of the word "reasonable" before the word "restrictions." This will bring clause (2) into line with clauses (3) to (6), all of which refer to laws imposing "reasonable restrictions." Certain consequential drafting changes have been made in the clause.')
22　*Chintaman Rao v. State of MP*, (1950) SCR 759. Although the Supreme Court's judgment was in the context of Article 19(6) and announced prior to the enactment of the First Amendment to the Constitution, the constitutional principle that the judgment developed applies equally to Article 19(2).
23　CAD, vol. X, p. 395.
24　Id., pp. 395–396.
25　*Indian Express Newspapers v. Union of India*, (1985) 1 SCC 641, para. 82.
26　Ibid.
27　Charles Henry Alexandrowicz, *Constitutional Developments in India* (New Delhi: Oxford University Press, 1957), p. 46. (Emphasis added) [hereinafter Alexandrowicz, *Constitutional Developments*].
28　Tripathi, 'Perspectives,' p. 90. (Emphasis added.)
29　Id., pp. 87–88.
30　Id., p. 89.
31　Seervai, *Constitutional Law*, p. 706.
32　Id., p. 705.
33　Id., p. 706.
34　*Mohd Arif v. Registrar, Supreme Court of India*, (2014) 9 SCC 737, para. 28 ('The wheel has turned a full circle. Substantive due process is now to be applied to the fundamental right to life and liberty.') (per R.F. Nariman, J.)
35　PD, 29 May 1951, column 9623. (Emphasis added.)
36　Ibid.
37　1958 SCR 308 [hereinafter *Virendra*].
38　Id., p. 313.
39　Id., p. 327.
40　Id., pp. 327–328. (Emphasis added.)

41 Id., pp. 323–324.
42 *Shayara Bano v. Union of India*, (2017) 9 SCC 1 [hereinafter *Shayara Bano*].
43 Id., para. 101.
44 Id., para. 87.
45 Id., para. 104.
46 See *Swiss Ribbons (P) Ltd v. Union of India*, (2019) 4 SCC 17, para. 38 (discussing all the cases in which laws have been struck down on the ground of manifest arbitrariness).
47 *Express Newspapers (P) Ltd v. Union of India*, (1959) SCR 12.
48 Id., p. 128. (Emphasis added.)
49 Ibid. (Emphasis added.)
50 *Sakal Papers*, p. 866.
51 Id., p. 866.
52 Ibid.
53 *Bennett Coleman & Co. v. Union of India*, (1972) 2 SCC 788.
54 Id., para. 34. (Emphasis added.)
55 Id., para. 80.(Emphasis added.)
56 Id., paras. 43.
57 Id., para 82. ('In the present case, it cannot be said that the newsprint policy is a reasonable restriction within the ambit of Article 19(2). The newsprint policy abridges the fundamental rights of the petitioners in regard to freedom of speech and expression. The newspapers are not allowed their right of circulation. The newspapers are not allowed right of page growth. The common ownership units of newspapers cannot bring out new papers or new editions. The newspapers operating above 10 page level and newspapers operating below 10 page level have been treated equally for assessing the needs and requirements of newspapers with newspapers which are not their equal. Once the quota is fixed and direction to use the quota in accordance with the newsprint policy is made applicable the big newspapers are prevented any increase in page number. Both page numbers and circulation are relevant for calculating the basic quota and allowance for increases. In the garb of distribution of newsprint the Government has tended to control the growth and circulation of newspapers. Freedom of the press is both qualitative and quantitative. Freedom lies both in circulation and in content. The newsprint policy which permits newspapers to increase circulation by reducing the number of pages, page area and periodicity, prohibits them to increase the number of pages, page area

and periodicity by reducing circulation. These restrictions constrict the newspapers in adjusting their page number and circulation.')
58   *Indian Express Newspapers (Bombay) (P) Ltd v. Union of India*, (1985) 1 SCC 641.
59   Id., para. 84.
60   See, generally, Soli J. Sorabjee, 'Constitution, Courts, and Freedom of the Press and Media,' in *Supreme but not Infallible: Essays in Honour of the Supreme Court of India*, eds. B.N. Kirpal, Ashok H. Desai, Gopal Subramanium, Rajeev Dhavan and Raju Ramachandran (New Delhi: Oxford University Press, 5th Impression, 2008), p. 341.

11: The Value of Political Speech

1   *Cohen v. California*, 403 US 15 (1971), para. 20 (SCC OnLine version).
2   *Shailabala Devi*, p. 661. Also see, pp. 663–664.
3   *New York Times*, para. 23.
4   *Robert Watts v. United States*, 394 US 705, para. 4 (SCC OnLine version).
5   Bickel, *Morality*, p. 65.
6   See generally, Bhatia, *Offend*, pp. 96–97.
7   *Kedar Nath Singh*, p. 809.
8   Bhatia, *Offend*, p. 95.
9   *Amish Devgan v. Union of India*, (2021) 1 SCC 1.
10 Id., para. 79. (Emphasis in the original.)
11 See generally, Singh, *Sedition*, pp. 225–309; Sinha, *Repression*, pp. 189–212.
12 *Balwant Singh v. State of Punjab*, (1995) 3 SCC 214.
13 Id., para. 2 ('The prosecution case against the appellants is that in a crowded place in front of the Neelam Cinema, on 31-10-1984, the day Smt Indira Gandhi, the then Prime Minister of India was assassinated, after coming out from their respective offices after the duty hours, raised the following slogans:
    "1. Khalistan Zindabad.
    2. Raj Karega Khalsa, and
    3. Hinduan Nun Punjab Chon Kadh Ke Chhadange, Hun Mauka Aya Hai Raj Kayam Karan Da."
    The prosecution examined Constable Som Nath, PW 2 and ASI Labh Singh PW 3, in support of its case besides PW 1, who proved the order of sanction for prosecution.')
14 Id., para. 8. ('…A plain reading of the above section would show that its application would be attracted only when the accused brings or attempts to bring into hatred or contempt or excites or attempts to

excite disaffection towards the Government established by law in India, by words either written or spoken or visible signs or representations etc. Keeping in view the prosecution evidence that the slogans as noticed above were raised a couple of times only by the appellant and that neither the slogans evoked a response from any other person of the Sikh community or reaction from people of other communities, we find it difficult to hold that upon the raising of such casual slogans a couple of times without any other act whatsoever, the charge of sedition can be founded. It is not the prosecution case that the appellants were either leading a procession or were otherwise raising the slogans with the intention to incite people to create disorder or that the slogans in fact created any law and order problem. It does not appear to us that the police should have attached much significance to the casual slogans raised by two appellants, a couple of times and read too much into them. The prosecution has admitted that no disturbance, whatsoever, was caused by the raising of the slogans by the appellants and that in spite of the fact that the appellants raised the slogans a couple of times, the people, in general, were unaffected and carried on with their normal activities. The casual raising of the slogans, once or twice by two individuals alone cannot be said to be aimed at exciting or attempting to excite hatred or disaffection towards the Government as established by law in India. Section 124-A IPC, would in the facts and circumstances of the case have no application whatsoever and would not be attracted to the facts and circumstances of the case.')

15 Sunstein, *Democracy*, p. 123.
16 Id., p. 127.
17 Ibid.
18 Ibid.
19 Ibid.
20 Id., pp. 127–128.
21 Id., p. 129.
22 Ibid.
23 See *Kaushal Kishore*, para. 38.

12: Beware the Ides of March

1 *Kedar Nath Singh*, p. 805.
2 Tobias T. Gibson, 'Bad Tendency Test', *The First Amendment Encyclopedia* (available at https://www.mtsu.edu/first-amendment/article/893/bad-tendency-test).

3   See generally, Singh, *Sedition*, p. 101.
4   Zinn, *A People's History*, p. 365
5   Ibid.
6   Ibid.
7   *Schenck v. United States*, 249 US 47 (1919) (SCC OnLine version).
8   Id., paras. 1–2.
9   Id., paras. 5–6.
10 Id., para. 6.
11 Ibid.
12 Ibid.
13 Zinn, *A People's History*, p. 366.
14 Ibid.
15 *Frohwerk v. United States*, 249 US 204 (1919) (SCC OnLine version).
16 Id., para. 2.
17 Id., paras. 5–6.
18 Id., para. 7.
19 Id., para. 9.
20 Id., para. 7.
21 Ibid.
22 Ibid. ('It may be that all this might be said or written even in time of war in circumstances that would not make it a crime. We do not lose our right to condemn either measures or men because the country is at war. It does not appear that there was any special effort to reach men who were subject to the draft; and if the evidence should show that the defendant was a poor man, turning out copy for Gleeser, his employer, at less than a day laborer's pay, for Gleeser to use or reject as he saw fit, in a newspaper of small circulation, there would be a natural inclination to test every question of law to be found in the record very thoroughly before upholding the very severe penalty imposed. But we must take the case on the record as it is, and on that record it is impossible to say that it might not have been found that the circulation of the paper was in quarters where a little breath would be enough to kindle a flame and that the fact was known and relied upon by those who sent the paper out. Small compensation would not exonerate the defendant if it were found that he expected the result, even if pay were his chief desire. When we consider that we do not know how strong the Government's evidence may have been we find ourselves unable to say that the articles could not furnish a basis for a conviction upon the first count at least. We pass therefore to the other points that are raised.')

23 *Debs v. United States*, 249 US 211 (1919) (SCC OnLine version).
24 Zinn, *A People's History*, pp. 279–281.
25 *Debs*, paras. 2–5.
26 Id., para. 5.
27 Id., para. 9
28 Ibid.
29 Harry Kalven, Jr., 'Ernst Freund and the First Amendment Tradition—Professor Ernst Freund and Debs v. United States,' *University of Chicago of Law Review*, vol. 40 (1973): p. 237 [hereinafter Kalven, 'First Amendment Tradition'].
30 Id., pp. 237–238.
31 *Schenk*, para. 6. ('We admit that in many places and in ordinary times the defendants in saying all that was said in the circular would have been within their constitutional rights. But the character of every act depends upon the circumstances in which it is done.')
32 Kalven, 'First Amendment Tradition,' pp. 235–239.
33 Id., p. 238.
34 Freund, '*Debs* case,' pp. 239–242.
35 Id., p. 239.
36 Ibid.
37 Ibid.
38 Id., p. 241.
39 Ibid. (Emphasis added.)
40 Id., p. 242.
41 Douglas H. Ginsburg, 'Afterword' in Harry Kalven, Jr., 'Ernst Freund and the First Amendment Tradition—Professor Ernst Freund and Debs v. United States,' *University of Chicago of Law Review*, vol. 40 (1973): pp. 243–247 [hereinafter Ginsburg, 'Afterword'].
42 *Abrams v. United States*, 250 US 616 (1919) (SCC OnLine version).
43 Id., para. 3.
44 Id., para. 6.
45 Id., paras. 40–41.
46 Id., para. 42.
47 Id., para. 44.
48 Kalven, 'First Amendment,' p. 238.
49 *Abrams*, para. 48. (Emphasis added.)
50 Ibid. (Emphasis added.)
51 Id., para 43.
52 Ginsburg, 'Afterword,' pp. 245–246. The letter from Justice Holmes to Harold Laski read:

'Freund's objection to a jury "guessing at motive, tendency and possible effect" is an objection to pretty much the whole body of the law, which for thirty years I have made my brethren smile by insisting to be everywhere a matter of degree. In *Nash v. United States*, 229 U.S. 373 the same objections were urged to criminal prosecutions under the Sherman Act in view of the interpretation of the Statute by the *Standard Oil & Tobacco Cases*—but I answered p. 377 that "the law is full of instances where a man's fate depends on his estimating rightly, that is, as the jury subsequently estimates it, from matters of degree," and illustrated by murder and manslaughter—showing that a man might be hanged for consequences that he neither intended nor foresaw (apart from statute of course).'

53 Ginsburg, 'Afterword,' p. 247 (internal citation omitted).
54 *Whitney v. People of State of California*, 274 US 357 (1927) (SCC OnLine version).
55 Kalven, 'First Amendment Tradition,' p. 238.
56 *Whitney*, para. 39.
57 Id., para. 38.
58 Ibid.
59 Ibid.
60 Id., para. 39.
61 Id., para. 40.
62 Ibid.
63 Ibid.
64 Ibid.
65 Bickel, *Morality*, p. 66.
66 *Schneider v. State*, 308 US 147 (1939).
67 *Dennis v. United States*, 341 US 494 (1951).
68 Bickel, *Morality*, p. 67.
69 Id., p. 67.
70 Ibid. (Emphasis added.)
71 Generally, see, Singh, *Sedition*, p. 114.
72 Kalven, 'First Amendment Tradition,' p. 236.
73 *Brandenburg v. Ohio*, 395 US 444 (1969) (SCC OnLine version).
74 Id., para. 1.
75 Id., para. 5. (Emphasis added.)
76 Id., para. 7. ('Accordingly, we are here confronted with a statute which, by its own words and as applied, purports to punish mere advocacy and to forbid, on pain of criminal punishment, assembly with others merely to advocate the described type of action. Such a statute falls

within the condemnation of the First and Fourteenth Amendments. The contrary teaching of Whitney v. California, supra, cannot be supported, and that decision is therefore overruled.')
77 Id., para. 6. ('Measured by this test, Ohio's Criminal Syndicalism Act cannot be sustained. The Act punishes persons who "advocate or teach the duty, necessity, or propriety" of violence "as a means of accomplishing industrial or political reform"; or who publish or circulate or display any book or paper containing such advocacy; or who "justify" the commission of violent acts "with intent to exemplify, spread or advocate the propriety of the doctrines of criminal syndicalism"; or who "voluntarily assemble" with a group formed "to teach or advocate the doctrines of criminal syndicalism." Neither the indictment nor the trial judge's instructions to the jury in any way refined the statute's bald definition of the crime in terms of mere advocacy not distinguished from incitement to imminent lawless action.')
78 Id., para. 17.
79 Id., para. 26.
80 Ibid.
81 Id., para. 37.
82 Ibid.
83 Id., para. 35. (Emphasis added.)

13: Truly Free Political Speech

1 *Shailabala Devi*, p. 661.
2 Id., p. 662.
3 Id., p. 663.
4 Ibid.
5 Id., p. 664
6 Id., p. 663.
7 *Ramji Lal Modi v. State of UP*, (1957) SCR 860.
8 Id., p. 865.
9 Id., p. 867.
10 *Virendra*, p. 317.
11 *Lohia* (I), p. 834.
12 Id., p. 835.
13 Id., pp. 834–835.
14 Id., p. 835.

15 Id., p. 836. (Emphasis added.)
16 Ibid.
17 Id., pp. 836–837.
18 Bhatia, *Offend*, p. 60.
19 *Ram Nandan*, para. 76.
20 Id., paras. 71–76.
21 See generally, Lawrence Liang, 'Free Speech and Expression,' in *The Oxford Handbook of the Indian Constitution*, eds. Sujit Choudhry, Madhav Khosla and Pratap Bhanu Mehta (New Delhi: Oxford University Press, 2016), pp. 827–828 [hereinafter Liang, 'Free Speech'].
22 *Kameshwar Prasad v. The State of Bihar*, (1962) (Supp) 3 SCR 369.
23 Id., p. 371.
24 Id., p. 370.
25 Id., p. 379.
26 Id., p. 381.
27 Id., pp. 382–384.
28 *S. Rangarajan v. P. Jagjivan Ram*, (1989) 2 SCC 574.
29 Id., para. 35.
30 Ibid.
31 Id., para. 36. (Emphasis added.)
32 Id., para. 41.
33 Id., para. 46. The decision of the Calcutta High Court is reported as *Kamal Krishan Sircar v. Emperor*, AIR 1935 Cal 636.
34 Id., para. 45. (Emphasis added.)
35 Ibid. (Emphasis added.)
36 See generally, Liang, 'Free Speech,' p. 828.
37 See generally, Bhatia, *Offend*, pp. 65–66.
38 *Shreya Singhal*, para. 13.
39 Singh, *Sedition*, p. 218.
40 See generally, Bhatia, *Offend*, p. 69 (proposing that the decision of the Indian Supreme Court in *Lohia* (I) contains principles similar to the ones enunciated by the US Supreme Court in the *Brandenburg* decision).
41 *Anuradha Bhasin v. Union of India*, (2020) 3 SCC 637, para. 50.
42 Id., para. 52.
43 *Amish Devgan*, para. 103.
44 Id., para. 26.
45 Id., para. 102.
46 Ibid.
47 Id., para. 26.

48 Id., para. 103.
49 *Vinod Dua v. Union of India*, (2021) SCC OnLine SC 414.
50 Id., paras. 23–35.
51 Id., paras. 58–59.
52 Id., paras. 60–70.
53 Id., para. 70.
54 Id., para. 69.

14: Avoiding a Pyrrhic Victory

1   The Constitution (Sixteenth Amendment) Act, 1963 (available at https://legislative.gov.in/constitution-sixteenth-amendment-act-1963).
2   See Section 2 of the Constitution (Sixteenth Amendment) Act, 1963. '2. Amendment of article 19. In article 19 of the Constitution,
(a) in clause (2), after the words "in the interests of", the words "the sovereignty and integrity of India," shall be inserted;
(b) in clauses (3) and (4), after the words "in the interests of", the words "the sovereignty and integrity of India or" shall be inserted.'
3   For a comprehensive history of how Parliament debated the Sixteenth Amendment, see Chandrachud, *Rhetoric*, pp. 98–110.
4   See Section 5 of the Sixteenth Amendment. Also see Chandrachud, *Rhetoric*, pp. 98–110.
5   Chandrachud, *Rhetoric*, pp. 98–101.
6   Id., p. 98.
7   See Austin, *Working*, p. 53; Chandrachud, *Rhetoric*, p. 106.
8   Preamble to the Unlawful Activities (Prevention) Act, 1967.
9   Ibid.
10 Section 2(1)(o): 'unlawful activity', in relation to an individual or association, means any action taken by such individual or association (whether by committing an act or by words, either spoken or written, or by signs or by visible representation or otherwise):
(i) which is intended, or supports any claim, to bring about, on any ground whatsoever, the cession of a part of the territory of India or the secession of a part of the territory of India from the Union, or which incites any individual or group of individuals to bring about such cession or secession; or
(ii) which disclaims, questions, disrupts or is intended to disrupt the sovereignty and territorial integrity of India; or
(iii) which causes or is intended to cause disaffection against India.

11 Singh, *Sedition*, p. 283.
12 See generally, Singh, *Sedition*, pp. 284–285.
13 *Thappar*, p. 602. (Emphasis added.)
14 See Anushka Singh, 'Criminalising Dissent: Consequences of UAPA,' *Economic and Political Weekly*, vol. 47 (2012): p. 15.
15 *Shreya Singhal*, para. 38.
16 *Lohia* (I), p. 836.
17 Ibid.
18 Preamble to the Constitution (Sixteenth Amendment) Act, 1963.
19 *Sakal Papers*, p. 845. ('Briefly stated the effect of the Act and of the impugned Order is to regulate the number of pages according to the price charged, prescribe the number of supplements to be published and prohibit the publication and sale of newspapers in contravention of any order made under Section 3 of the Act. The Act also provides for regulating by an order under Section 3, the sizes and area of advertising matter in relation to the other matters contained in a newspaper. Penalties are also prescribed for contravention of the provision of the Act or Order.')
20 Ibid. ('We may mention here that in the year 1952 the Government of India appointed a Press Commission for enquiring into a large number of matters concerning the press and one of the recommendations of the Commission was to enact a law such as the one impugned before us. This law is alleged by the respondent to have been made to give effect to that recommendation. Both the sides place reliance upon the findings of the Press Commission and have invited us to accept these findings, though not necessarily the recommendations.')
21 Id., p. 866. (Emphasis added.)
22 Ibid. (Emphasis added.)

Epilogue

1 Generally, see, *Kaushal Kishore*, para. 214 (per B.V. Nagarathna, J.)
2 Zinn, *A People's History*, p. 365.
3 Singh, *Sedition*, p. 148.
4 *Kedar Nath Singh*, p. 807.
5 Id., p. 805. (Emphasis added.)
6 In the case of *Ram Nandan* (1958), the Full Bench of the Allahabad High Court had used several such illustrations to highlight that

criticism of state activity cannot always fall within the net of Section 124A. See *Ram Nandan*, paras. 28–29, 33.
7   *Shreya Singhal*, para. 87.
8   Cass R. Sunstein, 'Ranking the Supreme Court's home run hitters', The Morning Call, 2 April 2014, (available at https://www.mcall.com/opinion/mc-xpm-2014-04-02-mc-supreme-court-justices-sunstein-web-20140402-story.html).
9   *West Virginia State Board of Education v. Barnette*, (1943) US SC 134, para. 35 (SCC OnLine version).

Index

Abrams v. United States, 249–250, 252–253, 258, 260
Adult suffrage, 185
Advisory Committee, 83, 85–87, 91, 96, 100, 148–149
Age of Consent Bill (1891), 28
Ahmed, Naziruddin, 141
Alexandrowicz, Charles Henry, 217
Ali, Saiyid Fazl (J), 109, 117, 119, 128, 154–155
Allahabad High Court, 42, 146, 172, 200, 270; in *Ram Nandan* case, 180
Alva, Joachim, xiv, 310n23
Alva, Violet, xiv, 310n23
Ambedkar, B.R., 83–84, 88, 90–91, 93, 96–101, 103, 106, 110, 138–140, 150–151, 157, 215: defending First Amendment,

137, 157; and Foreign Relations Act (1932), 129
Amish Devgan v. Union of India, 202, 236, 277
Amrita Bazar Patrika, into English publication, 45
Anderson, George William, 3
anti-war rhetoric, 242, 246
arbitrariness, doctrine of manifest, 222–223
Arendt, Hannah, 195–196
Arthur, Allan, 50
Asquith, Herbert Henry, 38–40: on Strachey, 41
Auckland, Lord, 3
Ayyangar, M. Ananthasayanam, 189–190, 208
Ayyangar, N. Rajagopala (J), 165, 271–272

Index

Ayyar, Alladi Krishnaswami, 83–84, 88–90, 92–96, 101
Azad, Maulana Abul Kalam, 83

Bal Gangadhar Tilak case 19, 36, 39, 47, 56–58, 60, 64, 68–70
Bangobasi, 27–28
Banker, Shankarlal, publisher of *Young India*, 59, 62
Batchelor, (J), 69–70
Batty, (J), 53–54, 56
Beg, N.U. (J), 146
Bentham, Jeremy, 6
Bhala 'A Durbar in Hell,' 53
Bhargava, Thakur Dass, 105, 136–137, 208, 210–216, 218–219
Bhasin, Anuradha, 277
Bhaskar Bhopatkar case, 53, 56
Bickel, Alexander, 196–197, 256–257
Bihar Land Reform Act (1950), 132, 134
Bill of Rights, 98, 241
Bombay Agriculture Debtors Relief Act (1939), 65
Bombay High Court, xiv, 19, 32–33, 36, 53, 55–58, 66, 69, 78, 103
Bombay Tenancy Act 1939, 65
Bose (Joginder Chunder) case, 27, 31, 33, 36–37, 42, 52, 55, 72, 105
Bose, Khudiram, 55
Brandeis, (J), 194, 253–256
Brandenburg v. Ohio, 257–258, 277–278, 280, 296, 305
Brennan, (J), 192–194

Brij Bhushan v. The State of Delhi, 109, 116–117, 119, 121, 123, 128, 130, 135, 154–155, 224, 228
Broomfield, Judge, 59–63, 80

Calcutta High Court, 28, 63, 65, 67, 89, 274
Cameron, Charles Hay, 3, 7, 13
Canning, Lord, 16–17, 44
Chafee, Zechariah, 244
Chagla, M.C. (JC), xiv, 59
Chalmers, M.D., 46–52
Charalu, Ananda, 51
Charter Act (1813), 1
Charter Act (1833), 1–3
Chaudhari, Rohini Kumar, 105
Chintaman Rao case, 215
Chitnavis, Gangadhar Rao Madhav, 50
civil disobedience, 200, 257
civil rights, 97–102, 107, 118, 149–151, 166, 211–213, 218–219; in Article 19, 218
Cochrane, J., 14, 27
Code of Criminal Procedure (1898), 63, 68
Coleman, Bennett, 226–227
Committee on National Integration and Regionalism, 296
Constituent Assembly, xv–xvi, 81–82, 86, 88–90, 93–94, 97–98, 102–103, 106, 108, 112–113, 118–119, 147–148, 150–153, 188, 211–212; against sedition, 137; amendments to Article 19, 131, 134–135, 144; list of

Fundamental Rights, 83; met in 1946, 81
Constitution of India x–xi, xv–xvi, xviii, 126, 161–162, 165, 200, 203, 208, 210, 217–219, 262, 264, 300–301, 304; Article 13(1) and 13(2), 133; Article 13(1), 113; Article 14, 223 287; Article 19, 107, 118 144, 290223, 287; Article 19(1)(a), 107, 153, 202, 209–210, 217, 226–228, 237, 276, 287–288, 344; Article 19(1)(b), 284; Article 19(1)(c), 118, 284; Article 19(1)(g), 118, 166, 216; Article 19(2), 111–115, 117–119, 121–124, 126–131, 136–137, 139–148, 152–157, 159–161, 169–172, 178–181, 210–211, 213–215, 220–222, 224–228, 267–268, 274, 276–277, 284–285, 288–292, 295–296; Article 19(3), 284; Article 19(4), 284; Article 21, 223, 287; Article 31, 132; Article 31A, 134; Article 31B, 132–134, 141; Article 246, 338n6; Article 366(10), 113; Article 372(1), 113, 331n16; birth of, xv; First Amendment (1951), xv–xvi, 125–128, 130–144, 146–147, 152, 154, 156–157, 159, 193–194, 215, 224–225, 228, 259, 261–262, 264; Ninth Schedule, 132–134, 138–139; political speech in, 209; Section 3(2), 141; sedition as crime in, 152; Sixteenth Amendment, 284, 289, 291–292, 296

constitutional: power, 161–174; principle of morality, 238; reason, 97, 162, 190, 237, 288
Council of Governor-General of India, 46
critical speech, 285–286
Cross Roads, Bombay, 109–110

Daily Newspaper (Price and Page) Order, 1960, 297
Das, Sajanikanta, 63–64
Das, Seth Govind, 105
Das, S.R. (CJ), 109, 221–222, 266–267
Daulatram, Jairamdas, 83
Davar, Justice, 56–58, 61
Debs v. United States, 245–249, 251–253
defamation, 6, 13, 50, 87, 94, 97, 107, 112, 124, 128, 239–240
defamatory speech, 239
'demand for *Swarajya*,' 55, 57, 69
democracy, xvii–xviii, 186, 189, 194, 201, 203, 208, 232, 238, 273, 299, 306; and criticism of government, 189; and law on sedition, 182
democratic process, and free speech, 200–202, 208, 270, 273
Desai, M.C. (J), 146
Devi, Shailabala, 121
Douglas, William (J), 258–259
Draft Article 13, 93–94, 98, 102, 104, 114, 149–151, 211–213
Draft Constitution, 88–90, 93–94, 96–98, 100–102, 149, 151–152
Drafting Committee, 88–97, 99–103, 106, 149–150, 152

Dua, Vinod, 279

East India Company, 1, 3-4, 8-9, 13; Standing Counsel of, 14, 27; and trade monopoly, 1
East Punjab Safety Act (1949), 117; Section 7(1)(c) of, 116
Edge, (CJ), 41-43, 47
elected representatives, ix, 186-188, 200, 202
Elliot, Daniel, 7, 13
Elphinstone, Mountstuart, 2
Emperor v. Sadashiv Narayan Bhalerao, 77-78, 159
England, Coroners and Justice Act, 194
English criminal law, 4, 6-7
Epidemic Diseases Act (1897), 184
expression of disapprobation, 46, 286-288

famine, 28
Farran, (CJ), 36, 38
Federal Court, 70-78, 80, 104, 143, 158, 175-176; against power abuse, 74
First Amendment Bill, 127-128, 130-135, 137, 139-141, 147, 210, 215; Select Committee, 127-128, 140-141, 215
Fletcher (J), 67
France, Royer-Collard and system of regulation, 248, *see also* French law
free speech and assembly, rights of, 255
freedom of association, 151, 211, 213

freedom of expression, as rule, 272
freedom of speech, 213; Bickel on, 257; concept of 'brigading,' action with 275; constitutional principle, 257; curbs on, 93, 95-96, 102, 107, 112, 115, 151, 153-154, 213-214, 261, 265, 267; and democracy, 269; principles of, 207, 227; protection of, 243; protection to, 256; as rights, xviii, 168, 237, 257, 260, 264, 278, 287; unreasonable restriction on, 281, 288; value of, 201, 239
freedom of speech and expression, xv-xviii, 85-88, 90-93, 102-103, 106-107, 121, 123-124, 149-150, 152, 163-164, 166-169, 182-183, 200-201, 203-204, 213-215, 224-226, 284-285, 287-288, 290-291, 293-294, 344-345n79; components of, 209
freedom of [the] press, x, xiii, 23, 40, 111, 116, 128, 166, 216, 224, 226-228
French law, 248
Freund, Ernst, 196, 248-249, 252
Frohwerk, Jacob, case 245, 247, 251
fundamental rights, xviii, 83-85, 95, 97-98, 100-101, 107-108, 110-111, 113, 131, 133-134, 167-168, 176-177, 211-212, 222-223, 300-301; to freedom of speech and expression, 81, 107, 182, 214
Fundamental Rights Committee, 103

Index

Fundamental Rights Sub-Committee, 83, 85–86, 96, 102

Gagging Act 1857 (Act XV of 1857), 16, 18–19, 44
Gandhi, Mahatma, xiii, 59; imprisonment of, 62; trial of, 59–63, 80
Gandhi, Gopalkrishna, xiv
Ghose, Aurobindo, letter of, 67
Ginsburg, Douglas H., 252
Gokhale, Gopal Krishna, 66
Golak Nath case, 142
Gopalaswami Ayyangar, N., 88
government, forms of, 189, 191, 193, 273–274
Government of India Act of 1935, 71, 78, 89, 113, 175; Sixth Schedule of, 82
Governor-General-in-Council, 2, 19
A Grammar of Politics, Laski, 252
Great Revolt of 1857, 16–20, 25, 44, 73, 105
Guha, Arun Chandra, 100
Gujarat High Court, 119
Gurtu, R.N. (J), 146
Gwyer, Maurice (CJ), 71, 73–74, 77, 79–80, 104, 176

Hanumanthaiya, K., 108
Haryana High Court, 119–120
hate speech, 184, 203, 240, 277
Hidayatullah, Justice, 142, 155, 336n61
Himatsingka, P.D., 139
The Hindu, found in 1878, 45

History of India, James Mill, 64
A History of the Criminal Law of England, Stephen, 75
Holmes, Oliver Wendell (J), 194, 242–253, 258–260
Holmwood, (J), 67
Home Rule, 68
homosexuality, decriminalization of, 223
House of Commons, 32, 45
Human Rights Act of 1998, 195

imminent harm, xix, 76, 254–256, 261, 266–267, 271, 281, 294; Brandeis on 255–256; free speech and, 254; Littledale on, 76
Imperial Legislative Council, 66
'incitement to an offence,' 127, 179, 181
India in Bondage: Her Right to Freedom, Sutherland, 63–65
Indian Councils Act of 1909, 66
Indian Express Newspapers case, 216, 227
Indian Independence Act (1947), 113
Indian Law Commission, xii, 2–5, 7–8, 11, 13–16
Indian National Congress, 45, 63, 132
Indian Penal Code (Amendment) Act (1898), 51
Indian Penal Code (IPC), xii, xv, 1, 3, 5–16, 19–22, 25, 28, 42–43, 46–47, 112, 114, 124–125, 283, 285; First Draft of, xii; imprint

of Bentham in, 6; as Macaulay's
Penal Code, 3; Section 9(1-A),
109–110, 163, 224; Section 66-
A, 170–171, 177–179, 291, 302,
340–341n51; Section 99A, 63,
112; Section 121A, 19–20, 25;
Section 124A, x–xiii, 25–30, 33–
37, 39–42, 46–59, 69–73, 77–82,
91–95, 102–107, 112–117,
119–120, 124–126, 143–146,
148–152, 156–161, 171–182,
281–283, 285–290, 292–294,
305–306, 309n15, 316n108;
Section 124A 'excitement of
disaffection,' 43, 50, 145, 180,
293, 300, 303, 321n100; Stephen
on, 5
Information Technology Act (IT
Act), 291, 302; amendment
2009, 177–178; Section 66A,
170, 178
Interim Report on Fundamental
Rights, 86, 148
Irish Constitution, 90, 149; free
speech clause of, 149

Jackson, Robret (J), 194
Jefferson, Thomas, 194
'Justiciable Fundamental Rights,'
charter of, 86–87, 148

Kamath, H.V., 102
Kania, Hiralal, (CJ), 109
Karmayogin of Ghose, 67
Kaur, Rajkumari Amrit, 83
Kedar Nath Singh v. State of Bihar,
125–126, 143, 146–147, 156,

158–159, 165, 168, 171–175,
177, 180, 232–234, 236,
270–271, 301–304
Kennedy, Pringle, 55
Kesari, 31, 39, 55; 'The Country's
Misfortune' in, 55; 'The
Remedies Are Not Lasting' in,
55
Kesavananda Bharati case, 139
Khaitan, D.P., 88
Khan Brothers (Amir and
Hashmadad Khan) trial of,
25–26
Khanna, Sanjiv (J), 202, 278
Kher, B.G., 88–89
Kingford, Douglas, 55
Kripalani, J.B., 83, 85
Krishnamachari, T.T., 88, 106,
208
Kunzru, H.N., 140–141

Lahiri, Somnath, 87
Lal, Shiv Charan, 138
Lalit, U.U. (J), 279–280
land reform laws, xv, 132–134,
138–139
Laski, Harold, 252
law on sedition, ix–xiv, xvi, xviii,
46–48, 50, 78, 81, 92, 178–180,
182, 192, 194, 235–236, 300–
301, 304–305, *see also* sedition
laws made in India, as 'Acts,' 2
Littledale, Judge, 76
Lohia, Ram Manohar. *See, Ram
Manohar Lohia* case
Lokur (J), xiv
Lytton, Lord, 44

Macaulay, Thomas Babington, xi–xiii, 3, 5–14, 21, 47–48: arrival of, xi, 6; Clause 113 of, 9, 15, 20, 22, 25; and Utilitarianism, 6, 9; utilitarian project, 23, 47
Macleod, John Macpherson, 3
Madison, James, 191, 193
Madras Maintenance of Public Order Act, 1949, 109–110, 112, 163, 224; Section 99A of, 112
Mahajan, M.C. (CJ), 109, 164, 262–263
Majumdar case, 70–71, 78, 104, 143, 158–159
manifest arbitrariness, 222–223
Manmohan Ghose v. Emperor, 67
Masani, M.R., 83
Meiklejohn, Alexander, 197–198, 273
Mill, James, 7
Minto, Lord, 66
Mitter, B.L., 88
Mookerjee, S.P., 136
Moradabad Sessions Court, 41
Morley, John, 58, 66
Morley–Minto Reforms, 66–67, 69
Mudholkar, J.R. (J), 165, 167–168
Mukherjea, Bijan Kumar (J), 109
Munshi, K.M., xv, 83–84, 88, 96, 103–107, 150, 188–190, 208, 281; against Section of 124A of IPC, 104

Nandan, Ram. *See Ram Nandan* case
Naoroji, Dadabhai, 'Grand Old Man of India,' 63–64

Nariman, R.F., (J), 171, 178–179, 209, 222–223, 276, 302
Nehru, Jawaharlal, xiii, 89, 116, 127, 131–132, 134–136, 140, 144–145, 157, 220, 224; on 1932 Act, 129; and laws of sedition, 144; in prison for sedition, xiv
Nehru, Motilal, 91
Nehru Report of 1928, 91
Newspaper (Price and Page) Act, (1956), 165, 201, 226, 297
Newsprint Import Policy, Coleman and, 227
New York Times, 59, 194, 231; 'GANDHI ARRESTED ON CHARGE OF SEDITION' in, 59
New York Times v. Sullivan, 192, 231
Niharendu Dutt Majumdar case, 70, 143
Ninth Schedule, Section 14, 133
non-violence, 62
Northern Ireland, common law of, 195
Norton, G., 14
Now It Can Be Told, Bali, 119

Pant, G.B., 83
Patel, Sardar Vallabhbhai, xv, 83, 86–88, 96, 116, 149, 176: and Advisory Committee's Interim Report, 86, 149
Patna High Court, 121–122, 128, 132, 262
peasantry mobilization, 65–66
Peel Acts (1829), 4

Petheram, W.C. (CJ), 28–31, 33–34, 37, 72: on Section 124A, 29
Phadke, Narayan, 65–66
plague, 28, 31, 35, 38
Plague Relief Committee, 31
Political Agent, 45
political change, xvi, 208–209, 253, *See* political speech
political speech, xvi–xix, 68, 70, 182–184, 188–192, 195–210, 230, 232, 234, 240–241, 249–250, 277, 281, 299–300, 304–306; conception of free, 202, 207–208; constitutional protection for, 234–237; for 'deliberative democracy,' 205; regulation of, 203, 206–207, 209, 237–239, 253; and State, 237–238; Sunstein on, 205, 239; value of, xvi, 204–205, 229–239, 253
population growth, 28
Poverty and Un-British Rule in India, Naoroji, 63
Prasad, Amba case. *See Queen-Empress v. Amba Prasad*
Prasad, Kameshwar case, 271
Prasad, Rajendra, 93
Prasad, Sarjoo (J), 122–124, 135, 262
Press (Emergency Powers) Act, 1931, 119, 121–122
Press and Registration of Books Act, 44
Preventive Detention Act 1950, 136
Privy Council, 38, 40–41, 71, 77–78, 158–159

Proclamation of 1858, of Queen Victoria, 16
prosecution, 11–12, 28, 31–32, 39–40, 43, 48, 53–54, 56, 58, 60, 62, *see also* trials
public disorder, 71, 74–75, 80, 159–160, 173, 175, 177, 180, 234–236, 264–265, 269, 271, 279
public interest, 60–61, 77, 213, 275
Public order, 109–110, 112, 117, 153–156, 158, 169–170, 172, 174, 180–181, 224, 261, 263, 265–266, 269–270, 272
Pugh, representing Tilak, 33, 37
Punjab High Court, 119–120, 145
Punjab Special Powers (Press) Act (1956), 221

Queen-Empress v. Amba Prasad, 41–43, 47, 52, 72, 105
Queen Victoria's Diamond Jubilee, 31
Quit India Movement (1942), 73

Rajagopalachari, C., 140
Ramji Lal Modi case, 264, 266–267, 270–271, 295
Ram Manohar Lohia case, 153, 169–170, 174, 200, 266–267, 270, 276, 287, 294–295, 305
Ram Nandan case, 146, 172, 180, 270–271
Rand, W.C., assassination of, 31–32, 39
Rangarajan, S.P., 272–275, 287

Rao, K. Subba (J), 153–156, 169–170, 200, 266–271, 276, 294–295, 305
Rao, N. Madhava, 88
Rasul, Begum Aizaz, 101
Rau, Benegal Narsing (Sir), 88–91, 149
R.C. Cooper case, 223
'reasonable restrictions,' 128, 131, 203, 210–213, 216–218, 220–221, 224, 228–229, 267–268, 274, 284–285, 296; and Article 19(2), 128, 215, 220, 268; in interests of public order, 265–266, 269, 271, 295; principle of, 223
Reform Bill of 1832, 11
Reform Scheme, 67–68
regulation of speech, 99, 241, 258
Report of the Fundamental Rights Sub-Committee, 102
restrictions on free speech, 86–87, 91–93, 97, 100, 143, 151
Roman Law, 8
Romesh Thappar v. State of Madras, 109–112, 116–117, 119–121, 123, 128, 130, 134–135, 144–145, 153, 153–155, 174–175, 224, 228, 279, 287
Royal Commission, 4
R v. Collins, 75–76

Saadulla, Saiyid Mohammad, 88
Sahib, Muhammad Ismail, 101
Sakal Papers v. Union of India, 165–166, 168, 174, 201, 224–225, 287, 297–298

Santhanam, K., 101
Sarkar, A.K. (J), 165
Sastri, Patanjali (J), 109, 111, 113–118, 163–164, 262: against sedition, 114
Schenck v. United States, 242–247, 251, 253, 258–259
'security of the State,' 119, 152, 154, 177, 264
sedition xi–xix, 10, 12, 27–36, 39–43, 46–48, 52–62, 67–69, 71–81, 87–89, 91–96, 102–107, 143–152, 177–181, 184–189, 191–195, 235–237, 279–280, 285–288, 300–306, 309n15; crime of, xii, 9–10, 12, 27, 34–35, 48, 102, 104, 185, 194–195, 303; and democracy, 191; life imprisonment for, x; Macaulay's law on, 12, 20–21, 23–24, 47; as 'political offence,' 11; reconstructing, 46–51; State Security and Public Order, 148–152; Stephen on, 21
seditious libel, 11, 21–22, 75–76, 194–195
seditious speech, 11, 22, 43, 48, 50, 53, 75, 159–160, 177, 179, 196
Seervai, H.M., 72, 203, 219
Setalvad, M.C., 120, 215
Seth, Damodar Swarup, 102, 151
Shah, Bahadur, 16
Shah, K.T. (J), 69, 83, 100
Shailabala Devi case, 122, 128, 135, 262
Shreya Singhal v. Union of India, 170, 178

Singh, Balwant case, 236
Singh, Harnam, 83–84
Singh, Kameshwar, case, 132, 134
Singhal, Shreya, 170, 177, 180, 209, 276, 287, 291, 302, 305
Sinha, B.P. (CJ), 125, 165, 169, 171–172, 188, 271; on Section 124A, 125
Sinha, Sachchidananda, 191
Sircar, Kamal Krishna case, 274
Sixteenth Amendment as Anti-Secession Bill, 284
sovereignty and territorial integrity of India, 284, 289–291, 294, 296, 345
speech and writings, 76, 230, 262–263
S. Rangarajan v. P. Jagjivan Ram, 272
Srivastava, J.P., 139
state security, xix, 122–123, 147, 150, 152–157, 230, 232–233, 238, 275–276, 303–304, 306
Stephen, James Fitzjames, 5, 7, 11–12, 19–24, 26, 30, 47, 75, 185–188, 301; amendments and sedition, 23, 25; father of sedition in India, 188, 301; on Section 124A, 30; and sedition, 21, 184; and 'The Phantom Wahabi,' 25
Strachey, John (J), 19, 33–39, 56–57, 70, 78: formulation of, 37, 64
Strangman, Thomas (Sir), 60–61
Sundaram, K.V.K., 133
Sunstein, Cass, 198–199, 204–206, 239; concept of political speech, 204; on right to free speech, 204; on Sedition Act, 199
suppression of speech, 255
Supreme Court: and free speech as right, 201; and Section 124A as unconstitutional, 114
Sutherland, 63
swadeshi movement, 68
swaraj (self-governance), 55, 57, 68–69
Sydenham, Lord, 58

Tagore, Rabindranath, 33
Tara Singh and sedition case, 119–121, 145
Thappar, Romesh case. See *Romesh Thappar v. State of Madras*
Third Census Report, 28
Thiruvenkatachari, V.K., 132
Tilak, Bal Gangadhar, xiii, 31–33, 36, 39, 42, 52, 55–61, 63, 68–70, 72, 105, 184; First Trial, 31–39, 47, 58, 78; first conviction for sedition, 57–58, 60; journalism of, 58; and Privy Council, 38–41; prosecution of, 39; release of, 32; Second Trial, 55–59; sedition trial in 1897 and 1908, 70; sentencing, 36, 58; Third Trial for Sedition, 68–70, *see also Bal Gangadhar Tilak* case
Treason-Felony Act, 21–22
trials, 29, 31, 36, 38, 41, 54–57, 59–61, 63, 76, 80, 136, *see also under separate entries*
Tripathi, P.K., 218
Triple Talaq case, 222–223

Unlawful Activities (Prevention) Act (UAPA), 283; expression of disaffection, 290, 292–293, 295, 303; provision on sedition, 292; to Section 2(1)(o), 285, 289, 291, 293–294, 298; Section 2(1)(o)(i), 289; Section 2(1)(o)(ii), 289; Section 2(1)(o)(iii) of, 285, 287–296, 298; sedition provision, 283, 293; version of sedition, 283

United States, 219, 242, 244, 246; anti-war speeches and, 246 (*see also* anti-war rhetoric); 'bad tendency test,' 241, 247, 278; Brandenburg decision, 277; clear and present danger test, 244–245, 247, 253, 258–259, 278; Espionage Act in 1917, 242, 245–246, 250, 300; police powers doctrine, 99–100; Act (1798), 65, 67, 113, 191–194, 199, 302; Sedition Act (1918), 191, 194, 242; 'shouting fire in a theater' analogy, 243–245, 247–249, 257, 259

United States Constitution, 83, 90, 98–99, 191–192, 194, 196–197, 199, 205–206, 208, 241, 249, 252–253, 257; 1st Amendment to, 98–99, 192, 194, 197, 199, 205, 241, 249, 252–253

United States Supreme Court, 99–100, 192, 194, 206, 230–231, 241–242, 247–248, 250, 256–259, 277, 303, 305

'unlawful activity,' 284–285, 289–294

UP Special Powers Act (1932), 169

Vernacular Press Act (1878), 44–45, 48

Viceroy's Council, 27, 30, 33

Virendra v. State of Punjab, 221, 224, 228, 266–267, 271, 295, 305

Wahabi Conspiracy, 24–25
Ward, Claire, 195
Weston, (CJ), xiv, 120
Whitney v. California, 253, 256, 258
Wilson, President Woodrow, 242

Young India, 59–60, 62; 'Tampering with Loyalty' in, 59

Zinn, Howard, 244, 300

Acknowledgements

To Nina, for everything.
To our children, Zarina and Cyrus, who, like the sunshine, light up our lives every day.

To my parents, Padma and Chittaranjan Alva, and my sister, Manisha Alva, without whom this book would never have been possible.

To my father-in-law, Rohinton Nariman, who gave me brilliant insights and ideas for the book, my mother-in-law, Sanaya Nariman, my sister-in-law, Khursheed Nariman, and my grandfather-in-law, Fali Nariman, for their untiring support.

To my uncle Vasanth Rao and my mother, who spent many weeks poring over the manuscript of this book.

To Faiz Tajuddin and Shiv Swaminathan for patiently looking over the manuscript and for all their helpful feedback. To Shaurya Upadhyay for taking time out of his holiday to spend time in the

British Library to pull out a treasure trove of archival material for this book.

Finally, to the superb team at HarperCollins including Swati Chopra, Kripa Raman, Paloma Dutta and Saurav Das for all their hard work for this book.

About the Author

ROHAN J. ALVA is a counsel practising in the Supreme Court of India and the High Court of Delhi. He graduated with an LLM from Harvard Law School, where he focused on constitutional law, and which he read for on numerous scholarships including as a Tata Scholar. He holds a BA in history from Loyola College, University of Madras, and an LLB from Campus Law Centre, University of Delhi, where he was editor of the *Delhi Law Review*. His debut book, *Liberty After Freedom: A History of Article 21, Due Process and the Constitution of India*, was published in January 2022.

30 Years *of*
HarperCollins *Publishers* India

At HarperCollins, we believe in telling the best stories and finding the widest possible readership for our books in every format possible. We started publishing 30 years ago; a great deal has changed since then, but what has remained constant is the passion with which our authors write their books, the love with which readers receive them, and the sheer joy and excitement that we as publishers feel in being a part of the publishing process.

Over the years, we've had the pleasure of publishing some of the finest writing from the subcontinent and around the world, and some of the biggest bestsellers in India's publishing history. Our books and authors have won a phenomenal range of awards, and we ourselves have been named Publisher of the Year the greatest number of times. But nothing has meant more to us than the fact that millions of people have read the books we published, and somewhere, a book of ours might have made a difference.

As we step into our fourth decade, we go back to that one word – a word which has been a driving force for us all these years.

Read.